Student Support and Benefits Handbook: England, Wales and Nort~~hern Ireland~~

. . . .

15th edit~~ion~~

David Mal~~colm~~ ~~and Angela Toal with Mike Rob~~erts

Child Povert~~y~~

Child Poverty Action Group works on behalf of the more than one in four children in the UK growing up in poverty. It does not have to be like this. We use our understanding of what causes poverty and the impact it has on children's lives to campaign for policies that will prevent and solve poverty – for good. We provide training, advice and information to make sure hard-up families get the financial support they need. We also carry out high-profile legal work to establish and protect families' rights. If you are not already supporting us, please consider making a donation, or ask for details of our membership schemes, training courses and publications.

Published by Child Poverty Action Group
30 Micawber Street
London N1 7TB
Tel: 020 7837 7979
staff@cpag.org.uk
www.cpag.org.uk

A CIP record for this book is available from the British Library
ISBN: 978 1 910715 45 1

Child Poverty Action Group is a charity registered in England and Wales (registration number 294841) and in Scotland (registration number SC039339), and is a company limited by guarantee, registered in England (registration number 1993854). VAT number: 690 808117

Cover design by Colorido Studios
Internal design by Devious Designs
Typeset by DLxml, a division of RefineCatch Limited, Bungay, Suffolk
Content management system by Konnectsoft
Printed and bound by CPI Group (UK) Ltd, Croydon CR0 4YY

The authors

David Malcolm is Head of Policy and Campaigns at the National Union of Students (NUS), where he has worked on student finance policy for over a decade. Previously, he was the sabbatical Vice President Welfare at the University of Strathclyde Students' Association.

Lynne Condell is Student Funds Manager at Liverpool John Moores University, and a former chair of the National Association of Student Money Advisers. She has worked in higher education funding for over 20 years, and in 2013 was awarded an MBE for services to higher education.

Angela Toal is a welfare rights worker with CPAG in Scotland, working on its Benefits for Students Project.

Alan Roberts is Policy Development Manager at NUS, working on student finance policy and other areas of education and social policy. Previously, Alan worked as an adviser at Liverpool Guild of Students, delivering academic and housing advice.

Acknowledgements

The authors would particularly like to thank Lindsey Fidler, Jayne Aldridge, Keith Houghton, Jeanette Jones and Carolyn George for their work on previous editions of this *Handbook*.

Grateful thanks are due to Connie Craig, Hannah Bundy and Gareth Davies for lending their time and expertise in checking and advising on this *Handbook*.

For editing the book and managing its production, thanks go to Alison Key. Thanks also to Kathleen Armstrong for proofreading the text and Anne Ketley for compiling the index.

The law covered in this book was correct on 1 September 2018 and includes regulations laid up to this date.

Contents

• • • •

Foreword

This fifteenth edition of CPAG's *Student Support and Benefits Handbook* is published at a time of continued uncertainty, austerity and change for both funding for education and social security provision.

Student poverty is a real issue. In England, students in further education can access little support for their maintenance or course costs, while many adult learners pay steep fees to access courses. In higher education, fees are now rising above £9,000 for full-time courses, while maintenance grants and bursaries for nursing and other healthcare courses have been scrapped and replaced with loans, causing student numbers to fall. The poorest young people graduate with the highest debts, part-time student numbers have plummeted and drop-out rates have increased. Funding for postgraduate study has finally improved – but this too is in the form of loans, rather than grants.

Elsewhere in the UK, students also struggle. In Northern Ireland, many grant and loan rates have been frozen for several years, with some rates inadequate even when they were set.

Wales shows that a different approach is possible: maintenance funding is substantially more generous than for new students in England or Northern Ireland. But here fees have risen, and further education students still receive less than those at university.

Meanwhile, the Department for Work and Pensions is undertaking an equally radical reform of social security, with the new universal credit now well on its way to replacing many benefits and tax credits, although its introduction has been far from smooth. Personal independence payment is replacing disability living allowance – but with a 20 per cent cut to total funding. Working-age benefits are frozen until 2020 and the benefit cap has been reduced still further.

In this context, it has never been more important to understand how both education funding and social security work, and how they interrelate.

Politicians, rightly, see education and work as crucial routes out of poverty, and vital to the economic health of the nation. Yet students from the poorest backgrounds are still hugely under-represented in further and higher education, even more so in the elite institutions.

Although we know that over the last two decades there has been a significant improvement – the majority of school leavers now continue in education – this expansion does not extend in anywhere near the same proportion to families living in poverty.

Low-income students still face formidable barriers to their participation and to their achievement. They often have to work more during term time, are able to rely less on family support (both financial and otherwise), and must navigate the ever-changing and quite bewildering student support and social security benefits systems, often with little or no guidance. The ongoing reductions in benefit entitlement for lone parents are likely to make matters worse.

And when people on low incomes do enter education, they tend to follow a more complicated path, taking more breaks, deferring enrolment and switching, repeating or restarting their courses for non-academic reasons. We know these people are also more likely to drop out or forego opportunities to progress to more advanced courses. All this complicates even further their financial support and adds to the pressures they face in determining their entitlement.

'How will study affect my benefits?' is a key question for anyone who is living on benefits and thinking about going into education. No one can make a decision to start or continue studying without knowing they can support themselves and their family.

Fair access to education – indeed, education itself – is about much more than money, but clear, relevant information on financial support for students is vital. This is why the National Union of Students (NUS) is proud to collaborate with CPAG in producing this *Handbook*.

Good advice is critical. Student support across England, Wales, Northern Ireland and Scotland differs and, as a devolved issue, these differences are ever more apparent. Advisers, therefore, need information that relates specifically to the different nations across the UK. This book covers students in England, Wales and Northern Ireland, complementing CPAG's *Benefits for Students in Scotland Handbook*. We hope it will aid advisers, act as a tool to help break down barriers and, in the process, help people from disadvantaged backgrounds enter and complete further and higher education courses.

Of course, this *Handbook* is no silver bullet. If the government seriously wishes to eradicate child poverty, education must be a priority. It must commit to action on a number of levels: fairer access to student support; increased capacity in the student advice sector; further development in childcare services; continued, far-reaching change in some of our older and larger educational institutions; a raising of aspirations and achievement in schools in disadvantaged areas; and more resources channelled into our community support services. All remain substantial challenges.

When access to education is truly equal for people from both poor and rich backgrounds, we will know that poverty is on its way to being eradicated. Until then, NUS is fully committed to supporting our members, breaking down financial barriers and fighting injustice in the education funding system.

Shakira Martin, NUS President
Eva Crossan Jory, NUS Vice President Welfare

How to use this *Handbook*

This *Handbook* is intended for those who advise students in England, Wales and Northern Ireland about their entitlement to student support, benefits, tax credits and other financial issues, such as tax and health benefits. It covers both further and higher education.

The *Handbook* covers rules affecting students studying in England, Wales and Northern Ireland who are eligible for support through English, Welsh and Northern Irish funding bodies. It does not cover the rules for students getting support from Scotland or elsewhere outside England, Wales or Northern Ireland.

Note: the benefits system in Northern Ireland is separate from that in the rest of the UK, though differences are usually minor. Any significant differences are highlighted. For the sake of simplicity, we refer to the Department for Work and Pensions as the responsible department in this *Handbook*, but this should be read as the Department for Communities in Northern Ireland.

CPAG publishes a companion volume entitled *Benefits for Students in Scotland Handbook*. Details can be found in Appendix 1.

Rates of government support

The *Handbook* is up to date at 1 September 2018 and is intended to be used for the academic year 2018/19, with information provided for 2019/20 where available.

Rates of student support, benefits and tax credits used are those for the 2018/19 academic year, and the 2019/20 year where available. Benefit and tax credit rates will be uprated in April 2019 (these rates are usually available from January, though the government has frozen many rates for the next few years), whereas student support rates will be uprated, where applicable, in September 2019.

Full-time students: definitions

Most full-time students are excluded from benefits – mainly those benefits for which entitlement relies on a means test. There is one definition of 'full-time student' used for income support, jobseeker's allowance and housing benefit. Other definitions are used for council tax, carer's allowance and employment and support allowance. And some students can still claim means-tested benefits, despite being classed as full time. So you should not assume that because a student is excluded from one benefit, s/he is excluded from them all. Who counts as a 'full-time student' is explained in detail in the relevant chapters.

Means testing students

Government support systems do not necessarily treat student income in the same way. Different means tests apply to means-tested benefits, tax credits, health benefits and student support. It is always worth checking across these systems when calculating a student's total entitlement to government support. To help students and their advisers do this, this *Handbook* has separate chapters covering the treatment of income.

Structure of the *Handbook*

Part 1 looks at students' entitlement to student support. **Part 2** covers students' entitlement to benefits and tax credits. **Part 3** considers how income affects the amount of benefits or tax credits, with a particular focus on how student support is treated. **Part 4** covers other matters, such as tax and taking time out from studying.

Chapters are endnoted with references to the legal authorities. Where an abbreviation is used in the endnotes or in the text, this is explained in Appendix 3 and on pxv. If you are appealing against a benefit or tax credit decision, you may want to refer to the law. Appendix 1 suggests where you can obtain copies of Acts, regulations and caselaw.

Your feedback counts

The National Union of Students (NUS) and CPAG hope that this publication will serve as a useful resource for students and their advisers to help them deal with the complexity of financial support. We are aiming for a publication that is clear and that responds to the needs of its audience. The book has expanded with every edition, and we would appreciate any comments on how it may be improved for future years. Please contact CPAG's publications department or David Malcolm at NUS: david.malcolm@nus.org.uk.

Abbreviations

BA	Bachelor of Arts	IB	incapacity benefit
BEd	Bachelor of Education	IS	income support
BSA	NHS Business Services Authority	JSA	jobseeker's allowance
BSc	Batchelor of Science	MA	maternity allowance
BTEC	Business and Technology Education Council	NHS	National Health Service
		NI	national insurance
CA	carer's allowance	NUS	National Union of Students
CTB	council tax benefit	NVQ	national vocational qualification
CTC	child tax credit	Ofsted	Office for Standards in Education, Children's Services and Skills
DfENI	Department for the Economy (Northern Ireland)		
		PAYE	pay as you earn
DipHE	Diploma of Higher Education	PC	pension credit
DoH	Department of Health (Northern Ireland)	PGCE	Postgraduate Certificate in Education
DLA	disability living allowance	PGDE	Postgraduate Diploma in Education
DWP	Department for Work and Pensions	PIP	personal independence payment
EEA	European Economic Area	RPI	retail price index
EHIC	European health insurance card	SAP	statutory adoption pay
ESA	employment and support allowance	SMP	statutory maternity pay
ESFA	Education and Skills Funding Agency	SPP	statutory paternity pay
EU	European Union	SSP	statutory sick pay
FE	further education	SSPP	statutory shared parental pay
HB	housing benefit	UC	universal credit
HMRC	Her Majesty's Revenue and Customs	UKCISA	UK Council for International Student Affairs
HNC	Higher National Certificate		
HND	Higher National Diploma	WTC	working tax credit

Means-tested benefit rates 2018/19

Universal credit
Standard allowance

		£pm
Single	Under 25	251.77
	25 or over	317.82
Couple	Both under 25	395.20
	One or both 25 or over	498.89

Elements

Eldest child		277.08
Second and each subsequent child who qualifies		231.67
Disabled child	Lower rate	126.11
	Higher rate	383.86
Limited capability for work (some claims only)		126.11
Limited capability for work-related activity		328.32
Carer		156.45

Childcare costs

One child	up to £646.35
Two or more children	up to £1,108.04
Percentage of childcare costs covered	85%

Income support and income-based jobseeker's allowance

Personal allowances		*£pw*
Single	Under 25	57.90
	25 or over	73.10
Lone parent	Under 18	57.90
	18 or over	73.10
Couple	Both under 18 (maximum)	87.50
	One 18 or over (maximum)	114.85
	Both 18 or over	114.85

Premiums		
Carer		36.00
Disability	Single	33.55
	Couple	47.80
Enhanced disability	Single	16.40
	Couple	23.55
Severe disability	One qualifies	64.30
	Two qualify	128.60
Pensioner	Single (jobseeker's allowance only)	89.90
	Couple	133.95

Pension credit		
Standard minimum guarantee	Single	163.00
	Couple	248.80
Severe disability addition	One qualifies	64.30
	Two qualify	128.60
Carer addition		36.00
Savings credit threshold	Single	140.67
	Couple	223.82

Income-related employment and support allowance

Personal allowances	Assessment phase £pw	Main phase £pw
Single		
Under 25	57.90	73.10
25 or over	73.10	73.10
Lone parent		
Under 18	57.90	73.10
18 or over	73.10	73.10
Couple		
Both under 18 (maximum)	87.50	114.85
Both 18 or over	114.85	114.85
Premiums		
Carer	36.00	36.00
Severe disability (one qualifies)	64.30	64.30
Severe disability (two qualify)	128.60	128.60
Enhanced disability		
Single	16.40	16.40
Couple	23.55	23.55
Pensioner		
Single, usual rate	89.90	60.85
Single, support group		52.25
Couple, usual rate	133.95	104.90
Couple, support group		96.30
Components		
Work-related activity (some claims only)		29.05
Support		37.65

Housing benefit

Personal allowances

Single	Under 25	57.90
	Under 25 (on main phase ESA)	73.10
	25 or over	73.10
Lone parent	Under 18	57.90
	Under 18 (on main phase ESA)	73.10
	18 or over	73.10
Couple	Both under 18	87.50
	Both under 18 (claimant on main phase ESA)	114.85
	One or both 18 or over	114.85
Children	Under 20	66.90
Over qualifying age for pension credit	Single under 65	163.00
	Single 65 or over	176.40
	Couple both under 65	248.80
	Couple one or both 65 or over	263.80

Premiums

Family	Ordinary rate	17.45
	Some lone parents	22.20
(only pre-1 May 2016 claims with a child already in the family)		
Carer		36.00
Disability	Single	33.55
	Couple	47.80
Disabled child		62.86
Severe disability	One qualifies	64.30
	Two qualify	128.60
Enhanced disability	Single	16.40
	Couple	23.55
	Child	25.48

Components

Work-related activity (some claims only)	29.05
Support	37.65

Non-means-tested benefit rates 2018/19

	£pw
Attendance allowance	
Higher rate	85.60
Lower rate	57.30
Bereavement benefits	
Bereavement payment (lump sum)	2,000
Bereavement allowance (maximum)	117.10
Bereavement support payment (maximum lump sum)	3,500
Bereavement support payment (maximum monthly rate)	350
Carer's allowance	64.60
Child benefit	
Only/eldest child	20.70
Other child(ren)	13.70
Disability living allowance	
Care component	
Highest	85.60
Middle	57.30
Lowest	22.65
Mobility component	
Higher	59.75
Lower	22.65
Employment and support allowance (contributory)	
Assessment phase	
Basic allowance (under 25)	57.90
Basic allowance (25 or over)	73.10
Main phase	
Basic allowance (16 or over)	73.10
Work-related activity component (some claims only)	29.05
Support component	37.65

Guardian's allowance   17.20

Jobseeker's allowance (contribution-based)

Under 25   57.90

25 or over   73.10

Maternity allowance

Standard rate   145.18

Variable rate   90% of earnings

Personal independence payment

Daily living component

Enhanced rate   85.60

Standard rate   57.30

Mobility component

Enhanced rate   59.75

Standard rate   22.65

Retirement pensions

State pension   164.35

Category A   125.95

Statutory adoption pay   145.18

Statutory maternity pay

Standard rate   145.18

Variable rate   90% of earnings

Statutory paternity pay   145.18

Statutory shared parental pay   145.18

Statutory sick pay   92.05

Tax credit rates 2018/19

Child tax credit	£ per day	£ per year
Family element (some claims only)	1.50	545
Child element	7.62	2,780
Disabled child element	8.98	3,275
Severely disabled child element	3.64	1,325

Working tax credit		
Basic element	5.37	1,960
Couple element	5.51	2,010
Lone parent element	5.51	2,010
30-hour element	2.22	810
Disabled worker element	8.47	3,090
Severe disability element	3.65	1,330
Childcare element		
Eligible childcare costs to a weekly maximum of:		
One child		70% of £175
Two or more children		70% of £300

Income thresholds	
Working tax credit only or with child tax credit	6,420
Child tax credit only	16,105

Student support rates 2018/19

Further education

	Maximum amounts
Care to Learn grant	
England (London)	£175 per child a week
England (outside London)	£160 per child a week
Northern Ireland	£165 per child a week
Education maintenance allowance	
Wales and Northern Ireland	£60 per fortnight
Further education award (Northern Ireland)	£2,092 per year
Welsh government learning grant	£1,500 per year
Vulnerable student bursary (England)	£1,200 per year (minimum)

Higher education

Full-time undergraduates

Adult dependants' grant	
England	£2,925 per year
Wales	£2,732 per year
Northern Ireland	£2,695 per year
Childcare grant	
One child:	
England	£164.70 per week
Wales	£161.50 per week
Northern Ireland	£148.75 per week
Two or more children:	
England	£282.36 per week
Wales	£274.55 per week
Northern Ireland	£255 per week
Disabled students' allowance	
England:	
Non-medical personal helper	£21,987 per academic year
Major items of specialist equipment	£5,529 for duration of course
Other expenditure	£1,847 per academic year
Additional expenditure on travel	Full reimbursement

Wales:

Non-medical personal helper	£21,181 per academic year
Major items of specialist equipment	£5,332 for duration of course
Other expenditure	£1,785 per academic year

Northern Ireland:

Non-medical personal helper	£20,938 per academic year
Major items of specialist equipment	£5,266 for duration of course
Other expenditure	£1,759 per academic year
Additional expenditure on travel	Full reimbursement

Maintenance grant (England and Northern Ireland)

England, 2012 cohort	£3,593 per year
Northern Ireland	£3,475 per year

Maintenance grant (Wales, 2018 cohort)

Base grant (all students)	£1,000 per year
Studying in London	£8,100 per year
Studying outside London	£10,124 per year
Living in parental home	£6,885 per year

Parents' learning allowance

England	£1,669 per year
Wales	£1,557 per year
Northern Ireland	£1,538 per year

Special support grant

England, 2012 cohort	£3,593 per year
Wales, 2012 cohort	£5,161 per year
Northern Ireland	£3,475 per year

Student loan for living costs

England, 2016 cohort:	*Full year*	*Final year*
Studying in London	£11,354	£10,518
Studying outside London	£8,700	£8,228
Living in parental home	£7,324	£6,892

Note: around 50% of the student loan is means tested.

England, 2016 cohort, eligible for benefits:	*Full year*	*Final year*
Studying in London	£12,382	£11,604
Studying outside London	£9,916	£9,479
Living in parental home	£8,640	£8,237

Note: these rates include a means-tested 'special support element' of £3,680 which is not included in benefit calculations. A proportion of the remaining 'maintenance element' is also means tested.

England, 2016 cohort, aged 60 or over:		£3,680 per year
England, 2012 cohort:	*Full year*	*Final year*
Studying in London	£8,702	£7,925
Studying outside London	£6,236	£5,800
Living in parental home	£4,960	£4,557

Note: 35% of the student loan is means tested. The rate of loan may be reduced if you are eligible for a maintenance grant.

Wales, 2018 cohort:

Studying in London	£10,250 per year
Studying outside London	£8,000 per year
Living in parental home	£6,650 per year

Note: the rate of loan is reduced £1 for every £1 of maintenance grant received. There is no final year rate of loan.

Wales, 2012 cohort:	*Full year*	*Final year*
Studying in London	£10,007	£9,112
Studying outside London	£7,143	£6,617
Living in parental home	£5,529	£5,006

Note: 25% of the student loan is means tested. The rate of loan may be reduced if you are eligible for a Welsh government learning grant.

Northern Ireland:	*Full year*	*Final year*
Studying in London	£6,780	£6,170
Studying outside London	£4,840	£4,480
Living in parental home	£3,750	£3,390

Note: 25% of the student loan is means tested. The rate of loan may be reduced if you are eligible for a maintenance grant.

Tuition fee grant (Wales, 2012 cohort)	£4,800 per year
Tuition fee loan	£9,250 per year
Welsh government learning grant (2012 cohort)	£5,161 per year

Part-time undergraduates

Course costs grant (Northern Ireland)	£265 per year

Maintenance grant (Wales, 2018 cohort)

Base grant (amount payable is pro-rated according to intensity of study)	£1,000 per year
Maintenance grant (maximum amount payable is pro-rated according to intensity of study)	£6,100 per year

Tuition fee grant
Wales, pre-2014 cohorts:
Course intensity equivalent to:
    50–59% of a full-time course   £690 per year
    60–74% of a full-time course   £820 per year
    75% or more of a full-time course   £1,025 per year
Northern Ireland:
Course intensity equivalent to:
    50–59% of a full-time course   £820 per year
    60–74% of a full-time course   £985 per year
    75% or more of a full-time course   £1,230 per year

Student loan for living costs   £5,650 per year
(Wales, 2018 cohort)
Maximum amount payable is pro-rated by intensity of study and loans are
reduced £1 for every £1 of maintenance grant payable

Tuition fee loan
England (post-2012 cohorts) and Wales for study
elsewhere in UK (post-2014 cohorts)   £6,935 per year
Wales for study in Wales, post-2014 cohorts   £2,625 per year
Northern Ireland   £3,022.50 per year

Welsh government learning grant   £1,155 per year

Healthcare students

Means-tested bursary
England and Wales (2012 system, 30-week rates):
    Studying in London   £3,191 per year
    Studying outside London   £2,643 per year
    Living in parental home   £2,207 per year
Northern Ireland:
    Living away from parental home   £2,355 per year
    Living in parental home   £1,920 per year

Non-means-tested grant
(England and Wales, 2012 system)   £1,000 per year

Nursing and midwifery bursary
(Northern Ireland)   £5,165 per year

Reduced-rate student loan

England:	Full year	Final year
Studying in London	£3,263	£2,498
Studying outside London	£2,324	£1,811
Living in parental home	£1,744	£1,324

Wales, 2018 cohort:

Studying in London	£5,125 per year
Studying outside London	£4,000 per year
Living in parental home	£3,325 per year

Note: there is no final year rate of loan.

Wales, 2012 cohort:

Studying in London	£4,920	£3,763
Studying outside London	£3,500	£2,727
Living in parental home	£2,625	£1,996
Northern Ireland:		
Living away from parental home	£2,324	£1,811
Living in parental home	£1,744	£1,324

Note: there is a range of supplementary grants for healthcare students not listed here. See Chapter 6 for further details.

Social work students

NHS Business Services Authority social work bursary (England)

Studying in London	£3,762.50 per year
Studying outside London	£3,362.50 per year

Social Care Wales social work bursary (Wales)	£2,500 per year
Office of Social Services social work bursary (Northern Ireland)	£4,000 per year

Teacher training students

Teacher training bursary (England and Wales)
Amount depends on subject studied and undergraduate degree classification held

Postgraduates

Postgraduate loan for doctoral degree (England and Wales)	£25,000 for duration of course

Postgraduate loan for master's degree

England	£10,609 for duration of course
Wales	£13,000 for duration of course

Postgraduate tuition fee loan (Northern Ireland)	£5,500

Other sources

Professional and career development loan	£300 to £10,000 for duration of course

Part 1

Student support

Chapter 1

Further education student support

This chapter covers:
1. Student support in England (below)
2. Student support in Wales (p13)
3. Student support in Northern Ireland (p16)

Basic facts
- Financial support available for further education students is generally split between that for students aged 16 to 19 and that for those aged 19 and over.
- The support is different in England, Wales and Northern Ireland. In England, most support is discretionary; you are not guaranteed any assistance. In Wales and Northern Ireland, support usually depends on your income, but may not be guaranteed.

In this chapter, the term 'student' is used to refer to someone on a further education course or programme. You may be referred to as a 'learner' by your college or learning provider, or by other agencies.

1. Student support in England

In England, funding for further education is largely in the form of discretionary awards made by individual colleges and local providers, along with a few national entitlement-based schemes. Many students aged 19 or over must pay fees for their courses, although they may be able to access loans to cover the cost.

Support for students in England is funded by the Education and Skills Funding Agency (ESFA).

Support for 16–19-year-olds

Tuition fees

Subject to certain residency conditions, which are broadly the same as for the 16–19 bursary fund (see p4), if you are under 19 on the 31 August prior to your enrolment and you are starting either a full- or part-time further education course funded by the ESFA, you do not have to pay tuition fees. Some private colleges or providers, however, may charge a fee.

16–19 bursary fund

The 16–19 bursary fund is the main form of support for the costs of learning for those aged 16 to 19. To be eligible, you must have been aged under 19 on the 31 August in the academic year you start your course.

The fund pays a guaranteed amount to a small number of students who meet specific criteria (see below). For most people, however, payment is at the discretion of the local learning provider – ie, your college, school or work-based learning provider. Amounts are not guaranteed, and funding is limited. If you are aged 19 or over, you may be able to get a discretionary bursary if you are continuing on a course you began before you turned 19 or if you have an education, health and care plan.

Who is eligible

You must be studying at a recognised school, sixth-form college, further education college or with a work-based learning provider. This can include traineeship programmes, but you cannot receive bursary funding if you are undertaking a waged apprenticeship. You must also meet certain residency requirements. You must be:

- a UK citizen or a person who is 'settled' in the UK within the meaning of the Immigration Act 1971 (ie, you have the right of abode or indefinite leave to enter or remain), and ordinarily resident in the UK for the three years prior to the start of the course; *or*
- a European Union (EU) citizen (or her/his spouse, civil partner or child) and ordinarily resident in the European Economic Area (EEA – see p22) or Switzerland for three years prior to the start of the course; *or*
- an EEA or Turkish migrant worker (or her/his spouse, civil partner or child) ordinarily resident in the UK at the start of the course and ordinarily resident in the EEA for the three years prior to the start of the course; *or*
- an officially recognised refugee (or her/his spouse, civil partner or child), or you must have been granted humanitarian protection; *or*
- the child of a diplomat.

Note: some temporary absences abroad may be disregarded when assessing your entitlement. Rules on residency are complicated, so if you are in doubt, speak to an adviser in the student services department in your college or contact either UKCISA or the National Union of Students (NUS). See Appendix 2 for the contact details.

There are special rules if a student from England studies in Wales or Scotland, and vice versa. If you are a student living in Wales, but travelling to England for your course, you should first apply for an education maintenance allowance in Wales (see p13) if you are eligible. You are not entitled to apply for the vulnerable students bursary (see below), although you can apply for a discretionary bursary. Any support received from Wales is taken into account when assessing need.

Students living in England and studying at a general further education college in Wales should apply for help through the Financial Contingency Fund (see p15). Students living in England and studying at a sixth-form college or special college in Wales should apply to their home local authority for help from the 16–19 bursary fund. Students living in England are not entitled to apply for a Welsh education maintenance allowance.

If you are a student living in Scotland, but travelling to England for your course, you should apply for an education maintenance allowance in Scotland. See CPAG's *Benefits for Students in Scotland Handbook* for more details. You are not entitled to support from the 16–19 bursary fund in England. Students living in England, but travelling to Scotland for their course, should apply to their home local authority for help from the 16–19 bursary fund, and are not entitled to apply for a Scottish education maintenance allowance.

Guaranteed funding

You can receive a bursary of at least £1,200 a year if you are:

- in local authority care, including if you are an unaccompanied asylum-seeking child; *or*
- a care leaver; *or*
- in receipt of universal credit (UC) or income support (IS) because you are financially supporting yourself and anyone dependent on and living with you, such as your child or partner; *or*
- a disabled young person getting both employment and support allowance (ESA) or UC and disability living allowance (DLA) or personal independence payment (PIP) in your own right.

You must provide evidence that you qualify – eg, a letter from your local authority confirming you were in care, or from Jobcentre Plus confirming you get a relevant benefit. **Note:** if you claim ESA in your own right while living with your parent(s), any child benefit s/he gets for you stops.

The bursary can be paid in one lump sum or in instalments. The total amount must be at least £1,200, although providers can pay more if they consider it appropriate. Payment may be made in one lump sum, regular cash payments, or in the form of travel passes or other in-kind support, or a combination of these. If your course lasts less than a year, your bursary payment is reduced pro rata. Payment is withheld if you stop attending your course.

Guaranteed bursaries for vulnerable students are not taken into account when calculating your entitlement to means-tested benefits (see Chapter 22).

General funds

For most students, support from the 16–19 bursary fund is not guaranteed. However, providers can make payments to support students who would otherwise face barriers to participation. This might include funding to meet the cost of books, equipment and transport, or other costs as appropriate.

Providers have the discretion to decide who should receive support, how much to pay and whether any conditions should be attached – eg, relating to attendance or behaviour.

Providers can also choose to buy books or equipment on behalf of individuals or groups of students, if they consider them to be in need (the fund should not be used to buy equipment for all students regardless of their situation). In other words, you may not receive any support in cash and you may have to return any books or equipment provided in this way.

If you are unhappy about a provider's decision, you can complain through its standard complaints procedure.

Armed forces bereavement scholarship scheme

The armed forces bereavement scholarship scheme provides additional support for children of servicemen/women killed on active duty since 1990. The scheme offers an annual grant of £1,500 per year (2018/19 rates) to help with the costs of learning on further education courses lasting up to three years. It does not pay for repeat years.

To qualify, your parent must have died while in service with the UK armed forces and her/his death must be attributable to that service.

Parent

A person counts as your '**parent**' if s/he was your biological or adoptive parent, or you were the subject of a special guardianship order, or if s/he was your step-parent and had financial responsibility for you. A foster parent does not count.

If your parent dies while you are in further education, support can be backdated to the start of the current term. It starts from the next term if s/he dies during a vacation.

Support is not means tested. You must study at an institution in the UK, although you do not have to be resident in the UK. If you go on to university, you can receive further help from the scheme (see p104).

Further information is at www.gov.uk/support-military-bereaved-children.

Care to Learn

Care to Learn is a scheme funded by the ESFA to help young parents in England pay for their childcare costs while in full-time or part-time further education, Foundation Learning or other non-employed work-based learning schemes. If you are eligible, the scheme pays for the costs of registered childcare while you are at school, college or on placement, including fees that must be paid during holidays, deposits and registration fees, 'taster' sessions for up to five days, plus the cost of transport to and from the childcare provider. You can claim up to a maximum of £175 a week per child if you live in London or up to £160 a week per child if you live elsewhere.

The amount you receive is not taken into account as income when working out your entitlement to social security benefits and tax credits.

However, if you are in receipt of childcare help through UC, working tax credit or a learning programme funded by the European Social Fund, you cannot get help from Care to Learn. You are also expected to take up your full entitlement to a government-funded early education place, but Care to Learn can pay for any additional costs. Your local authority can advise you on your entitlement.

You can apply if you were aged under 20 at the start of your course, living in England and caring for your own child(ren). You must want to start or continue a publicly funded course at school or sixth-form college, or to start a course at a further education college. If you are studying on a course in Scotland or Wales, you can receive help, but your usual place of residence must be in England.

The scheme only funds registered or approved childcare. If you are uncertain whether or not your childcare is registered or approved, speak to your college's student services department. If you have informal childcare arrangements, you can apply for support through the discretionary support funds (see p11).

You must meet residency conditions similar to those for higher education support (see p21). However, there are some differences – eg, asylum seekers under the age of 18 can receive help from Care to Learn, and asylum seekers aged 18 and 19 can receive help if they are also care leavers.

For further information, including how to apply, see www.gov.uk/care-to-learn or phone 0800 121 8989 (textphone 0800 917 6048).

Transport

Local authorities have responsibility for ensuring appropriate provision of home-to-school or home-to-college transport for those aged 16 to 18.[1] This might not be free of charge. Contact your college or local authority for further information, or see www.gov.uk/subsidised-college-transport-16-19 for details of local policies. Many colleges and sixth-form colleges provide subsidised transport – ask them for details.

Meals

Further education providers are required to provide free meals to disadvantaged young people. You are eligible if you meet the residency conditions for learner support (see p4), and are aged 16–18 on the 31 August prior to the academic year. To receive free meals, you must be regarded as 'disadvantaged'. This means that either you or your parents receive certain benefits or your/their income is below

£16,190 for the purposes of child tax credit (see Chapter 19). From 1 April 2018, you are eligible for free meals if you or your parents get UC and your/their net earnings do not exceed £7,400 a year.

If you started your course before 1 April 2018 and were eligible for free meals, you can continue to receive them until you complete your course, even if your/ your family's income is more than this amount.

The free meal does not have to be a lunch if, because of the pattern of your course, breakfast would be more suitable. Ask your college or learning provider for more information on its policy. Guidance for colleges and providers is at www.gov.uk/guidance/16-to-19-funding-free-meals-in-further-education-funded-institutions.

Residential bursaries

If a course you want to do is not available locally, you may be able to get help with accommodation for one further afield. Some specialist colleges that concentrate on agriculture, horticulture or art and design offer residential bursaries through the discretionary support funds. There are 50 of these colleges – a list is available at www.gov.uk/guidance/16-to-19-education-financial-support-for-students. See p11 for more information about assistance from the discretionary support funds. The bursaries are available for full-time study and are also for travel costs if you have to live at home but travel significant distances to college.

If you wish to study a course not on the above list, but which is not available locally, you may be able to receive help under the residential support scheme. This offers up to £3,458 a year (£4,079 in London) for accommodation costs, provided the course is your first level two or level three qualification, requires 15 hours' attendance a week, is at least 10 weeks long and is not available within 15 miles or a two-hour return journey of your home. You must also be ordinarily resident in England and, to receive support in the 2018/19 academic year, you must be aged 16 or over but under 19 on 31 August 2018. If you are 19 or over, you are eligible for a bursary if you are continuing on a course you began when you were under 19, or you have special educational needs and have an education, health and care plan. The amount you receive depends on your family income – in general, colleges must ensure that support is targeted at those students 'facing the most significant financial barriers to participation'. More information is available from www.gov.uk/residential-support-scheme.

Disabled students

Colleges administer funds for students with learning difficulties or disabilities. If you have additional needs or costs related to a learning difficulty or disability, ask your college or learning provider for information about how to access extra help.

Asylum seekers

Although most public funds are not available to you, if you are an unaccompanied asylum seeker aged under 18, you can apply to the 16–19 bursary fund (see p4) for assistance. This can only be in-kind support and not cash. If you are under 18 (or under 20 and a care leaver) and have childcare costs, you can also apply for help from the Care to Learn scheme (see p6).

For other sources of funding, contact the the Ruth Hayman Trust at www.ruthhaymantrust.org.uk.

Support for students aged 19 and over

Tuition fees

In general, students who are 19 and over must pay tuition fees for further education.

Subject to residency conditions, free tuition is available in certain circumstances, including if you are:

- studying a basic literacy or numeracy course;
- aged 19 or over and undertaking GCSE maths and/or English, provided you do not already hold these at grades A–C or at level four or higher;
- aged 19–23 at the start of a course of vocational training that leads to your first level two qualification (the equivalent of five GCSEs at grades A*–C or at level four or higher), but note that the GCSEs themselves are not funded under this provision;
- aged 19–23 at the start of a course for your first full level three qualification;
- aged 19–23 at the start of your course and you are a level four 'jumper' – ie, you have a level two qualification and are moving directly onto your first level four course without having studied for a level three qualification;
- aged 19–23 at the start of your course and undertaking an apprenticeship (intermediate, advanced or higher level);
- aged 24 or over at the start of your course and undertaking an apprenticeship;
- aged 19–24 and have an education, health and care plan, or a section 139a learning difficulty assessment, for certain courses that meet the aims of the plan/assessment;
- aged 19 or over at the start of your course and you get jobseeker's allowance, or ESA and you are in the work-related activity group, or UC and you must undertake skills training;
- aged 19 or over at the start of your course and you get another social security benefit in addition to the ones in the bullet point above, at the discretion of your college or learning provider;
- aged 24 or over and you have left the British armed forces after 10 years' service or you have been medically discharged due to injury in active service, for the first full level two or level three qualification; *or*
- studying an English as a second or other language qualification, in certain circumstances.

If you qualify, the ESFA pays your tuition fees for the course. The rules are complicated, so check whether you are eligible with your college or learning provider. Detailed guidance is also available at www.gov.uk/guidance/sfa-funding-rules.

If you are not in any of the groups on p9, you may have to pay tuition fees. Students aged 19–23 taking courses above level three, or courses at level two and three after their first such course (other than apprenticeships), and students aged 24 or over at the start of the course and undertaking qualifications at level two or above (other than apprenticeships), must pay fees in most cases. There are loans available to help (see below). If you have difficulty meeting the costs of your fees, get advice from your student services department on your options.

Advanced learner loan

If you are aged 19 or over (or aged 24 or over if your course started before 1 August 2016) at the start of your further education course and are charged fees, you may be eligible for a student loan to cover the cost. Loans are available for courses at levels three, four, five and six (levels three and four only if you started your course before 1 August 2016).

Note: if you are aged 19–23 and have not yet completed a full level two or full level three course, you should not be charged tuition fees for your first such course.

The loans are administered by the Student Loans Company on behalf of the ESFA.

You can take out up to four loans, either concurrently in the case of A levels (ie, you can have four at once, if you are taking up to four A levels in one year), or consecutively (ie, four separate years of loan funding) for other qualifications. The minimum loan you can get is £300; the maximum cannot exceed the 'funding rate' stipulated by the ESFA for the course, which can be several thousand pounds. You may also be restricted to the amount your college or learning provider is willing or able to make available, and your loan may therefore be lower than the fees you are charged.

The residency rules that apply to higher education student support (see p21) also apply. The rules can be complicated, so if you are in any doubt about your entitlement, get advice from your student services department.

Repayment terms and conditions are the same as those for loans in higher education taken out by students who started their courses on or after 1 September 2012 (see p31). Repayments start once you have completed your course. Although it is possible to make voluntary repayments, you should consider whether this is of financial benefit to you, given that outstanding loans are written off after 30 years and many people may not repay their loans in full. Ask your student services department for advice.

If you take out one or more advanced learner loans in order to pay for an 'access to higher education' course, these are written off if you proceed to higher education and complete the course. However, if you take out loans for other further education courses, these are not written off if you go on to complete a higher education course.

More information on advanced learner loans, including links to the application form and guidance documents and resources for advisers and other intermediaries, is available at www.gov.uk/advanced-learner-loan.

Disabled students

Colleges administer funds for students with learning difficulties or disabilities. If you have additional needs or costs related to a learning difficulty or disability, ask your college or learning provider for information about how to access extra help. **Note:** additional funding for disabled students in receipt of an advanced learner loan should come from the Loan Bursary Fund instead (see p12).

Discretionary support funds

You may be able to get additional help for your living or course costs through discretionary learner support funds. These are amounts of money given to colleges and other providers by the ESFA for students in need. You must meet the same residency criteria as for students in higher education to receive any support (see p21). If you get an advanced learner loan, you must apply to a separate bursary scheme (see p12), although in practice the rules of both schemes are similar. You can receive help from these funds if you are undertaking a traineeship, but not if you are receiving help for childcare and/or travel through Jobcentre Plus. There are three types of payments:

- hardship funds (see below);
- residential bursaries (see p8); *and*
- childcare support (see below).

Hardship funds

These are general funds to enable students to access a course or stay on a course, or to encourage attainment. They can pay for books and equipment, transport, course-related trips, emergencies or, in exceptional circumstances, tuition fees.

Your college or learning provider has discretion on how to prioritise spending and on the assessment criteria, so the support available to you depends on your college. If you want to challenge a decision, your college or learning provider must have an appeals procedure.

Childcare support

Support can be offered to meet the costs of any registered childcare for students aged 20 or over. The support available is unlikely to be more than that available through the Care to Learn scheme (approximately £5,000 a child), but this may differ between colleges and providers. Funds are often oversubscribed and no particular sum is guaranteed. Payments can be made directly to the childcare provider or to you, depending on your college's/provider's policy. If you are aged under 20 and starting a new course, apply to the Care to Learn scheme (see p6) for help with registered childcare.

Loan Bursary Fund

The Loan Bursary Fund provides support for disadvantaged and vulnerable students. All students who have had a loan approved by Student Finance England and have registered for their course are potentially eligible to apply, depending on their needs and circumstances.

The Fund provides discretionary support for students in hardship and for other expenses, such as childcare and travel. It can be used at the discretion of the provider to cover a student's needs in an emergency. Additional learning support is also available – eg, for teaching assistant support, specialist equipment, technology and necessary adjustments under the Equality Act 2010.

The bursaries are granted at the discretion of each college.

Meals

Some students aged 19–25 who are subject to a learning difficulty assessment or an education health and care plan may be entitled to free meals. You must be regarded as 'disadvantaged'. This means that either you or your parents receive certain benefits or your/their income is below £16,190 for the purposes of child tax credit (see Chapter 19). From 1 April 2018, you are eligible for free meals if you or your parents get UC and your/their net earnings do not exceed £7,400 a year.

If you started your course before 1 April 2018 and were eligible for free meals, you can continue to recieve them until you complete your course, even if your/ your family's income is more than this amount.

The free meal does not have to be a lunch if, because of the pattern of your course, breakfast would be more suitable. Ask your college or learning provider for more information on its policy. Guidance for colleges and providers is at www.gov.uk/guidance/16-to-19-funding-free-meals-in-further-education-funded-institutions.

Other grants

City and Guilds bursary

A small number of bursaries are available to help with the costs of study for students on qualifying City and Guilds or former National Proficiency Tests Council courses. To qualify, you must be living in the UK and intending to study in the UK. Applications are considered twice a year, in April and September. For more information, see www.cityandguildsgroup.com/bursaries.

Work Programme training allowance

If you are on the Work Programme, you may be able to get a training allowance to help you gain qualifications to improve your employability. You are exempt from work-related activity requirements for benefits while you are in receipt of the training allowance.

Apprenticeships

If you are undertaking an apprenticeship at any level, your employer must pay you at least the minimum wage for apprenticeships. If you are under 19, this is £3.70 per hour. If you are aged 19 or over, the minimum wage is £3.70 an hour for the first year of the apprenticeship, after which you must be paid at the standard rate for your age. This is at least £5.90 an hour if you are aged 20, at least £7.38 an hour if you are aged 21 or over, or at least £7.83 an hour if you are aged 25 or over. See www.gov.uk/topic/further-education-skills/apprenticeships for further information. These minimum wage rates apply from 1 April 2018 and are reviewed annually. **Note:** these are the minimum wage rates and many employers offer more. However, some employers pay less, particularly in otherwise low-paid sectors like hairdressing and social care. If you are being paid less than the correct minimum wage rate, this is illegal, and you should contact Acas. See www.gov.uk/pay-and-work-rights for more information.

Professional and career development loan

Students on further education courses can apply for a professional and career development loan (see p104). However, consider carefully whether or not this is the most affordable option for you and get financial advice.

---

2. Student support in Wales

Support for 16–19-year-olds

Tuition fees

Subject to certain residency conditions, if you are under 19 on the 31 August prior to your enrolment and you are starting either a full- or part-time further education course funded by the Welsh government, you do not have to pay tuition fees. Some private colleges or providers, however, may charge a fee.

Education maintenance allowance

The education maintenance allowance is a payment of £30 a week (paid fortnightly) to eligible students who meet certain course, residence and income conditions.

To receive an education maintenance allowance:
- you must be participating in a programme of full-time education (at least 12 guided learning hours for at least 10 weeks) at a recognised school, sixth-form college or further education college;
- you must meet certain residence conditions (see p47). You do not have to study in Wales to qualify, provided you live in Wales and your school or college is participating in the scheme;
- you must have been aged between 16 and 18 on 31 August 2018.

In addition, your gross (before tax) household income must be below £20,817 if you are the only child in the household, or £23,077 if there are additional young people studying full time and eligible for child benefit in the household. The income assessed is usually that of your parents or guardians. If you live with only one parent, your other parent's income is not assessed and any maintenance s/he pays is not counted as income. Benefits (including child benefit) and tax credits are disregarded when calculating your household income. The household income figure used is that for the previous tax year. For applications for 2018/19, this is the 2016/17 tax year. Any income you have (eg, from a part-time job) is not included.

Provided you meet the other standard conditions, if you are an 'independent student' (see below), you automatically receive the full allowance of £30.

Independent students

You count as an '**independent student**' if you:
– are responsible for a child; *or*
– live apart from your parents and are estranged from them, and you are not under the care of the local authority; *or*
– are under the care of the local authority – eg, with foster parents; *or*
– are classed as a young person in custody.

Payments are available for up to three full academic years and depend on your meeting the conditions set out in your agreement (see below).

Applications made after the start of the course can only be backdated for 28 days, so it is important to apply within 28 days of the start of your course.

Education maintenance allowance payments are disregarded when calculating your family's entitlement to means-tested benefits. Therefore, you can receive an education maintenance allowance in addition to any benefits you or your family are claiming.

Education maintenance allowance agreement

To receive your weekly payments, you are required to sign an education maintenance allowance agreement provided by your college or learning provider (this may be referred to as a contract or something similar). It sets out what you are expected to achieve in terms of attendance and academic work and is signed by you, your parents (or another responsible adult) and the college/learning provider. If you fail to meet part of the contract in any week (eg, you do not attend classes or hand in homework), you are not paid your allowance for that week.

Although payments depend on 100 per cent attendance, some types of absence are permitted or 'authorised'. However, it is advisable to notify your college or learning provider of any absences if you want to be considered for your payment and any bonuses, particularly if you know in advance that you will be absent.

Authorised absences can include sickness, unavoidable medical appointments, religious holidays, emergency caring duties, driving tests, family funerals or representative duties such as a college governors' meeting. **Note:** jury service is not normally considered to be an authorised absence, as the guidance states you should seek to defer your service to a holiday period or until after the course.

Holidays are not generally considered acceptable reasons for absence. Colleges make the final decision on authorised absences, and you should discuss with your own provider any absence you may have to take.

Passport to Study grant

A small number of local authorities in Wales offer extra funding for young people in further education whose parents are not in paid work, or who are receiving benefits because of having a low income or a disability. The funding was previously called Passport to Study. Contact your local authority to see whether it offers any grants, and what terms and conditions apply.

Financial Contingency Fund

If you are studying at a college, you may be able to get additional help for your living or course costs from the Financial Contingency Fund. This is similar to the discretionary support funds in England (see p11).

Support for students aged 19 and over

Tuition fees

There is no guaranteed help with fees if you are aged 19 or over. However, some colleges may run schemes providing full or partial remission if, for example, you are on a low income, are disabled or are in receipt of means-tested benefits. Ask your college what it provides.

Welsh government learning grant

If you are aged 19 or over on 1 September 2018 and on a low income, you may be eligible for a means-tested Welsh government learning grant of up to £1,500.[2] A grant of at least £450 is available if you are on a full-time course (500 contact hours or more a year) and your household income is below £18,371. If your household income is below £12,236, £750 is available. The full £1,500 is available if your household income is less than £6,121. Part-time students (those who have between 275 and 499 contact hours a year) can receive a reduced grant of £300, £450 or £750 on the same income bands. The household income figure used is that for the previous tax year. For applications in 2018/19, this is the tax year 2016/17.

You are not entitled if you have previously received a Welsh government learning grant for a course at the same level.

The grants are administered through Student Finance Wales, but students may attend any institution in the UK. More information is available at www.studentfinancewales.co.uk/fe.

Financial Contingency Fund

If you are studying at a college, you may be able to get additional help for your living or course costs from the Financial Contingency Fund. This is similar to the discretionary support funds in England (see p11).

Other grants

Work Programme training allowance

Welsh students may be able to receive the Work Programme training allowance (see p12).

Apprenticeships

Apprentices in Wales must be paid the minimum wage at the appropriate rates (see p13). Apprentices in Wales do not pay tuition fees. More information is available from Careers Wales at www.careerswales.com.

Professional and career development loan

Students on further education courses can apply for a professional and career development loan (see p104). However, consider carefully whether or not this is the most affordable option for you and obtain financial advice.

---

3. **Student support in Northern Ireland**

Support for 16–19-year-olds

Tuition fees

If you are a full-time student, your tuition fees are paid in full. If you are a part-time student, concessionary tuition fees may apply.

Education maintenance allowance

In Northern Ireland, the education maintenance allowance scheme is similar to that in Wales (see p13). However, there are some differences. Students in Northern Ireland are entitled to an education maintenance allowance if they turned 16, 17, 18 or 19 between 2 July 2017 and 1 July 2018. Your course must comprise at least 15 guided learning hours a week.

You are eligible for a payment of £30 a week if you are the only young person in your household or are an 'independent' student (see p14) and your gross (before tax) annual household income is £20,500 or less. If you have one or more siblings either aged under 16, or under 20 and in full-time education or training, your gross (before tax) annual household income must be £22,500 or less.

You are paid fortnightly.

Two £100 bonus payments are available if you have met the goals in your education maintenance allowance agreement (see p14). These are usually provided in January and June.

More information on Northern Irish education maintenance allowances is at www.nidirect.gov.uk/articles/education-maintenance-allowance-explained.

Care to Learn

The Department for the Economy's Care to Learn scheme is designed to help young parents in Northern Ireland pay their childcare costs while in full- or part-time further education. If you are eligible, the scheme pays for the costs of registered childcare while you are at school, college or on placement, including fees that must be paid during holidays, plus the cost of transport to and from the childcare provider, up to a maximum of £165 per child a week. It does not affect, nor is it affected by, any benefits and tax credits you may receive.

You can apply if you are aged 16 or over but under 20 at the start of your course, live in Northern Ireland and fulfil certain residency requirements, and you care for your own child(ren). You must wish to start or continue a publicly funded course at school or a sixth-form college, or to start a further education or higher education course at a further education college. If you are already receiving childcare funding from other government sources (eg, through working tax credit), you are not eligible for this scheme and should apply to the college's support fund if you need further help.

The scheme only funds childcare from a provider registered with the Health and Social Care Trust.

More details are available at www.nidirect.gov.uk/articles/care-learn-scheme.

Support for students aged 19 and over

Tuition fees

You are not charged tuition fees if you are studying a full-time eligible vocational course up to level three – eg, NVQ level three.

Full-time course

A 'full-time course' is defined as a course lasting for a minimum of 30 weeks and comprising at least 15 hours and at least seven sessions a week, or 21 hours a week with no sessional requirement. GCSE, A level or AS level subjects are not eligible, except when studied in combination with a relevant vocational qualification at a similar level.

If your course does not qualify for tuition fee remission, you may be able to receive discretionary help from your college support fund.

Further education awards

If you are on a full-time further education course, you can apply to the regional Education Authority office for a non-repayable maintenance grant, called a further education award. This can also provide additional help with tuition fees, if required. There are also extra allowances, similar to those available in higher education (see p68), for students with dependants, disabled students and care leavers. All these grants (except for disabled students' allowances) are means tested.

There are residency requirements, and you cannot be in receipt of another award, such as an education maintenance allowance (see p16) or a Department of Agriculture, Environment and Rural Affairs grant (see p19), at the same time. Further education awards are discretionary – there are insufficient funds to provide all applicants with grants, so you should apply as soon as possible.

Note: the closing date for applications for each year is the 1 September prior to the start of the course for full-time students, and the end of September for part-time students.

For further information, see www.eani.org.uk/i-want-to/apply-for-a-further-education-award, or contact The Education Authority, Further Education Awards Section, 1 Hospital Road, Omagh, Co Tyrone BT79 0AW, tel: 028 8225 4546 or email: feawards-wr@eani.org.uk.

Maintenance grant

You may qualify for a means-tested maintenance grant of up to £2,092. The maximum amount is available if your household income is less than £21,331, and a partial amount if your household income is between £21,331 and £38,805. No maintenance grant is payable if your household income exceeds £38,805.

Childcare grant

If you have children and incur childcare costs, you can claim a childcare grant. How much you receive depends on your household income and the number of children you have. See www.eani.org.uk for more details.

If you are aged under 20 at the start of the course, you should apply to the Care to Learn scheme in Northern Ireland to cover your childcare costs (see p17).

Disabled students

Disabled students who require additional support should apply to their college or learning provider for assistance. Contact the disability adviser at the college in the first instance.

Part-time courses

Part-time courses attract funding at lower levels. If fees are charged, you may qualify for fee support of up to £465 a year. A means-tested course costs grant of up to £265 is available. You cannot receive any help if your income exceeds £25,000 a year. See www.eani.org.uk for more details.

Support funds

There are two discretionary funds administered by colleges that offer additional help if you are a part-time or full-time further education student aged 19 or over. Support funds are aimed at those experiencing financial difficulties and may include help with living costs and/or fees. Eligibility criteria apply. The additional support funds are aimed at students with learning difficulties who are not in receipt of other help for disabled students, such as a disabled students' allowance, and can be used to pay for additional support, such as IT hardware or assistance with notetaking.

Other grants

Department of Agriculture, Environment and Rural Affairs grant

If you are attending a further education course at the Enniskillen, Greenmount or Loughry campuses of the College of Agriculture, Food and Rural Enterprise, you may be eligible for financial support from the Department of Agriculture, Environment and Rural Affairs.

To be eligible, you must be ordinarily resident in Northern Ireland and meet certain other residency requirements. You can be any age.

A means-tested living costs grant of up to £1,659 is available if you live in your parents' home, or up to £2,362 if you do not. Further allowances may be available if you have children or adult dependants, or if you are a care leaver or have a disability.

Further information can be found at www.cafre.ac.uk/study-at-cafre/financial-support.

Professional and career development loan

Students on further education courses can apply for a professional and career development loan (see p104). However, consider carefully whether or not this is the most affordable option for you and obtain financial advice.

Notes

1. Student support in England
1 s509 EA 1996

2. Student support in Wales
2 E(ALGS)(W) Regs

Chapter 2

Undergraduate student support: England

This chapter covers:
1. Full-time undergraduates (p21)
2. Part-time undergraduates (p35)
3. How income affects student support (p39)
4. Discretionary and institutional funds (p44)

There are different systems of undergraduate student support in England, Wales, Northern Ireland and Scotland. See Chapter 3 for details of the system in Wales, Chapter 4 for Northern Ireland and CPAG's *Benefits for Students in Scotland Handbook* for details of the system in Scotland.

Students living in England who wish to study in Wales, Northern Ireland or Scotland receive the same package of support as though they were studying in England.

Basic facts
– Undergraduate students can apply for a mixture of grants and loans, depending on their personal circumstances.
– The type of financial support available depends on several factors, including when the course starts, its length, the discipline and whether the course is full time or part time.
– Separate provision is available for social work, initial teacher training and some healthcare students.
– Institutions should have funds to help students in hardship and to support retention and progression.

Future changes
The Higher Education and Research Act 2017 introduces some significant changes to the higher education sector. However, the proposal of different rates of fees, directly linked to institutional outcomes of the Teaching Excellence Framework, has been put on hold until

an independent review has taken place. The Act allows the introduction of an alternative student finance product that is compliant with Islamic finance laws. The timetable for its introduction is still unclear – it will not be available until 2020/21 at the earliest.

1. Full-time undergraduates

Full-time undergraduates in England on eligible courses (see p24), and who are personally eligible (see below), can apply for financial assistance from the Department for Education. Funding is administered by Student Finance England on its behalf. There have been a number of changes to student funding and support over the last 10 years, and so the tuition fees you can be charged and the support you can receive for both your fees and living costs depends on when you started your course.

Separate provision is available for part-time undergraduates (see p35) and students studying vocational courses (see Chapter 6).

Who is eligible for support

To receive any type of student support, you must be 'personally eligible' by meeting residence conditions (see below) and be studying an eligible course (see p24).

Residence conditions

To be eligible for support, you must meet residence conditions.[1] This usually means that you must:

- be settled in the UK within the meaning of the Immigration Act 1971 (this includes those with British citizenship, right of abode or indefinite leave to enter/remain in the UK); *and*
- be resident in England on the first day of the first academic year; *and*
- have lived in the 'UK and islands'[2] for three years immediately before the start of the course, although temporary absences for reasons such as vacations or temporary employment abroad can be disregarded. Service abroad in the regular UK armed forces is always disregarded; *and*
- not have spent any of the three years in the 'UK and islands' mainly for the purpose of receiving full-time education. If you were in full-time education during the three years, you can still receive support if you can prove this was not the main reason for your being in the UK.

Following a ruling by the Supreme Court in 2016, you are also eligible if you are currently resident in England and:[3]

* you are either under 18 and have spent seven years living in the UK prior to the start of the course or you are 18 and over and have spent at least half your life (or at least 20 years) living in the UK; *and*
* you have had three years' lawful residence in the UK prior to the start of the course for purposes other than full-time education.

If you meet the residence conditions, you are known as a 'home student'. You are charged lower fees than students from overseas and you qualify for full student support, including loans for fees and maintenance, for courses which start on or after 1 August 2016.

Residency rules are very complex. If you are unsure whether or not you are eligible, you may wish to speak to an adviser in your institution or students' union.

European Union nationals

Broadly, if you are a European Union (EU) national, you can count as a home student and be eligible for support with both tuition fees and living costs if you have been resident in the UK for the five years immediately before the start of the course and you are resident in England or Wales on the first day of the first academic year. If any of this time was spent mainly for the purpose of receiving full-time education, you must have been ordinarily resident in the UK, elsewhere in the European Economic Area (EEA) or Switzerland immediately before the five-year period began.[4] **Note:** this rule was amended in 2016 and the five-year residency rule applies to students starting a course for the first time on or after 1 August 2016. If your course began before this date, or after this date but you applied for support before 25 March 2016, only three years of residence are required.[5]

The European Economic Area

The '**European Economic Area**' comprises the member states of the EU plus Norway, Liechtenstein and Iceland.

The current member states of the EU are: Austria, Belgium, Bulgaria, Croatia, Cyprus, Czech Republic, Denmark, Estonia, Finland, France, Germany, Greece, Hungary, Ireland, Italy, Latvia, Lithuania, Luxembourg, Malta, Netherlands, Poland, Portugal, Romania, Slovenia, Slovakia, Spain, Sweden and the UK.

Alternatively, if you have permanent residence after having become settled in the UK, you may qualify as a home student. This can also be granted if you are a 'relevant family member' of a person with permanent residence and you have been resident in the UK for three years or more.[6] However, if any of this time was spent mainly for the purpose of full-time education, you must have been resident in the UK or elsewhere in the EEA or Switzerland immediately before the three-year period.

If you are a national of an EU member state (or a 'relevant family member' of an EU national) and coming to the UK to undertake higher education, you may be eligible for help with fees only. You must have lived in the EEA and/or Switzerland for three years before the start of your course, and no part of the three-year period should have been mainly for the purposes of full-time education.

Relevant family member

A **'relevant family member'** includes children, grandchildren, a spouse or civil partner or, in some cases, dependent direct 'ascendants', such as parents or grandparents. If you are an eligible direct descendant of an EEA worker who is no longer working in the UK, you may still be eligible for student support if you came to the UK to accompany your parent.

If a new country joins the EU, it is considered to have always been in the EEA when determining the three- or five-year period. For example, although Croatia joined the EU on 1 July 2013, it is regarded as having always been part of the EEA for the purposes of assessing support.

Following the result of the referendum on the UK's membership of the EU, the Department for Education has stated that students from other EU countries who started their courses before 2018/19, or who commence a course in 2018/19 or 2019/20 and who have been assessed as eligible for funding, will continue to receive funding as normal until they complete their course. Rules for students starting courses in future years are uncertain – check the Student Finance England website.

Migrant workers

If you are a non-UK, EEA or Swiss migrant worker and are, or have been, working in the UK (employed, self-employed or as a frontier worker), or you are a 'relevant family member' (see above) of such a migrant worker, you may be eligible for support with both tuition fees and living costs as a home student. You must also have three years' residence in the EEA and/or Switzerland.

If you are a UK national or the relevant family member of a UK national and have been living in another EEA country or Switzerland and you return to the UK to study, you may be eligible for support as a home student if you were ordinarily resident and settled in the UK immediately prior to leaving, and you are now settled and ordinarily resident in the UK on the first day of the first year of your course. You or your family member must have been resident in another EEA country as a student, worker, self-sufficient or self-employed person. You must apply for support in the part of the UK in which you were living before you left.[7]

If you are the child of a Turkish migrant worker, you can also pay home fees and receive support if your parents have been ordinarily resident in the UK and lawfully employed, and if you are ordinarily resident in the UK on the first day of the first academic year of the course and have been ordinarily resident in the EEA, Switzerland and/or Turkey for the three years before the start of the course.[8]

If you are the child of a Swiss worker still living in the UK as a worker, student, self-employed or self-sufficient person, you may qualify for student support if you have been resident in the UK or elsewhere in the EEA/Switzerland for the three years before the first day of the first academic year of your course, and you are ordinarily resident in the UK by that date. If, during the three years, your main purpose for being in the UK or EEA/Switzerland was for full-time education, you must have been ordinarily resident before this date.

Note: Student Finance England checks the 'worker' status of either the student or relevant family member each term before releasing the next term's payment.

Refugees

If you are recognised as a refugee by the UK government and have lived in the 'UK and islands' since being granted this status, or you are a 'relevant family member' of such a person (see p23), you should be treated as a home student and be eligible for support with both your tuition fees and living costs (see pp27–34).[9]

If you applied for asylum and have been granted humanitarian protection or discretionary (or exceptional) leave, you may be treated as a home student for support purposes. If you have been given humanitarian protection, this need not have been by the first day of the first academic year but you must have had lawful residence before your humanitarian protection was granted.

If you have discretionary (or exceptional) leave:[10]

- and are under 18, you must have lived in the UK for at least seven years on the first day of the first year of the course;
- and are 18 or over, you must have lived in the UK for either half your life, or 20 years, on the first day of the first year of your course. **Note:** you cannot add separate periods of residency together to make up this period;
- in all cases, your residency must have been lawful and you must have had ordinary residence for three years before the first day of the first year of the course.

Residency is complex and you should speak to an adviser in your student union or university.

What is an eligible course

To be eligible for support, broadly the course must be full time (as defined by the education provider) and be:[11]

- a first degree (including foundation degrees);
- a diploma of higher education;

- a BTEC Higher National Certificate (HNC) or Higher National Diploma (HND);
- a course of initial teacher training;
- a course for the further training of teachers, or youth or community workers;
- a course to prepare for certain professional examinations of a standard higher than A level, or HNC/HND where a first degree is not required for entry;
- a course not higher than a first degree, but higher than those described in the above bullet point.

Note: some courses, particularly in art and design, can require students to undertake a foundation year or course. This is different from a foundation degree. A foundation course is normally a course of one academic year in length which you would normally be required to complete before you are offered a place on a higher education degree course.

Support for these foundation courses is often limited, as they do not usually come within the definition of 'higher education'. You may be eligible for support as a further education student (see Chapter 1). Speak to an adviser in your students' union or institution for further guidance.

Some courses particularly in science, engineering or technology, can have an integrated foundation year which forms part of the higher education course, and these consequently attract higher education funding. If in doubt about your entitlement, speak to an adviser.

Pre-registration courses in subjects allied to healthcare, such as nursing, midwifery, physiotherapy and radiography, are eligible for standard funding from Student Finance England if the course begins on or after 1 August 2017. Previously, such courses were funded via NHS bursaries, but these have now been abolished for most new students (see p86). Funding for these courses is available even if you already hold a degree or have had previous experience of higher education (see p26). Some additional support is available through the NHS in certain circumstances (see Chapter 6).

Which system of student support applies

The student support to which you are entitled depends on when you started your course. In this *Handbook*:

- students who started their course in the 2006/07 or 2007/08 academic year are referred to as **'2006 cohort'** students;
- students who started their course in the 2008/09 academic year are referred to as **'2008 cohort'** students;
- students who started their course in the 2009/10, 2010/11 or 2011/12 academic year are referred to as **'2009 cohort'** students;
- students who started their course in the 2012/13, 2013/14, 2014/15 or 2015/16 academic year are referred to as **'2012 cohort'** students;
- students who started their course in the 2016/17, 2017/18 or 2018/19 academic year are referred to as **'2016 cohort'** students.

Students in the 2006, 2008, 2009 and 2012 cohorts can apply for a package of support, which includes:
- a loan for tuition fees (see p27);
- either a maintenance grant (see p28) or special support grant (see p29);
- a loan for living costs (see p29);
- supplementary grants in particular circumstances (see p32).

2016 cohort students can apply for a package of support, which includes:
- a loan for tuition fees (see p27);
- a loan for living costs, including an enhanced rate for those eligible for benefits (see p29);
- supplementary grants in particular circumstances (see p32).

Previous study

If you have previously attended a higher education course, the amount of support you can receive on any subsequent course may be affected.[12]

If you hold an honours degree and are studying for a new qualification, unless you are covered by one of the exceptions (see below), you can only apply for a supplementary grant for travel costs, a grant for any dependants and a grant for disability-related costs.[13] You are not entitled to any other kind of support. This is regardless of where in the world you may have studied previously and how your first course was funded.

In addition, if you wish to study for a qualification of an equivalent or lower level to the one you already hold, financial support may be further restricted. Check your entitlement with an adviser.

There are some exceptions.
- Students who hold an honours degree and are undertaking a Postgraduate Certificate in Education (PGCE) or Postgraduate Diploma in Education (PGDE) course receive full funding.
- Students undertaking a further undergraduate course in certain professional subjects, such as medicine, veterinary science, architecture and social work, can receive a loan for their living costs,[14] although not a loan for tuition fees or a maintenance or special support grant, if applicable. For further details of medicine and dentistry courses, see p28.
- From the 2017/18 year, students domiciled in England who wish to start a pre-registration course in a subject allied to healthcare, such as nursing, midwifery, physiotherapy or radiography, have any previous study disregarded, including any previous degree awards. They can therefore apply for full support, subject to the usual rules on residency and income.[15]
- Students who started healthcare courses before 2017/18 and who are eligible for a means-tested NHS bursary continue to be eligible for a reduced-rate loan, whether or not they already hold an equivalent or higher level qualification.

If you do not already hold an honours degree, but have studied before, in general the maximum number of years of tuition fee loan and maintenance or special support grant funding you can receive is equivalent to the ordinary length of your course plus one year, less any years of study previously undertaken.[16] If you have studied part of a year, you are treated as if you have undertaken a full year of study. Loans for living costs are, however, unaffected.

If you are transferring courses, or undertaking an 'end-on' course (topping up from one qualification to another), these previous study rules affect you. You may be able to secure additional years of 'full' funding if you were unable to complete a previous year or course for 'compelling personal reasons', such as illness or caring responsibilities.[17] You must provide evidence of this to Student Finance England.

Further information on previous study is available from www.gov.uk/student-finance or from your student adviser.

Loan for tuition fees

All students are charged tuition fees for each year of their course. The amount you are charged depends on where you study, whether your institution has an approved 'access and participation plan' with the Office for Students, whether your institution received a rating of 'meets expectations' under the Teaching Excellence and Student Outcomes Framework, and which cohort of student you are in.

Publicly funded institutions can charge 2012 and 2016 cohort students tuition fees of up to £9,250 per academic year in 2018/19 (or up to £6,000 a year if they do not have an approved 'access and participation plan'). If you choose to study outside England, the same fees and funding arrangements apply: you may be charged up to £9,250 a year to study in Scotland, Wales and Northern Ireland.

If you are undertaking a sandwich (placement) year, fees are restricted to 20 per cent of the maximum fee (you can be charged a maximum of £1,850). If you are on an Erasmus placement, fees are restricted to 15 per cent of the maximum fee (£1,385 per year).

Continuing students who started their courses between 1 September 2006 and 31 August 2012 (2006, 2008 and 2009 cohorts) can be charged fees of up to £3,465 a year.

Note: if you transfer from one course or institution to another, this may affect the fee you are charged. Speak to an adviser if this affects you.

If you are a home (see p22) or EU student, you can apply for a loan to cover all, or part, of the cost of the fees.[18] Your income is not assessed for this. There is no requirement to take out a tuition fee loan. If you wish, you can pay all, or part of, the fee in advance. Your institution generally expects some indication of how you intend to pay your fees when you register.

The repayment terms of a tuition fee loan are the same as for an income-contingent loan for living costs (see p31).

Medicine and dentistry students

There are different fee arrangements for medicine and dentistry students, depending on whether you are undertaking a standard five-year undergraduate medicine or dentistry course, or the four-year graduate entry course.[19]

If you are on a standard five-year undergraduate course, you pay fees at the rate charged by the institution until the fifth year of study, after which you move to the NHS bursary scheme (see Chapter 6). The NHS then pays your fees in the fifth and any subsequent years. For example, if you started in 2012/13 or later your maximum fee is £9,250 in years one to four, in line with other students, and is paid in the fifth and subsequent years by the NHS.

If you are on the four-year graduate entry course and started your course in 2011/12 or earlier, you must pay the fee charged by the institution upfront in your first year, up to a maximum of £3,465. There is no loan available to help with your fees for this year. However, after the first year, you are then funded through the NHS bursary scheme.

If you started a four-year graduate entry course in 2012/13 or later, the maximum fee is £9,250 a year. In your first year, you must pay the first £3,465 of your fees. A student loan is available to cover any amount charged above this level. In your second and subsequent years, the NHS pays the first £3,465 (rising with inflation), and a student loan for fees is available for any amount charged above this.

Note: different arrangements for both standard five-year undergraduate and graduate-entry students may be introduced for those starting in 2019/20 or later. Check with your institution.

Students who hold an honours degree and who wish to study the standard undergraduate course do not have access to fee support until they reach the NHS bursary-funded stage of the course in year five.

Maintenance grant

A maintenance grant is available to pre-2016 cohort students from low-income backgrounds.[20] This grant is for your living costs. The maximum amount in 2018/19 is £3,299 if you are in the 2009 cohort and £3,593 if you are in the 2012 cohort.[21]

Part of the grant substitutes part of the loan for living costs (see below). How this is done depends on which cohort you are in.

If you are a 2009 cohort student, 50 pence of the loan is substituted for every pound of maintenance grant paid. This means that if you are eligible for the maximum maintenance grant, your loan is reduced by £1,649.[22]

Students in the 2012 cohort receive a higher grant, with a maximum payment of £3,593. They also have 50 pence of the loan substituted for every pound of maintenance grant paid, so that the maximum substitution is £1,796 if the full maintenance grant is paid.[23]

If you are eligible for means-tested benefits, the maintenance grant is taken into account as income when working out your entitlement, so if possible, make sure you apply for the special support grant instead (see below). An adviser in your university can help you with this.

Special support grant

A special support grant is available to students who started their courses before 1 September 2016 and who are eligible for means-tested benefits, such as universal credit (UC), income support and housing benefit.[24] The maximum amount in 2018/19 is £3,229 for the 2009 cohort and £3,593 for the 2012 cohort.[25] This grant is intended for course-related costs and is not taken into account as income when working out your entitlement to means-tested benefits.

The special support grant does not have a loan substitution and can be paid in addition to the loan for living costs.

Loan for living costs

In addition to a loan for tuition fees, eligible students can also apply for a loan to help with their living costs, such as food and rent. Unlike the loan for tuition fees, part of the loan for living costs depends on an income assessment (see p39). This varies, depending on which cohort you are in (see p25). You may be entitled to an additional amount of loan if your course exceeds 30 weeks and three days in the year (see p30).

Note: 'mortgage-style loans' were available to students who were eligible to receive mandatory awards before 1998. These are no longer available, but see p32 for information on repayment.

Because students starting in 2016/17, 2017/18 or 2018/19 (2016 cohort students) are not eligible for a maintenance grant or a special support grant, they can get a larger loan. Students who are aged over 60 on the first day of the first academic year of their course can receive a means-tested, reduced-rate loan of £3,680 if they are not entitled to a standard loan because of their age.[26]

Students who would have previously been entitled to the special support grant and are entitled to a means-tested benefit can receive a higher amount of loan, part of which is called the 'special support element'. This is disregarded when working out student income for benefit purposes. If you declare that you are eligible for benefits when you apply for your funding, you should be awarded this. You are then asked to provide evidence you are eligible for benefits to Student Finance England.

If you are unsure about your eligibility or whether you are receiving the correct amount of loan, speak to an adviser in your university or students' union.

Maximum amount of loan for living costs 2018/19

2016 cohort, eligible for benefits[27]

	Full-year special support element	Maintenance element	Final-year special support element	Final-year maintenance element
London	£3,680	£8,702	£3,680	£7,924
Elsewhere	£3,680	£6,236	£3,680	£5,799
Parental home	£3,680	£4,960	£3,680	£4,557
Overseas rate	£3,680	£7,410	£3,680	£6,439

2016 cohort, not eligible for benefits[28]

	Full year	Final year
London	£11,354	£10,518
Elsewhere	£8,700	£8,228
Parental home	£7,324	£6,892
Overseas rate	£9,963	£8,918

2012 cohort[29]

	Full year	Final year
London	£8,702	£7,925
Elsewhere	£6,236	£5,800
Parental home	£4,960	£4,557
Overseas rate	£7,410	£6,440

2009 cohort[30]

	Full year	Final year
London	£7,855	£7,152
Elsewhere	£5,614	£5,195
Parental home	£4,352	£3,948
Overseas rate	£6,682	£5,810

Long courses loan

You may be entitled to an additional amount of loan for any extra weeks of attendance over the standard 30 weeks and three days. Your institution can clarify whether your course has additional weeks.

If you started your course before 1 September 2008, this additional amount is simply added to the standard amount of loan paid. For 2008, 2009, 2012 and 2016 cohort students, it is known specifically as the long courses loan and is treated differently in the income assessment (see p41). Any additional amount is paid with other forms of support at the start of each term, and is repaid in the same way as other student loan debt.

The table below shows the amount paid for each week your course exceeds the standard length. If your course is 45 weeks or more, you are paid for a full 52 weeks of attendance. However, you will not be eligible for a long courses loan for any extra weeks that fall in the same quarter of the year as the long vacation.

Amount of long courses loan 2018/19[31]

	Weekly amount
London	£120
Elsewhere	£93
Parental home	£61
Overseas rate	£129

Repaying your loan

Loans are repayable at the end of your studies. The amount of money you pay back each month depends on your earnings and when you started your course. **Note:** if you were overpaid while studying, see p35.

If you started your course in 2011/12 or earlier, you begin to make repayments from the April after you graduate or otherwise leave your course, once you earn above £18,330 a year. Repayments start at a rate of 9 per cent of all income above that threshold.[32] For example, if you earn £19,330 a year, you pay back 9 per cent of the £1,000 of income over the threshold – ie, £90 a year or £7.50 a month.

If you started your course before 2012/13, interest is set at the rate of inflation, measured by the retail price index (RPI) in March, applied for a year from the following September, with a cap of 1 per cent above the base rates of certain nominated banks.

If you started your course in 2012/13 or later, you begin to repay your loan from the April after you graduate or otherwise leave your course, at a rate of 9 per cent of any income above £25,000 a year. **Note:** the government has frozen this threshold until at least April 2021.

Interest on loans for 2012 cohort students is variable. During the period of study, up to the April following graduation or otherwise leaving the course, the interest rate is set at the rate of inflation, measured by the RPI in March, plus 3 per cent. Thereafter, it is at:

- RPI if you earn less than the repayment threshold of £25,000;
- RPI plus 3 per cent if you earn more than £45,000 a year before tax;
- an amount on a sliding scale between RPI and RPI plus 3 per cent if you earn between £25,000 and £45,000 a year.

Your liability to repay a loan can be cancelled if you die or if you become permanently unable to work because of a disability.

If you started your course before 2012/13, your liability is cancelled 25 years after the April following graduation or when you otherwise left the course.[33] If you are a 2012 or 2016 cohort student, your liability is cancelled 30 years after the April following graduation or when you otherwise left the course.

If you started your course between 1 September 1998 and 1 September 2006, your liability is also cancelled when you reach the age of 65.

Mortgage-style loans

If you were eligible to receive a mandatory award before 1998, you may have had a 'mortgage-style loan'. These are normally repaid over 60 fixed monthly instalments from the April following your graduation or the point you otherwise leave your course, or over 84 fixed monthly instalments if you had loans for five or more years.[34] However, you can request that repayments be deferred if you earn less than 85 per cent of the national average wage. In 2018/19, repayments can be deferred if your gross earnings are not more than £30,737 per year or £2,562 per month.

Liability to repay mortgage-style loans can be cancelled if:[35]
* you die;
* you are permanently incapacitated from work because of a disability;
* you reach the age of 50 (or 60 if you were 40 or over when you last took out a loan);
* 25 years have passed since the April following your graduation or the point at which you otherwise left your course,

whichever comes first.

Interest on mortgage-style loans is set at the rate of inflation, measured by the RPI in March, applied for a year from the following September. All mortgage-style loans have now been sold to one of three private companies (Thesis Servicing, Honours Student Loans, or Erudio Student Loans), which should have written to you with their contact details. The repayment terms of the loans remain the same.

Supplementary grants

A number of additional grants are available to students in certain circumstances. **Note:** if you are a student on a pre-registration healthcare course starting on or after 1 August 2017, you may also be eligible for extra support from the NHS for your child(ren) (see Chapter 6).

Adult dependants' grant

If you have an adult dependant(s) who is 'wholly or mainly financially dependent' on you, you may be eligible for an adult dependants' grant.[36] Eligible adult dependants include your spouse or civil partner, or (if you are aged 25 or over) a cohabiting partner. The maximum grant is £2,925 in 2018/19, but the amount you receive depends on your situation and the income of your dependant(s). The amount you are eligible to receive is halved if your spouse/partner receives any student support as a full-time student.

Parents' learning allowance

If you are a parent with a dependent child(ren), you may be eligible for a parents' learning allowance to help cover your course-related costs.[37] How much you get depends on your income and that of your partner, spouse and any other dependants. The allowance is not counted as income when assessing your benefit and tax credit entitlement.

The maximum amount in 2018/19 is £1,669. If a couple are both full-time students, both can claim the full allowance, subject to their household income.

Childcare grant

If you have responsibility for a child under the age of 15 (or 17 if s/he has special educational needs) and you use registered or approved childcare, you can apply for a childcare grant.[38] You cannot receive the childcare grant if you receive the childcare element in UC (see Chapter 18) or working tax credit (WTC – see Chapter 20). You are also ineligible if your partner receives the childcare allowance in an NHS bursary (see p89).

Registered and approved childcare

A 'registered childcare provider' is a person who is registered under the Children Act and who provides daycare.[39] The person must care for one or more children aged under eight for more than two hours a day for payment. The care must be provided on domestic premises used wholly or mainly as a private dwelling. A relative who provides childcare for your child qualifies, provided s/he is registered with the Office for Standards in Education, Children's Services and Skills (Ofsted) and s/he is also looking after other children who are unrelated to her/him. Nurseries, out-of-hours school clubs and holiday playschemes also count.

'Approved childcare' covers provision for children aged eight or over. The childcare must be approved by an accredited organisation under the Working Tax Credit (Entitlement and Maximum Rate) Regulations 2002 (as amended). This definition includes carers who are approved under the voluntary childcare approval scheme. This covers childcare in the parent's home for children of any age, and childcare for children aged eight or over provided by a childminder in her/his own home or other domestic premises.

The grant can cover up to 85 per cent of your actual costs for childcare. In 2018/19, the maximum amount you can receive is £164.70 a week for one child or £282.36 a week for two or more children. The maximum amount of grant available annually in 2018/19 is £8,564.40 for one child and £14,682.72 for two or more children.

The amount you receive depends on your income and the income of any dependants.

Grant for travel costs

If you are a medical or dental student undertaking clinical placements, or if you have to study abroad as a compulsory part of your course, you may be able to claim help with your travel costs if they are more than £303 in the year. The amount you get depends on your household income (see p39).

Disabled students' allowance

If you incur additional course-related costs as a consequence of a disability, you can apply for disabled students' allowance.[40] This is a needs-based allowance and you must provide medical evidence of your disability, such as a letter from your doctor, educational psychologist or other specialist, when you apply to Student Finance England for assistance. If Student Finance England accepts this proof, it (and/or the adviser in your university or college) helps you to arrange a needs assessment with a recognised assessor. It then recommends what additional support or equipment you should be supplied with.

Maximum amount of disabled students' allowance 2018/19[41]

Non-medical personal helper(s)	£21,987 per academic year
Major items of specialist equipment	£5,529 for the duration of the course
Other expenditure	Up to £1,847 per academic year
Extra travel expenditure resulting from disability	Full reimbursement

Note: students may be expected to pay the first £200 towards any IT equipment, although some institutions have hardship funds or bursaries to help with this cost. Some non-medical help and other support may be provided by the institution. Speak to an adviser in your institution for more information.

Erasmus and other study or work placements

Funding rules can be different if you are studying abroad or are on a work placement (sometimes known as a 'sandwich year'). Fees may be reduced, but in some circumstances student support for living costs may also be limited.

If you are on an Erasmus study exchange or work placement, you can claim support for living costs as usual, and may qualify for an additional Erasmus grant. See the British Council website for more details (www.britishcouncil.org/study-work-abroad//outside-uk/erasmus).

The funding rules for study abroad and sandwich years are different and can be complex. Ask your university or students' union advice centre for more information.

Overpayments

If you have been overpaid student support by Student Finance England, the overpayment will be recovered.[42] This is the case even if the overpayment was the result of a mistake made by Student Finance England.

Usually, any overpayment of student support is recovered by reducing the support you are due to receive in future instalments. If you are not due to receive any further instalments, Student Finance England can use any other methods available to it. In practice, this means either asking you to repay the money in full directly, agreeing a repayment plan with you or adding the overpayment to your student loan debt.

If you have been overpaid tuition fee support, Student Finance England normally recovers this money from your institution directly and sometimes retrospectively. This may make you in debt to your institution.[43]

If you have received equipment through the disabled students' allowance and it is subsequently decided that you have been 'overpaid', it may be acceptable to return the equipment rather than repay its cash value.[44]

Contact your students' union or advice service for help checking whether an overpayment has been made, and for help negotiating with Student Finance England or your institution if this is the case.

2. Part-time undergraduates

Part-time students who started their course before the 2018/19 academic year can apply for support for their tuition fees and, for those started before 2012, course-related costs. The support available depends on when you started your course. The same course and residence requirements apply as for full-time students (see pp21–25).[45]

A new pro rata loan for living costs is available for undergraduates starting certain part-time courses from the 2018/19 academic year. You are eligible if your course meets certain requirements (see p36).

Note: students with an honours degree from a previous course who want to study certain science, technology, engineering and maths subjects part time can receive a loan for their tuition fees, even though they would not receive funding for an equivalent full-time course. Speak to an adviser in your institution for more information.

Grant for tuition fees: pre-September 2012 entrants

If you started your course in 2011/12 or earlier and are a part-time undergraduate student (including a student from the European Union (EU – see p22), you may be eligible for an income-assessed tuition fee grant.[46] The maximum amount of grant for which you are eligible depends on the intensity of study (compared to a full-time course) for each academic year of the course.

Maximum grant for part-time fees 2018/19

Course intensity	Maximum grant available
Less than 60%	£907
60–74%	£1,088
75% or more	£1,363

Part-time students whose tuition fees are higher than the amount covered by the grant for fees should apply to their institution for help from its hardship fund. Although hardship funds were part of the Access to Learning Fund, which is no longer funded by the former Higher Education Funding Council for England, many institutions offer transitional protection for continuing part-time students. Ask your advice centre or students' union for further information.

Loan for tuition fees: 2012 entrants or later

Student loans for tuition fees are available for part-time students (including students from the EU – see p22) starting from September 2012/13. The intensity of your course must be at least 25 per cent of the equivalent full-time course (ie, it should take no more than four times the amount of time to complete), and you can receive support for a maximum of 16 years.[47]

In 2018/19, you can receive a loan of up to £6,935 to cover the cost of the fees charged.[48] From 1 September 2012, part-time fees for new students have been regulated, so your fees should not exceed this amount. Loans to part-time students must be repaid in the same way as loans to full-time 2012 cohort students, with the same arrangements for interest (see p31).

Tuition fee loans for part-time students are not means tested, so your income and the income of your parents or partner do not affect your entitlement.

Loan for living costs

If you start your part-time undergraduate course in the 2018/19 academic year or later, in addition to a tuition fee loan you can apply for a loan to help cover your living costs.[49] The amount you can borrow depends on the intensity of your study, where you live and your household income (see p39).

Not all courses/qualifications are eligible. The following qualifications/courses are eligible:[50]
- a bachelor's degree (with or without honours) – eg, a BA or BSc;
- an integrated master's course – eg, an MEng or BEng;
- a Postgraduate Certificate in Education (PGCE) or Postgraduate Diploma in Education (PGDE), provided you do not already have qualified teacher status;

- a graduate diploma or graduate certificate, provided a degree is not required to do the course;
- a foundation degree in dental hygiene or dental therapy;
- a Diploma of Higher Education (DipHE) in dental hygiene or dental therapy or operating department practice.

Other lower level (level 4 or 5) courses, such as foundation degrees, DipHEs, Higher National Certificates (HNCs) and Higher National Doplomas (HNDs), are not eligible. However, you can apply for a loan if you are 'topping up' a course that you started before 2018/19 with one that you are starting in the 2018/19 academic year, provided the new qualification meets the criteria. For example, if you complete an HND in summer 2018 and then want to top this up to a part-time degree starting in September 2018, you can apply for a loan for the new course.

You must attend the course to be eligible; distance learning courses do not count, unless you are doing a distance learning course because you have a disability.[51] You must provide evidence of your disability when you apply.

To be eligible for the new loan, you must attend for a minimum number of hours, equivalent to 25 per cent of the intensity of a full-time course, each year – ie, the course takes no more than four times the amount of time to complete. The number of years of available funding is capped at four times the length of the equivalent full-time course.[52] Institutions are required to confirm the intensity of your course each year. Ask your university or college if you are uncertain what this is.

Amount of loan for living costs 2018/19[53]

Course intensity	Maximum loan	Minimum loan
London		
100%	£11,354	£5,684
75–100%	£8,515	£4,240
66.6–75%	£7,561	£3,765
50–66.6%	£5,677	£2,827
33.3–50%	£3,780	£1,882
25–33.3%	£2,838	£1,413
Elsewhere		
100%	£8,700	£4,054
75–100%	£6,525	£3,040
66.6–75%	£5,794	£2,699
50–66.6%	£4,350	£2,027
33.3–50%	£2,897	£1,349
25–33.3%	£2,175	£1,013

Parental home

100%	£7,324	£3,224
75–100%	£5,493	£2,418
66.6–75%	£4,877	£2,147
50–66.6%	£3,662	£1,612
33.3–50%	£2,438	£1,073
25–33.3%	£1,831	£806

Special support element

Loans for living costs for part-time students include a special support element, which is disregarded for means-tested benefits. You do not have to provide any evidence you are eligible for benefits to receive this. The amount of the special support element is based on a full-time rate of £3,680 in 2018/19, pro-rated by intensity of study, and is not affected by your household income.[54] However, if your household income would reduce your standard loan entitlement below the relevant rate of the special support element, you receive the reduced rate, payable entirely as a special support element.

Repaying your loan

The loan is repaid in the same way as the loan for living costs for full-time students (see p31), except that repayments start in the April after you graduate or leave your course *or* the April four years after you start your studies, whichever is the soonest. This means that, in some cases, if you earn over the threshold, you may be repaying your loan while you are still studying.

Grant for course costs: pre-September 2012 entrants

A grant of up to £297 is available for students from low-income backgrounds to help with the costs of books, equipment and travel.[55] The amount of grant available is not affected by the intensity of your study. This is not available for EU students.

Disabled students' allowance

If you are a part-time student and studying at an intensity of at least 50 per cent (pre-2012 entrants) or 25 per cent (2012 or later entrants) of an equivalent full-time course and have a disability, you can apply for a disabled students' allowance. However, the amount Student Finance England can award for non-medical help and other general expenditure is reduced according to the workload of a part-time course.

Maximum amount of disabled students' allowance 2018/19[56]

Non-medical personal helper(s)	£16,489 per academic year
Major items of specialist equipment	£5,520 for the duration of the course
Other expenditure	Up to £1,385 per academic year
Extra travel expenditure resulting from disability	Full reimbursement

Note: students may be expected to pay the first £200 towards any IT equipment, although some institutions have hardship funds or bursaries to help with this cost. Some non-medical help and other support may be provided by the institution. Speak to an adviser in your institution for more information.

---

3. How income affects student support

How your income is assessed

Student support for living costs depends on an income assessment.[57] You may be assessed as either an independent student (see below) or a dependent student (see p40).

In all cases, your household income is assessed. This means your own income (excluding your income from part-time work) is always assessed, plus that of your:

- parent(s), unless you are an independent student (see below); *or*
- spouse, if you are married; *or*
- civil partner, if you are in a civil partnership; *or*
- cohabiting partner, if you are aged 25 or over.

If you are a part-time student, only your and your partner's income is taken into account as household income. Your parents' income is ignored, regardless of your age.[58] See p43.

Independent students

You are assessed as an independent student if:[59]

- you are either aged 25 before the beginning of the academic year in which your course begins or you become 25 during the academic year (in which case, you are assessed as an independent student from the beginning of the following academic year); *or*
- you are married or in a civil partnership before the course begins, or you marry or form a civil partnership during the course (in which case, you are assessed as an independent student from the beginning of the following academic year); *or*
- you have been financially self-reliant for any three years before the academic year in which your course begins (this qualifying period can include periods of

unemployment and participation in training schemes for the unemployed, such as apprenticeships); *or*
- you have responsibility for at least one child; *or*
- you are 'irreconcilably estranged' from your parents (see below); *or*
- you have been in the care of a local authority for a certain period; *or*
- your parents cannot be found; *or*
- your parents are not in the UK and it is not reasonably practicable for them to send parental contributions to the UK, or they would be placed in jeopardy if they did so; *or*
- you have no living parents; *or*
- you are a member of a religious order living in a house of that order, and you started your course before 1 September 2009.

If you are considered to be an independent student, your parents' income is *not* taken into account. Your gross taxable income for the academic year, less various disregards (all earnings from part-time work are disregarded), is taken into account. If you have a spouse or partner, her/his income may be taken into account (see p41).

Estrangement

If your relationship with your parents has completely broken down, and you do not meet any of the other criteria for independent status, you can apply for 'estrangement' status so that their income is not taken into account.

If you can provide evidence that you have had no contact with either of your parents for at least a year, you should be treated as estranged. If you have become estranged but have had contact within the last 12 months, you can still use other evidence to prove your estrangement – eg, letters from social services or medical or other professionals.[60] You cannot usually be assessed as estranged part way through the year. Instead, you must wait until you reapply the next academic year and provide evidence of your circumstances at that time.

Your students' union or institution advice centre can assist you to apply for estrangement status.

Dependent students

If you do not meet the criteria for being an independent student (see p39), you are considered to be a dependent student. Student Finance England looks at your parents' gross taxable income over the previous full tax year (for the academic year 2018/19, this is 6 April 2016 to 5 April 2017), then subtracts pension scheme and superannuation payments, which attract tax relief. A further £1,130 is deducted for each additional dependent child or if your parent is a student her/himself.[61]

The remaining amount is added to your estimated gross taxable income for the 2018/19 academic year (if any). This is your household income figure.[62] When calculating your gross income, certain income, including all your earnings from part-time or casual work, is disregarded.

The household income figure is then used to determine how much the household is expected to contribute to your costs and, therefore, how much support you can receive from the government.

Note: if the level of your parents' income falls by at least 15 per cent during the academic year, you can request a reassessment (called a 'current year income assessment') from Student Finance England.[63]

If your parents are separated, divorced or widowed and you are not deemed to be an independent student, the income of the parent with whom you live is taken into account. If you do not live with either parent, Student Finance England decides which parent's income is the most appropriate to use.

If your parent has a partner with whom s/he lives, the partner's income is also included in the assessment, even if that person is not your parent.

Spouses and partners

If your spouse or civil/cohabiting partner is considered part of the assessable household, her/his income is assessed in a similar way to that of a student's parents (see p40).[64]

Any income from your spouse or civil/cohabiting partner is added to your income to form the household income to be taken into account. However, if you have separated from your spouse or civil partner, her/his income is not assessed.

The household income figure is used to determine how much the household is expected to contribute to your costs and, therefore, how much support you can receive from the government.

How your student support is affected

2016 cohort students

If your household income is £25,000 or less, you qualify for the maximum amount of loan for living costs.

If your household income is more than £25,000 and you are not entitled to benefits, your living cost loan is reduced by the appropriate rate for your circumstances:

London	£1 for every £7.87 over £25,000, up to the minimum amount of loan (£5,654 – 49.8 per cent of the maximum loan)
Elsewhere	£1 for every £8.01 over £25,000, up to £4,054 (46.6 per cent of the maximum loan)
Parental home	£1 for every £8.10 over £25,000, up to the minimum amount of loan (£3,224 – 44 per cent of maximum loan)
Overseas rate	£1 for every £8.18 over £25,000

If your household income is more than £25,000 and you are entitled to benefits, your assessed income reduces the amount of your loan. The special support element of your loan is reduced first before the standard maintenance element. Your loan is then reduced by the appropriate rate for your circumstances:

London	£1 for every £5.418 between £25,001 and £42,875
	£1 for every £7.87 over £42,875, up to the minimum amount of loan (£5,654 – 45.7 per cent of the maximum loan)
Elsewhere	£1 for every £5.185 between £25,001 and £42,875
	£1 for every £8.01 over £42,875, up to £4,054 (40.9 per cent of the maximum loan)
Parental home	£1 for every £5.075 between £25,001 and £42,875
	£1 for every £8.10 over £42,875, up to the minimum amount of loan (£3,224 – 37.3 per cent of maximum loan)
Overseas rate	£1 for every £8.18 over £25,000

Other income-assessed support is reduced in a different way. Support is reduced at a rate of £1 for every £8.73 of income above £39,796.[65] Any supplementary grants for dependants are reduced first, then any long courses loan payable and, finally, any grant for travel costs.[66]

Students aged 60 or over
If you start your course on or after 1 August 2016 and you were aged 60 or over on the first day of your first academic year, your assessed income reduces the amount of the over-60 rate of loan you get. In 2018/19, the following applies.[67]
- If your household income is £25,000 or less, you qualify for the maximum amount of loan.
- If your household income is between £25,001 and £43,695, your loan is reduced by £1 for every £5.15 of income over £25,000.
- If your household income is over £43,695, you do not qualify for a loan.

2012 cohort students
- If your household income is £25,000 or less, you receive the maximum maintenance or special support grant.
- If your household income is between £25,001 and £42,645, you receive a reduced amount of the applicable grant (the minimum amount is £50). For every £4.98 of household income above £25,000, £1 is deducted from the grant until the maximum household income of £42,645 is reached.
- No grant is payable if your household income is more than £42,645.

Any income above £42,875 reduces the income-assessed 35 per cent of the applicable basic rate of student loan (see p30) at a rate of £1 for every £8.84 of additional income.[68]

Other income-assessed support is reduced in a different way. Support is reduced at a rate of £1 for every £8.73 of income above £39,796.[69] Any supplementary grants for dependants are reduced first, then any long courses loan payable and, finally, any grant for travel costs.[70]

2009 cohort students

- If your household income is £25,000 or less, you receive the maximum maintenance or special support grant.
- If your household income is between £25,001 and £50,706, you receive a reduced amount of the applicable grant (the minimum amount is £50).
  - For every £4.70 of household income between £25,001 and £34,264, £1 is deducted from the grant.
  - For every £12.86 of household income above £34,264, £1 is deducted from the grant until the maximum household income of £50,706 is reached.
- No grant is payable if your household income is more than £50,706.

Income above £50,778 reduces the income-assessed 28 per cent of the applicable basic rate of student loan (see p30) at a rate of £1 for every £4.42 of additional income.[71]

Other income-assessed student support is reduced in a different way. Support is reduced at a rate of £1 for every £8.73 of income above £39,796.[72] Any supplementary grants for dependants are reduced first, then any long courses loan payable and, finally, any grant for travel costs.[73]

Part-time students

If you are a part-time student and you started your course before 1 September 2012, your grant for tuition fees and course costs is means tested in the following way.

- If your income is below £16,845, you are eligible for the maximum grant for fees and course costs.
- If your income is between £16,846 and £25,422, you receive some help with fees and course costs.
- If your income is between £25,423 and £28,064, you receive some help with course costs, but not with fees. The exact amount you receive depends on your income.
- If your income is £28,065, you receive a course grant of £50. If your income is above this amount, you receive no support.

Only your and your partner's income is taken into account as household income. Your parents' income is ignored, regardless of your age.[74]

If you are married or in a civil partnership, or aged 25 or over and living with a partner (including a same-sex partner) or have dependent children, the following amounts are deducted from your income:[75]

* £2,000 for your partner;
* £2,000 for your eldest child;
* £1,000 for every other child.

4. Discretionary and institutional funds

Institutions are expected to provide funds to alleviate student hardship and to support retention and progression. These funds are not provided or reported on centrally, and do not have common assessment criteria. You should therefore contact your institution for information on how to apply and how you are assessed.

Note: in exceptional cases, students on a pre-registration healthcare course may be eligible for additional hardship funding from the NHS (see p86).

Additional fee support scheme

All institutions are expected to provide funds to support retention and progression, and so funds should still be available to help part-time 'home' and European Union students who started their course before 1 September 2012 to meet the costs of their tuition fees, where these fees are higher than the amount covered by the tuition fee grant. Local fund administrators have discretion on how much assistance to pay and to whom. For more information, speak to an adviser in your university or college or contact the fund administrator.

Institutional bursaries

If you are a full-time student and you started your course in 2011/12 or earlier, you are receiving the full maintenance or special support grant of £3,299 in 2018/19 and your university or college charges fees of more than £3,299, you are eligible for a minimum non-repayable bursary.

The Office for Students (formerly the Office for Fair Access), which governs bursary rules, has stated that the minimum mandatory bursary must be equivalent to 10 per cent of the tuition fees charged by the university or college. Therefore, in 2018/19, if the fee charged is £3,465, the mandatory minimum bursary is £347.[76] However, many institutions offer more than this. Contact your university or college for more information.

There is no minimum bursary for students who started in 2012/13 or later.

Notes

1. Full-time undergraduates
1 Sch 1 Part 2 E(SS) Regs
2 'Islands' in this context are the Channel Islands and the Isle of Man.
3 Sch 1 para 13 E(SS) Regs
4 Sch 1 para 10A E(SS) Regs
5 Sch 1 para 9 E(SS) Regs and reg 1 Education (Student Support) (Amendment) Regulations 2016, No.270
6 For a definition of 'relevant family member', see Sch 1 para 1 E(SS) Regs
7 Sch 1 para 8 E(SS) Regs
8 Sch 1 para 12 E(SS) Regs
9 Sch 1 para 4 E(SS) Regs
10 Sch 1 para 17 E(SS) Regs
11 Reg 5 and Sch 2 E(SS) Regs
12 Regs 21-23 E(SS) Regs
13 Regs 20, 56, 60 and 67 E(SS) Regs
14 Reg 67 E(SS) Regs
15 Regs 12(4A) and 13(2A) E(SS) Regs
16 Regs 20 and 21 E(SS) Regs
17 Regs 19(10) and 30(2) E(SS) Regs
18 Reg 19 E(SS) Regs
19 Letter from David Willetts and Andrew Lansley to the British Medical Association, 28 June 2011
20 Reg 56 E(SS) Regs
21 Regs 57, 58 and 60 E(SS) Regs
22 Reg 72(8)-(10) E(SS) Regs
23 Reg 76 E(SS) Regs
24 Reg 61 E(SS) Regs
25 Regs 62, 63 and 65 E(SS) Regs
26 Reg 80C E(SS) Regs
27 Reg 80B E(SS) Regs
28 Reg 80A E(SS) Regs
29 Reg 76 E(SS) Regs
30 Reg 74 E(SS) Regs
31 Reg 81 E(SS) Regs
32 Reg 44 E(SL)(R) Regs
33 Reg 19 E(SL)(R) Regs
34 Sch 2 para 5 E(SL) Regs. If you have taken out more than five student loans, you repay your loan in 84 monthly instalments.
35 Sch 2 para 12 E(SL) Regs
36 Reg 44 E(SS) Regs
37 Reg 46 E(SS) Regs
38 Reg 45 E(SS) Regs
39 s79(f) CA 1989
40 Reg 40 E(SS) Regs
41 Reg 41 E(SS) Regs
42 Regs 117-19 E(SS) Regs
43 Reg 157 E(SS) Regs
44 Regs 117, 156 and 168 E(SS) Regs

2. Part-time undergraduates
45 Reg 137 E(SS) Regs
46 Reg 141 E(SS) Regs
47 Reg 144 E(SS) Regs
48 Reg 145 E(SS) Regs
49 Reg 157A-157R E(SS) Regs
50 Reg 139 E(SS) Regs
51 Reg 157B E(SS) Regs
52 Reg 157B E(SS) Regs
53 Reg 157F-157J E(SS) Regs
54 Reg 157G E(SS) Regs
55 Reg 142 E(SS) Regs
56 Reg 147 E(SS) Regs

3. How income affects student support
57 Sch 4 E(SS) Regs
58 Reg 142 E(SS) Regs
59 Sch 4 para 2 E(SS) Regs
60 Sch 4 para 2(1)(e) E(SS) Regs
61 Sch 4 para 3 E(SS) Regs
62 Sch 4 paras 3 and 4 E(SS) Regs
63 Sch 4 para 5(3)-(4) E(SS) Regs
64 Sch 4 para 6 E(SS) Regs
65 Sch 4 para 9 E(SS) Regs
66 Regs 99 and 100 E(SS) Regs
67 Reg 80C E(SS) Regs
68 Reg 76 E(SS) Regs
69 Sch 4 para 9 E(SS) Regs
70 Regs 99 and 100 E(SS) Regs
71 Reg 72 E(SS) Regs
72 Sch 4 para 9 E(SS) Regs
73 Regs 97 and 100 E(SS) Regs
74 Reg 142 E(SS) Regs
75 Reg 143 E(SS) Regs

4. Discretionary and institutional funds
76 Letter from the Office for Fair Access to higher education institutions, 23 July 2009

3

Chapter 3

Undergraduate student support: Wales

This chapter covers:
1. Full-time undergraduates (below)
2. Part-time undergraduates (p55)
3. How income affects student support (p59)
4. Discretionary hardship funds (p61)

There are different systems of undergraduate student support in England, Wales, Northern Ireland and Scotland. See Chapter 2 for details of the system in England, Chapter 4 for Northern Ireland and CPAG's *Benefits for Students in Scotland* for details of the system in Scotland.

Students living in Wales who wish to study in England, Northern Ireland or Scotland receive the same package of support as though they were studying in Wales.

In 2018/19, the student support package for new students in Wales changed significantly. Students who started before 2018/19 continue on the same arrangements as when they started their course. This chapter does not cover those who started their course before 2012/13. If you think this applies to you, see an adviser in your university or students' union.

Basic facts
- Undergraduate students can apply for a mixture of grants and loans, depending on their personal circumstances.
- The type of financial support available depends on several factors, including when the course starts, its length, the discipline and whether the course is full time or part time.
- Separate provision is available for social work, healthcare and initial teacher training students.
- Support from hardship funds may be available for those in financial difficulty.

1. Full-time undergraduates

Full-time undergraduates in Wales on eligible courses (see below) and who are personally eligible (see below) can apply for financial assistance from the Welsh government. Separate provision is available for part-time undergraduates (see p55). There have been a number of changes to student funding and support during the last 10 years, and so the support you can receive depends on when you started your course.

Who is eligible for support

To receive financial support, you must be 'personally eligible' by meeting residence conditions (see below) and be studying an eligible course (see below).

Residence conditions

To be personally eligible for support from the Welsh government, you must meet residency conditions.[1] These are generally the same as for England (see p21), except that, where appropriate, you must be normally resident in Wales on the first day of the first academic year. In addition, in Wales, students with certain forms of leave to remain can receive support, unlike in England. Ask an adviser for information.

Following the result of the referendum on the UK's membership of the European Union (EU), the Welsh government has stated that students from other EU countries who start their courses in 2018/19 or 2019/20 and who have been assessed as eligible for funding will continue to receive it as normal until they complete the course. Rules for students starting courses in future years are uncertain – check the Student Finance Wales website.

What is an eligible course

To be eligible for support, broadly the course must be full time (as defined by the education provider) and be:[2]

- a first degree;
- a higher education diploma;
- a BTEC Higher National Certificate (HNC) or Higher National Diploma (HND);
- a course of initial teacher training;
- a course for the further training of teachers, or youth or community workers;
- a course to prepare for certain professional examinations of a standard higher than A level, or HNC/HND where a first degree is not required for entry;
- a course not higher than a first degree, but higher than those described in the above bullet point.

Note: some courses, particularly in art and design, can require students to undertake a 'foundation' year or course. This is different from a foundation degree. It is normally a course of one academic year in length which precedes the main higher education degree course. Support for foundation courses is often limited as they do not come within the definition of 'higher education'. You may be eligible for support as a further education student (see Chapter 1). Speak to an adviser in your students' union or institution for further guidance.

Which system of student support applies

The student support to which you are entitled depends on when you started your course. In this *Handbook*:
- students who started their course between the 2012/13 academic year and the 2017/18 academic year are referred to as '**2012 cohort**' students;
- students who started their course in the 2018/19 academic year are referred to as '**2018 cohort**' students.

Students in the 2012 cohort can apply for a package of support, which includes:
- a grant to pay part of their tuition fees (see p49);
- a loan for any remaining tuition fees (see p49);
- either a Welsh government learning grant (see p51) or a special support grant (see p51);
- a loan for living costs (see p53);
- supplementary grants in particular circumstances (see p55).

2018 cohort students can apply for a different package of support, which includes:
- a loan for tuition fees (see p49);
- a 'base' grant of £1,000 (see p50);
- a maintenance grant (see p50), which may include a special support payment if you are entitled to claim social security benefits (see p50);
- a loan for living costs (see p52);
- supplementary grants in particular circumstances (see p55).

Previous study

If you have previously attended a higher education course, the amount of support you can receive may be affected by the rules on previous study.[3] The rules are broadly the same for both 2012 and 2018 cohort students.

If you hold an honours degree from a UK institution and are studying for a new qualification, unless you are covered by one of the exceptions (see below), you can only apply for a supplementary grant for travel costs, a grant for any dependants and a grant for disability-related costs.[4] You are not entitled to any other kind of support.

There are some exceptions:
- Students who hold an honours degree and who are undertaking a Postgraduate Certificate in Education (PGCE) course receive full funding.

- Students undertaking a further full-time undergraduate course in certain professional subjects, such as social work, medicine, dentistry, architecture, town planning or veterinary science, can receive a loan for their living costs,[5] although not a loan for tuition fees or a maintenance grant, a special support grant or special support payment.
- Students who hold an honours degree who wish to study certain courses part time can receive full funding.[6]

If you do not already hold an honours degree, in general the maximum number of years of tuition fee loan and maintenance, special support grant or special support payment funding you can receive is equivalent to the ordinary length of your course plus one year, less any years of study previously undertaken.[7] If you have studied part of a year, you are treated as if you have undertaken a full year of study. Entitlement to loans for living costs is unaffected.

If you are transferring courses, or undertaking an 'end-on' course (topping up from one qualification to another), these previous study rules affect you.

You may be able to secure additional years of 'full' funding if you were unable to complete a previous year or course for 'compelling personal reasons', such as illness or caring responsibilities.[8] You must provide evidence of this to Student Finance Wales.

Further information on previous study is available from your student adviser or www.studentfinancewales.co.uk.

Grant and loan for tuition fees

If you started your course on or after 1 August 2018 (2018 cohort) and you are an eligible Welsh-domiciled student studying in Wales, or a non-UK EU student studying in Wales, you may be charged fees of up to £9,000 a year. A loan is available to cover this cost. Eligible Welsh-domciled students studying elsewhere in the UK may be charged up to £9,250. You can take out a loan to cover this cost.[9]

If you started your course on or after 1 September 2012 but before 1 August 2018 (2012 cohort) and you are an eligible Welsh-domiciled student studying in Wales, or you are a non-UK EU student studying in Wales, you may be charged fees of up to £9,000 a year. Eligible Welsh-domiciled students studying elsewhere in the UK may be charged up to £9,250. In 2018/19, if you are charged more than £4,200 in Wales or £4,450 elsewhere in the UK, you can apply for a fee grant from the Welsh government of up to £4,800 so that your liability does not exceed £4,200 or £4,450.[10] You can then take out a loan to pay for all, or part, of the remaining amount.[11]

The maximum loan available matches the fee you are charged, less any fee grant where this applies. The loan is not means tested on your income or the income of anyone in your household. However, it is added to your total student loan debt (including any loan taken out for your living costs). You must start your repayments once you have graduated or otherwise left the course, and are earning at least £25,000 a year and are working in the UK. If you live and work abroad following graduation, the thresholds may be different – contact the Student Loans Company for more details.

If you wish to pay all, or part, of your fees in cash in advance, you can do so. Your institution will generally expect some indication of how you intend to pay your fees when you enrol.

Help with tuition fees for part-time courses is also available (see p56).

Base grant: 2018 cohort students

In 2018/19, if you are a 2018 cohort student, you receive a £1,000 'base grant' as part of your living costs support.[12] Student Finance Wales may refer to this as a 'minimum grant'. This grant is non-means tested and non-repayable. If you are entitled to apply for means-tested benefits, the base grant is treated as part of your special support payment (see below) and is not taken into account as income when working out your entitlement to benefit. You should ensure that you apply for the special support payment in your student support application.

Maintenance grant: 2018 cohort students

In addition to a base grant, 2018 cohort students may also receive a maintenance grant for their living costs.[13] How much you get depends on where you study or live and your household income.

Maximum maintenance grant 2018/19

London	£9,124
Elsewhere	£7,100
Parental home	£5,885

If you are a care leaver, you automatically receive the maximum rate of the grant. Otherwise, you receive the full grant if your annual household income is £18,370 or less, and a partial grant on a sliding scale up to a household income of £59,200 a year. See p59 for details of the income assessment. Any grant you receive reduces the amount of your loan for living costs pound for pound – see p52 for details of loan amounts. However, the total cash support you can receive, whether by loan or a combination of loan and grant, should always remain the same.

Special support payment

A special support payment is available to provide extra support for 2018 cohort students who are regarded as particularly vulnerable. You must be a full-time student eligible for means-tested benefits to qualify.[14] Most full-time students cannot receive universal credit (UC) or other means-tested social security benefits. Some students, however, can claim – eg, if you are a lone parent, or if you and your partner are both full-time students and have a child, or if you get the housing element in UC, or you receive disability living allowance (DLA) or personal independence payment (PIP). See the relevant benefits chapter for details of which students can claim UC or means-tested benefits.

If you are entitled to UC or means-tested benefits, you should claim the special support payment as part of your maintenance grant. The special support payment comprises the £1,000 base grant and up to £4,161 of any maintenance grant (£5,161 in total) which is then disregarded as income when calculating your entitlement to UC or means-tested benefit. Claiming the special support payment also entitles you to a higher minimum rate of loan for your living costs (see p52), which means that your overall cash support is usually higher than students who claim the standard maintenance grant.[15] **Note:** Student Finance Wales may not make clear the grant's different elements. If this causes problems, contact an adviser.

Welsh government learning grant: 2012 cohort students

In 2018/19, the Welsh government learning grant for 2012 cohort students is a non-repayable, means-tested allowance of up to £5,161.[16] The maximum amount is payable to students with a household income of less than £18,371 a year, and a partial amount is paid on a sliding scale to students with a household income of up to £50,020.

Part of the grant substitutes the student loan for living costs. If you receive a Welsh government learning grant, the amount of loan for living costs you can receive is reduced by 50 pence for every £1 you receive, up to a maximum of £2,580. See p52 for more details on loans for living costs.

Example
Rhys receives an Welsh government learning grant of £1,540. The maximum amount of loan for living costs he can receive is reduced by £770.

If you are entitled to apply for means-tested benefits, the Welsh government learning grant is taken into account as income when working out your (or your partner's) entitlement, so you should apply for a special support grant instead (see below).

Special support grant: 2012 cohort students

A special support grant is available to provide extra support for 2012 cohort students who are regarded as particularly vulnerable. You must be a full-time student eligible to claim means-tested social security benefits.[17]

Note: most full-time students cannot receive UC or other means-tested benefits. Some students, however, can claim – eg, if you are a lone parent, or you and your partner are both full-time students and you have a child, or you get the housing element in UC, or you receive DLA or PIP. See the relevant benefits chapter for details of which students can claim UC or means-tested benefits.

If you are entitled to UC or means-tested benefits, you should claim the special support grant rather than the Welsh government learning grant. Like the Welsh government learning grant, the special support grant is a non-repayable, means-tested allowance of up to £5,161.[18] The special support grant is based on the same income scales as the maintenance grant for each cohort (see p50).

Unlike the Welsh government learning grant, however, the special support grant does not substitute any part of the student loan, and it is not taken into account as income when calculating your entitlement to means-tested benefits.

Loan for living costs

2018 cohort students

Student loans for living costs are available to eligible Welsh-domiciled 2018 cohort students. The amount of loan you can receive varies, depending on your place of study. It is reduced pound for pound by any maintenance grant you receive, but not by the base grant.

Maximum amount of loan 2018/19[19]

London	£10,250
Elsewhere	£8,000
Parental home	£6,650

The loan is not further reduced by your household income. You may be entitled to additional amounts if your course length exceeds 30 weeks and three days in the year (see p54).

If you receive the special support payment (see p50), your loan is not reduced below a certain minimum level, regardless of the total grant received.

Minimum amount of loan for special support payment recipients 2018/19[20]

London	£5,125
Elsewhere	£4,000
Parental home	£3,325

In many cases, the amount of loan to which you are entitled will be higher. Your exact loan entitlement is calculated by subtracting the special support payment from either a notional 'applicable amount' of living costs support (see p53) *or* the total base and maintenance grant you are eligible for, plus the minimum rate of loan – whichever of these two figures is higher. Any amount of grant paid that is not a special support payment is then subtracted from this figure to give the amount of loan to which you are entitled.[21]

- -

'Applicable amount' 2018/19

London	£11,250
Elsewhere	£9,000
Parental home	£7,650

- -

- -

Example

Gwyneth is a new student at the University of Swansea in 2018/19. She is claiming UC as a single parent, and is entitled to the special support payment. She has no additional household income and receives full support as a student living away from home outside London. Her loan entitlement is calculated as follows.

Step 1   Gwyneth is entitled to a special support payment of £5,161, comprising her £1,000 base grant and the first £4,161 of her maintenance grant.

Step 2   The total base and maintenance grant she is entitled to is £8,100. The minimum rate of loan for Gwyneth is £4,000. £8,100 + £4,000 = £12,100. This amount is more than the 'applicable amount' of £9,000. Her notional maximum support is therefore £12,100.

Step 3   Gwyneth's special support payment of £5,161 is subtracted from her notional maximum support of £12,100, giving £6,939. The amount of maintenance grant that is not the special support payment (£8,100 – £5,161 = £2,939) is then subtracted from this figure: £6,939 – £2,939 = £4,000.

Step 4   Gwyneth's total loan for living costs entitlement in 2018/19 is £4,000. This is equal to the minimum rate of loan possible.

- -

If you are getting a special support payment, you may also be entitled to additional amounts of loan if your course length exceeds 30 weeks and three days in the year (see p54).

2012 cohort students

Student loans for living costs are available to eligible Welsh-domiciled 2012 cohort students. Part of the loan is subject to an income assessment (see p59). If you receive a Welsh government learning grant, the loan is reduced by 50 pence for every £1 of grant you receive (see p51). If your course requires attendance in excess of 30 weeks and three days, you may be able to receive additional amounts of loan (see p54).

Maximum amount of loan 2018/19[22]

	Full year	Final year
London	£9,697	£8,830
Elsewhere	£6,922	£6,412
Parental home	£5,358	£4,851
Overseas rate	£8,253	£7,179

Extra weeks allowance

Both 2012 and 2018 cohort students may be entitled to additional amounts of loan for any extra weeks of attendance over the standard 30 weeks and three days. Your institution can clarify whether your course has additional weeks.

The table below outlines the amount paid for each week your course exceeds the standard length. If your course year lasts 45 weeks or more, you are paid for a full 52 weeks of attendance.

Amount of extra weeks allowance 2018/19

	Weekly amount
London	£153
Elsewhere	£120
Parental home	£80
Overseas rate (2012 cohort only)	£166

Repaying your loan

Repayment terms are the same as for English students. The rules differ, depending on whether you started your course before or after 1 September 2012 (see p31).

Partial cancellations

Eligible Welsh-domiciled students who have taken out a maintenance loan since 2010/11 may be able to have up to £1,500 of the loan cancelled when they reach the point when they begin making repayments. This cancellation can only be applied once, and is not multiplied by the number of academic years in which you took out a loan. If the balance of your loan is less than £1,500, the cancellation is equal to the loan balance less the first repayment you make. **Note:** cancellation is not automatic and you should speak to Student Finance Wales to ensure it is applied; a manual payment of at least £5 is required.

If you have any outstanding penalties or charges on your loan, are in breach of your loan agreement or 'are shown by your conduct to be unfit to receive a cancellation', it will be refused. You might be considered 'unfit' if, for example, you provided false information when applying for the loan.

See www.studentloanpayment.co.uk for more details.

Supplementary grants

A number of additional grants and allowances are available to both 2018 and 2012 cohort students who have extra needs.

Students with dependants

Students with dependent children may be able to receive a **parents' learning allowance**[23] of up to £1,557 and/or a **childcare grant**[24] of 85 per cent of the actual costs of their childcare, up to a maximum of £161.50 a week for one child, or 85 per cent of the actual costs up to a maximum of £274.55 a week for two or more children.

If you have an adult dependant(s) 'wholly or mainly financially dependent' on you, you may be eligible for a means-tested **adult dependants' grant** up to a maximum of £2,732.[25] Students with children should also apply for child benefit (see Chapter 8), and either child tax credit (see Chapter 19) or UC (see Chapter 18).

Disabled students' allowance

If you are disabled and have extra costs associated with your course because of your disability, you may be entitled to extra help to pay for them. This is awarded on the same basis as in England (see p34). **Note:** there are lower rates in Wales – the maximum general allowance is £1,785; the maximum grant for equipment is £5,332; and the maximum non-medical helper allowance is £21,181 per year.[26]

Grant for travel costs

Medical and dental students on placement and students who must travel abroad may be entitled to help with the cost of travel. This is awarded on the same basis as in England (see p34).[27]

Erasmus and other study or work placements

Funding rules can be different if you are studying abroad or are on a work placement (sometimes known as a 'sandwich year'). Fees may be reduced, but in some circumstances support for living costs may also be limited.

If you are on an Erasmus study exchange or work placement, you can claim support for your living costs as usual, and may qualify for an additional Erasmus grant. See the British Council website for more details (www.erasmusplus.org.uk).

The funding rules for study abroad and sandwich years can be complex. Ask your university or students' union advice centre for more information.

2. **Part-time undergraduates**

Support for part-time students is different from that available to full-time students. New and existing part-time undergraduate students can qualify for support for fees and living costs. The course and personal eligibility requirements are the same as for full-time students (see p47), except that students who already hold honours degrees can still receive funding for a further degree at part-time intensity, if the course starts on 1 September 2017 or later and the subject is one of the following disciplines:[28]

- engineering;
- technology;
- computer science;
- subjects allied to medicine;
- biological sciences;
- veterinary sciences;
- agriculture and related subjects;
- physical sciences or mathematical sciences;
- Welsh.

The support offered depends on when you started your course. For students starting after 1 August 2018, living costs support is more generous.

Grant for tuition fees

If you are a part-time undergraduate student (including a student from the European Union (EU) – see p22), and you started your course before 1 September 2014, you may be eligible for a means-tested grant for your tuition fees.[29] You must be studying a course that is at least 50 per cent intensity of a full-time course – ie, it takes no longer than twice the time of the equivalent full-time course to complete. The maximum amount of grant to which you are eligible depends on the intensity of study for each academic year of the course (see below).

Maximum grant for part-time fees 2018/19

Course intensity	Maximum grant available
Less than 60%	£690
60–74%	£820
75% or more	£1,025

Loan for tuition fees

Welsh-domiciled part-time students who started their course on 1 September 2014 or later can apply for a non-means-tested loan to help pay their tuition fees. These are similar to the loans for part-time students in England since 2012/13 (see p36), but with some differences. In particular, the maximum loans for study in Wales are lower, and there is no regulation of part-time fees in Wales. This means that the fee charged may be higher than the loan you can receive.

Eligible Welsh-domiciled and non-UK EU students can get a loan of up to £2,625 a year.[30] If your course is at an institution in England, Scotland or Northern Ireland, the loan can be up to £6,935 a year.[31] If your course fee is lower than these amounts, you can take out a loan up to the value of your fees. Repayment arrangements are the same as for full-time students starting their course after 1 September 2012 (see p31).

If you started your course before 1 September 2014, see p56 for information on tuition fee grants.

Grant and loan for living costs: 2018 cohort students

If you start your part-time course in 2018/19 and are studying at course that is at least 25 per cent the intensity of an equivalent full-time course, you are entitled to a base grant, maintenance grant, special support payment (if this applies) and a loan for living costs on a similar basis to full-time students (see pp49–51 and p52). However, there are differences: the total amount you can receive is adjusted by the intensity of your study, it is not affected by where you study, and the minimum income threshold for support is different.

Base grant

All eligible part-time students, regardless of income, can receive a base grant. Student Finance Wales may refer to this as a 'minimum grant'. The amount you receive is £1,000 pro rata, based on the intensity of study.[32] For example, if you are studying at 50 per cent intensity (your course takes twice as long as the full-time equivalent), you receive £500.

Maintenance grant

You are entitled to a maintenance grant if your household income is less than £59,200. If your your household income is £25,000 or less or you are a care leaver, the maximum grant you can get is £5,000 pro rata by intensity of study. If your household income exceeds £25,000, your grant is calculated by subtracting £1 for every £6.84 of household income above £25,000 from the maximum £5,000. The remaining amount is then multiplied by the intensity of study to give the pro-rata amount.[33]

If you are entitled to claim benefits as a part-time student, you should claim the maintenance grant as a special support payment (see p50). This does not affect the amount you receive, but ensures it is not taken into account as income when calculating your benefit entitlement.[34]

Loan for living costs

If you start your course in 2018/19, you are entitled to a loan for your living costs. The amount you receive is not affected by your household income, but is reduced by any amount of maintenance grant you are entitled to, pound for pound. Like other part-time support, your entitlement to a loan is based on a notional maximum figure, pro rata according to the intensity of study. The maximum loan amount in 2018/19 is £5,650.[35]

Example

James is a part-time student at Trinity St David University, studying at 50 per cent intensity of a full-time course. His household income is £35,000 and he is not entitled to a special support payment. His entitlement to living costs support is calculated as follows.

Step one   Calculate his base grant, based on the intensity of study:

   £1,000 x 50 per cent intensity = £500

Step two   Calculate his maintenance grant, based on his income and the intensity of study:

   James' income (£35,000) is £10,000 over the threshold of £25,000.

   £10,000 ÷ £6.84 = £1,462

   Maximum maintenance grant of £5,000 – £1,462 = £3,538

   £3,538 x 50 per cent intensity = £1,769

Step three Calculate his loan, based on the intensity of study and offset by his maintenance grant:

   £5,650 x 50 per cent intensity = £2,825

   £2,825 – £1,769 = £1,056

   James' total support = £500 base grant + £1,769 maintenance grant + £1,056 living costs loan = £3,325

Grant for course costs: pre-2018 cohort students

If your course started in the 2017/18 academic year or earlier, a grant for course costs of up to £1,155 is available to students from low-income backgrounds to help with the costs of books, equipment and travel.[36] You must be studying a course that is at least 50 per cent intensity of a full-time course – ie, it takes no longer than twice the time of the equivalent full-time course to complete. The exact amount you receive depends on your household income (see p59). This grant is not available to EU students. It does not affect your entitlement to means-tested benefits.

Maximum grant for part-time course costs 2018/19

Course intensity	Maximum grant available
Less than 60%	£1,155
60–74%	£1,155
75% or more	£1,155

Chapter 3: Undergraduate student support: Wales
3. How income affects student support

3

Disabled students' allowance

All part-time students who are are studying at an intensity of at least 25 per cent of an equivalent full-time course and have a disability can apply for a disabled students' allowance.[37] The amount Student Finance Wales can award for non-medical help and other general expenditure is, however, reduced according to the workload of a part-time course.

Grants for dependants

All part-time students who are studying at an intensity of at least 50 per cent of an equivalent full-time course and have dependent children or an adult dependant can apply for the **childcare grant**, **parents' learning allowance** or **adult dependants' grant**.[38] See p55 for further information. The amount you can receive depends on your income and that of your household.

The amount Student Finance Wales can award is reduced pro rata according to the workload of the part-time course.

Fee waiver

This is available to part-time students undertaking no more than 20 credits in the academic year, who are in receipt of a means-tested benefit, and whose sole income is benefits or who are registered jobseekers. Students who already have a first degree are not eligible. This scheme is administered by universities and colleges.

3. **How income affects student support**

How your income is assessed

Much of the support you receive is based on your household income. The definition of household income in Wales is the same as that in England (see p39).

Once your household income is assessed, it first reduces any maintenance grant or special support grant you are due to receive. The assessment is different, depending on whether you are a full-time or part-time student and which cohort of students you are in.

Full-time students

2018 cohort students

In 2018/19, the following applies:[39]

- Regardless of your household income, you receive the base grant of £1,000.
- If your household income is £18,370 or less, you receive the maximum additional maintenance grant which applies.

- If your household income is between £18,371 and £59,200, you receive a reduced amount of the maintenance grant.
  - If you are entitled to the parental home rate, for every £6.937 of your income that exceeds £18,370, your grant is reduced by £1.
  - If you are entitled to the London rate, for every £4.475 of your income that exceeds £18,370, your grant is reduced by £1.
  - If you are entitled to the elsewhere rate, for every £5.570 of your income that exceeds £18,370, your grant is reduced by £1.
- If your household income is £59,200 or more, you do not receive a maintenance grant. Income above £59,200 may also reduce any supplementary grants for dependants,[40] and may reduce the grant for travel by up to £1,000, if the total amount payable to you exceeds £303.[41]

2012 cohort students
In 2018/19, the following applies.[42]
- If your household income is £18,370 or less, you receive the maximum maintenance or special support grant.
- If your household income is between £18,371 and £50,020, you receive a reduced amount of the applicable grant (the minimum amount is £50).
  - For every £3.653 of household income between £18,371 and £26,500, £1 is deducted from the grant.
  - For every £4.18 of household income between £26,501 and £34,000, £1 is deducted from the grant.
  - For every £14.67 of household income above £34,000, £1 is deducted from the grant until the maximum household income of £50,020 is reached.
- No grant is payable if household income is £50,021 or more.

Income above £50,753 reduces other support at a rate of £1 for every £5 of additional income.[43] Any supplementary grants for dependants are reduced first, then the 25 per cent of the student loan that is means tested, and finally any grant for travel costs.[44]

Part-time students
If you started your course on or after 1 September 2014 but before 1 August 2018, your course is at least 50 per cent intensity of an equivalent full-time course, the following applies.[45]
  If you are single and have no dependents:
- If your income is below £26,095, you receive the full course costs grant.
- If your income is between £26,096 and £28,180, you receive a partial grant.
- If your income exceeds £28,180, you do not receive any grant.

If you started your course before 1 September 2014, the following applies.[46]
  If you are single and have no dependants:
- If your income is £16,864 or less, you are eligible for the maximum grant for fees and course costs.

- If your income is between £16,865 and £25,435, you receive some help with fees and course costs.
- If your income is between £25,436 and £28,180, you receive some help with course costs, but not with fees. The exact amount you receive depends on your income.
- If your income exceeds £28,180, you cannot receive support for fees or course costs.

Your taxable income and the taxable income of your partner is taken into account when determining how much support you receive. Your parents' income is ignored.

The above also applies if you are married or in a civil partnership, or aged 25 or over and living with a partner (including a same-sex partner) or have dependent children, but the following amounts are deducted from your income:[47]

- £2,000 for your partner;
- £2,000 for your eldest child;
- £1,000 for every other child.

If you are entitled to a grant for a dependant (see p59), a different income assessment applies.

Student Finance Wales has published further information on its website at www.studentfinancewales.co.uk.

4. **Discretionary hardship funds**

Higher education institutions usually provide discretionary hardship funds for 'home' (see p22) undergraduate and postgraduate students in financial difficulty. The funds issue both repayable loans and non-repayable grants. They are sometimes known as Financial Contingency Funds in Wales.

Non-repayable grants may be available on a needs-assessed basis if you are experiencing financial difficulty serious enough to mean you may have to leave your course.

In most cases, hardship funds can help with living and study costs, such as childcare, rent, course costs and utility bills, or with large one-off and exceptional costs, such as major housing repairs and emergency situations such as fire or bereavement. Generally, hardship funds do not assist with the payment of tuition fees. The institution has discretion and makes the final decision.

Priority is usually given to students with children, mature students, students from low-income families, disabled students, final-year students and those who have left care. Usually, you must have applied for your full entitlement of a student loan, if you are eligible for one.

Individual institutions have different application processes and different pressures on the funds available and no sum is guaranteed. However, there is normally an appeals process if you want to challenge the fund administrator's decision.

Notes

1. **Full-time undergraduates**
   1 Sch 2 E(SS)(W) Regs; Sch 1 E(SS)(W) Regs 2017
   2 Regs 5-8 E(SS)(W) Regs; reg 5 and Sch 2 E(SS) Regs 2017
   3 Regs 14-18 and 24 E(SS)(W) Regs; regs 6 and 7 E(SS)(W) Regs 2017
   4 Reg 24 E(SS)(W) Regs; reg 7 E(SS)(W) Regs 2017
   5 Reg 54 E(SS)(W)Regs; reg 7(5) E(SS)(W) Regs 2017
   6 Reg 25 E(SS)(W) Regs; reg 81 E(SS)(W) Regs 2017
   7 Regs 14-15 E(SS)(W) Regs; reg 6 E(SS)(W) Regs 2017
   8 Reg 15 E(SS)(W) Regs; reg 6 E(SS)(W) Regs 2017
   9 Reg 40 E(SS)(W) Regs; reg 19 E(SS)(W) Regs 2017
   10 Reg 16 E(SS)(W) Regs 2017
   11 Reg 19 E(SS)(W) Regs 2017
   12 Regs 43-45 E(SS)(W) Regs
   13 Reg 46 E(SS)(W) Regs
   14 Reg 51 E(SS)(W) Regs
   15 Regs 50-52 and 56 E(SS)(W) Regs
   16 Reg 38 E(SS)(W) Regs 2017
   17 Reg 38 E(SS)(W) Regs 2017
   18 Reg 39 E(SS)(W) Regs 2017
   19 Reg 55 E(SS)(W) Regs
   20 Reg 56 E(SS)(W) Regs
   21 Reg 56 E(SS)(W) Regs 2017
   22 Regs 41-52 E(SS)(W) Regs 2017
   23 Reg 74 E(SS)(W) Regs; reg 28 E(SS)(W) Regs 2017
   24 Reg 76 E(SS)(W) Regs; reg 27 E(SS)(W) Regs 2017
   25 Reg 72 E(SS)(W) Regs; reg 26 E(SS)(W) Regs 2017

   26 Reg 63 E(SS)(W) Regs; reg 24 E(SS)(W) Regs 2017
   27 Regs 64-67 E(SS)(W) Regs; regs 32-34 E(SS)(W) Regs 2017

2. **Part-time undergraduates**
   28 Reg 21 E(SS)(W) Regs; reg 81(28) E(SS)(W) Regs 2017
   29 Reg 85 E(SS)(W) Regs
   30 Reg 86(3) E(SS)(W)Regs
   31 Reg 86(4) E(SS)(W)Regs
   32 Reg 45 E(SS)(W) Regs
   33 Reg 47 E(SS)(W) Regs
   34 Reg 52 E(SS)(W) Regs
   35 Reg 58 E(SS)(W) Regs
   36 Regs 85 and 87 E(SS)(W) Regs 2017
   37 Reg 63 E(SS)(W) Regs; reg 88 E(SS)(W) Regs 2017
   38 Reg 77(2) E(SS)(W) Regs; regs 89-93 E(SS)(W) Regs 2017

3. **How income affects student support**
   39 Reg 46 E(SS)(W) Regs
   40 Reg 46 E(SS)(W) Regs
   41 Reg 65 E(SS)(W) Regs
   42 Regs 36 and 39 E(SS)(W) Regs 2017
   43 Sch 5 E(SS)(W) Regs 2017
   44 Reg 56 E(SS)(W) Regs 2017
   45 Reg 85(5) E(SS)(W) Regs 2017
   46 Reg 85(5) E(SS)(W) Regs 2017
   47 Reg 9(8) E(SS)(W) Regs 2017

Chapter 4

Undergraduate student support: Northern Ireland

This chapter covers:
1. Full-time undergraduates (p64)
2. Part-time undergraduates (p69)
3. How income affects student support (p71)
4. Discretionary support funds (p72)

There are different systems of undergraduate student support in England, Wales, Northern Ireland and Scotland. See Chapter 2 for details of the system in England, Chapter 3 for Wales, and CPAG's *Benefits for Students in Scotland Handbook* for details of the system in Scotland.

Students living in Northern Ireland who wish to study in England, Wales or Scotland receive the same package of support as though they were studying in Northern Ireland.

Basic facts
- Undergraduate students can apply for a mixture of grants and loans, depending on their personal circumstances.
- The type of financial support available depends on several factors, including when the course starts, its length, the discipline, whether the course is full time or part time, and any previous study undertaken.
- Separate provision is available for social work, healthcare and initial teacher training students.
- Discretionary funds are available for those in financial difficulty, but funding is not guaranteed.

1. **Full-time undergraduates**

Student awards for Northern Irish-domiciled students studying in Northern Ireland, mainland Britain or the Republic of Ireland are administered by the Department for the Economy (DfENI). Applications for support are processed by the Education Authority, under the 'brand' of Student Finance NI. You should apply via the Student Finance NI website, or to the Education Authority regional office that covers the area in which you normally live, rather than where you intend to study. A list of offices is at www.studentfinanceni.co.uk.

Who is eligible for support

In order to receive financial support, you must be 'personally eligible' by meeting residence conditions (see below) and be studying an eligible course (see below).

Residence conditions

To be eligible for support from Student Finance NI, you must meet the residence conditions.[1] These are the same as for England (see p21), except that, where appropriate, you must be normally resident in Northern Ireland on the first day of the first academic year. Also, in Northern Ireland, students from overseas with certain forms of leave to remain can receive support, unlike in England. Ask an adviser for information.

Following the result of the referendum on the UK's membership of the European Union (EU), the DfENI has stated that students from other EU countries who started their courses before 2019/20, or who commence a course in 2019/20, and who have been assessed as eligible for funding will continue to receive it as normal until they complete the course. Rules for students starting courses in future years are uncertain. You should check the Student Finance NI website.

Course eligibility

To be eligible for support, broadly the course must be full time (as defined by the education provider) and be:[2]

- a first degree;
- a higher education diploma;
- a BTEC Higher National Certificate (HNC) or Higher National Diploma (HND);
- a course of initial teacher training;
- a course for the further training of teachers, or youth or community workers;
- a course to prepare for certain professional examinations of a standard higher than A level, or HNC/HND where a first degree is not required for entry;
- a course not higher than a first degree, but higher than those described in the above bullet point.

Note: some courses, particularly in art and design, can require the student to undertake a foundation year or course. This is different to a foundation degree. It is normally a course of one academic year in length which precedes the main higher education degree course.

Support for foundation courses is often limited as they do not usually come within the definition of 'higher education'. You may be eligible for support as a further education student (see Chapter 1). Contact an adviser in your students' union or institution for further guidance.

Previous study

If you have previously attended a higher education course, the amount of support you can receive may be affected by the rules on previous study.[3]

If you hold an honours degree and are studying for a new qualification, unless you are covered by one of the exceptions (see below), you can only apply for a supplementary grant for travel costs, a grant for any dependants and a grant for disability-related costs.[4]

There are some exceptions.

- Students who hold an honours degree and who are undertaking a Postgraduate Certificate in Education (PGCE) or social work course receive full funding.
- Students undertaking a further undergraduate course in certain professional subjects, such as medicine or veterinary science, can receive a loan for their living costs,[5] although not a loan for tuition fees or a maintenance or special support grant.

If you do not already hold an honours degree, in general the maximum number of years of tuition fee loan and maintenance or special support grant funding you can receive is equivalent to the ordinary length of your course plus one year, less any years of study previously undertaken.[6] If you have studied part of a year, you are treated as if you have undertaken a full year of study. Loans for living costs are unaffected.

If you are transferring courses, or undertaking an 'end-on' course (topping up from one qualification to another), these previous study rules affect you. You may be able to secure additional years of 'full' funding if you were unable to complete a previous year or course for 'compelling personal reasons' such as illness or caring responsibilities.[7] You must provide evidence of this to Student Finance NI.

Further information on previous study is available from your students' union or institution.

Loan for tuition fees

Eligible Northern Irish-domiciled students studying in Northern Ireland pay variable fees of up to £4,160 in the 2018/19 academic year. You are eligible for a loan to cover these.[8]

If you started your course on 1 September 2012 or later and study in England, Scotland or Wales, you are charged up to £9,250 in the 2018/19 academic year. You are eligible for a loan to cover these fees.[9]

If you started your course in the Republic of Ireland on or after 1 September 2013, you are charged a student contribution of €3,000 in 2018/19. You can apply for a student contribution loan to cover the cost. The terms and conditions of student contribution loans are identical to those for tuition fee loans for students studying in the UK (see p68).[10] You can also apply for a maintenance grant or loan for your living costs (see below and p68).

The maximum fee loan or student contribution loan available matches the fee or contribution you are charged. Neither loan is means tested on your household income. However, the loan is added to your total student loan debt (including any loans taken out for living costs – see p68) and you must start repayments once you have graduated, or otherwise left the course, and are earning at least £18,330 a year.

If you wish to pay all or part of the fee upfront yourself, you can do so. Your institution will expect some indication of how you intend to pay your fees when you register.

Help with tuition fees for part-time courses is also available (see p69).

Maintenance grant

The maintenance grant is a non-repayable, means-tested allowance of up to £3,475. The maximum amount is payable to students with a household income of £19,203 or less a year, and a partial amount is paid on a sliding scale up to a household income of £41,065.[11]

If you are entitled to apply for means-tested benefits, the maintenance grant is treated as income when working out your (or your partner's) entitlement, so you should apply for the special support grant instead (see p67).

Part of the maintenance grant substitutes part of the student loan for living costs (see p68). This means that if you receive any maintenance grant, the amount of loan for living costs you can receive is reduced, up to a maximum of £1,887.[12] The formula for this can be complex, so get advice if you are uncertain whether it has been applied correctly.

If you get a full maintenance grant of £3,475, the maximum amount of student loan for living costs is reduced by £1,887. If you get a maintenance grant of more than £1,318 but less than £3,475, your loan is reduced by an amount equal to £1,887 less £1 for every £17.25 that your household income exceeds £19,203. If your grant is £1,318 or less, the loan is reduced by the amount of maintenance grant paid.

See p39 for how your household income is calculated and p71 for how it affects your student support.

The way the grant affects a loan is slightly different for teacher training students. Check with Student Finance NI, or your students' union or university advice service.

Examples

Laura is a single, independent student studying in Belfast. She starts her course in October 2018. Her household income is £2,000. She receives the maximum grant of £3,475 and can take out a student loan of up to £2,953 (the maximum rate of £4,840 *less* £1,887).

Anne is 18 and lives with her parents in Armagh. She starts her course in Belfast in October 2018. Her household income is £21,500, which means she receives a maintenance grant of £2,921.
Her household income is £2,297 above the lower limit of £19,203. This £2,297 is divided by 17.25 to give £133. This is subtracted from the maximum loan deduction of £1,887 to give £1,754.
Anne's maximum loan entitlement is therefore £3,750 – £1,754 = £1,996

Iain is 19 and starts his course in Coleraine in October 2018. He receives a maintenance grant of £800. The maximum amount of loan he can receive is reduced by £800.

Special support grant

The special support grant is available to full-time students entitled to claim means-tested benefits who are regarded as particularly vulnerable.[13]

Most full-time students are not entitled to means-tested benefits. However, you may be entitled if, for example, you are a lone parent, or you and your partner are both full-time students and have one or more children, or you receive disability living allowance or personal independence payment, or you are deaf. See Chapters 10, 12, 13, 14 and 18 for details of which students can claim means-tested benefits.

If you get a means-tested benefit, you should claim the special support grant instead of the maintenance grant. Like the maintenance grant, the special support grant is a non-repayable, means-tested allowance of up to £3,475. The maximum amount is payable to students with a household income of £19,203 or less a year. A partial amount is paid on a sliding scale up to a household income of £41,065.

Unlike the maintenance grant, however, the special support grant does not substitute any part of the student loan and it is not taken into account as income when calculating your entitlement to means-tested benefits.

Loan for living costs

Students can apply for a means-tested student loan to help cover their living costs and other expenses. A quarter of the loan is means tested on your household income.

Maximum amount of loan 2018/19[14]

	Full year	Final year
London	£6,780	£6,170
Elsewhere	£4,840	£4,480
Parental home	£3,750	£3,390
Overseas rate	£5,770	£5,015

You may be entitled to an additional amount of loan for any extra weeks of attendance over the standard 30 weeks and three days. Your institution can clarify whether your course has additional weeks.

The table below shows the amount paid for each week your course exceeds the standard length. If your course year lasts 45 weeks or more, you are paid for a full 52 weeks of attendance.

Amount of extra weeks allowance 2018/19

	Weekly amount
London	£108
Elsewhere	£84
Parental home	£55
Overseas rate	£117

If you get a maintenance grant, up to £1,887 of the loan may be substituted for the maintenance grant paid. See p66 for details. If you receive a special support grant, no part of your loan is substituted.

The loan is repayable at the end of your studies. The amount of money you pay back each month depends on your earnings. Once you earn above £18,330 a year, repayments begin at the rate of 9 per cent of all income above this threshold. For example, if you earn £19,330 a year, you pay back 9 per cent of £1,000 – ie, £90 a year or £7.50 a month.

Supplementary grants

The **childcare grant**, **parents' learning allowance**, **adult dependants' grant** and **disabled students' allowance** are all available to Northern Irish undergraduates on the same basis as for students in England (see p32).[15]

Except for the disabled students' allowance, all these grants are means tested. **Note:** the rates for some of these grants are slightly different in Northern Ireland from what they are in England.

Maximum amounts of supplementary grants 2018/19

Parents' learning allowance	£1,538 a year
Childcare grant (one child)	£148.75 a week
Childcare grant (two or more children)	£255 a week
Adult dependants' grant	£2,695 a year
Disabled students' allowance (non-medical personal help)	£20,938 a year
Disabled students' allowance (equipment)	£5,266 for the duration of the course
Disabled students' allowance (general allowance)	£1,759 a year

Medical and dental students on placement and students who must travel abroad may be entitled to help with the cost of travel. This is awarded on the same basis as in England (see p34).

Erasmus and other study or work placements

Funding rules can be different if you are studying abroad or are on a work placement (sometimes known as a 'sandwich year'). Fees may be reduced, but in some circumstances student support for living costs may also be limited.

Students on Erasmus study exchanges or work placements can claim support for living costs as usual, and they may qualify for an additional Erasmus grant. See the British Council website for more details (www.britishcouncil.org/study-work-abroad/outside-uk/erasmus).

The funding rules for study abroad and sandwich years can be complex. Ask your university or students' union advice centre for more information.

2. Part-time undergraduates

Support for part-time students is different from that available for full-time students, although the course and personal eligibility requirements are the same (see p64).[16]

Grant for tuition fees

Part-time undergraduate students (including students from the European Union (EU) – see p22) may be eligible for an income-assessed grant for tuition fees.[17] The maximum amount of grant for which you are eligible depends on the intensity of study for each academic year of the course and your household income (see below). You must be studying at at least 50 per cent intensity of an equivalent full-time course to receive a fee grant.

Maximum grant for part-time fees 2018/19

Course intensity	Maximum grant available
Less than 60%	£820
60–74%	£985
75% or more	£1,230

Fee grants can be topped up with a tuition fee loan (see below) if the fee charged by the institution is higher than the grant received.

Loan for tuition fees

From the 2017/18 academic year, loans for tuition fees became available for part-time study. This includes students who started their course in previous academic years. A loan for tuition fees can be combined with a tuition fee grant (see above), if you are eligible for one.

Eligible Northern Irish-domiciled and non-UK EU students can access a non-means-tested loan for part-time study in the UK of up to £3,120 a year in 2018/19, provided they are studying at at least 25 per cent intensity of a full-time course.[18] If your course fee is lower than this amount, you can take out a loan up to the value of the fees charged, less any fee grant received. If the fees charged are higher than your fee loan (and fee grant, if applicable) and your support does not cover the total cost of the course, you must pay the difference. You can receive fee loans for up to 16 years of study in total.[19]

Repayment arrangements are the same as for full-time students (see p68), except that repayments start after four years of a part-time course, provided your income is above the repayment threshold, even if you have not yet completed the course.

Grant for course costs

A grant of up to £265 is available to students from low-income backgrounds to help with the costs of books, equipment and travel.[20] You must be studying at at least 50 per cent intensity of an equivalent full-time course. This grant is not available to EU students.

Disabled students' allowance

If you are studying at an intensity of at least 25 per cent of an equivalent full-time course and have a disability, you can apply for a disabled students' allowance. The amount that can be awarded for non-medical help and other general expenditure is, however, reduced according to the workload of a part-time course.

Maximum amount of disabled students' allowance 2018/19[21]

Non-medical personal helper(s)	£15,703 per academic year
Major items of specialist equipment	£5,266 for the duration of the course
Other expenditure	Up to £1,319 per academic year
Extra travel expenditure resulting from disability	Full reimbursement

---

3. How income affects student support

Full-time students

Much of the support you receive is based on your household income. The way your household income is assessed is the same as that in England (see p39).

Once your household income is assessed, it first reduces any maintenance grant or special support grant you are due to receive.

In 2018/19, the following applies.[22]

- If your household income is £19,203 or less, you receive the maximum maintenance or special support grant.
- If your household income is between £19,204 and £41,065, you receive a reduced amount of the applicable grant (the minimum amount is £50).
  - For every £4.55 of household income between £19,204 and £29,019, £1 is deducted from the grant.
  - For every £9.50 of household income above £29,019, £1 is deducted from the grant until the maximum household income of £41,065 is reached.
- No grant is payable if your household income is £41,066 or more.

Income above £41,540 reduces other support at a rate of £1 for every £9.50 of income above that figure.[23] Any supplementary grants for dependants are reduced first, then the 25 per cent of the student loan that is means tested and, finally, any grant for travel costs.[24]

Part-time students

Loans for tuition fees and the disabled students' allowance are not means tested. Other support depends on your household income.

In 2018/19, the following applies.

- If your income is below £16,843, you are eligible for the maximum grant for fees and course costs.

- If your income is between £16,843 and £24,420, you receive some help with fees and course costs.
- If your income is between £25,421 and £28,067, you receive some help with course costs, but not with fees. The exact amount you receive depends on your income.
- If your income is £28,067, you receive a course grant of £50. If your income is above this amount, you receive no support.

Only your and your partner's income is taken into account when assessing your household income. Your parents' income is ignored, regardless of your age.[25]

If you are married or in a civil partnership, or are aged 25 or over and living with a partner (including a same-sex partner), or have dependent children, the following amounts are deducted from your income:[26]

- £2,000 for your partner;
- £2,000 for your eldest child;
- £1,000 for every other child.

---

4. Discretionary support funds

Higher education institutions are allocated money to provide hardship funds for 'home' (see p22) undergraduate and postgraduate students in financial difficulty. In Northern Ireland these are known as 'support funds'. Repayable loans and non-repayable grants can be issued, although support is not guaranteed. Additional hardship funds may be available – check with your institution or students' union.

Non-repayable grants may be available on a needs-assessed basis if you are experiencing financial difficulty serious enough to mean you may have to leave your course. The funds can help with living and study costs such as childcare, rent, books and utility bills, or with large one-off and exceptional costs, such as major housing repairs and emergency situations, such as fire or bereavement.

Priority is usually given to students with children, mature students, students from low-income families, disabled students, final-year students and those who have left care. However, all students who meet the personal and course requirements for undergraduate student support can apply, including healthcare students. You must, however, have applied for your full entitlement of a student loan, if you are eligible for one.

The funds cannot be used to meet the costs of tuition fees or to make up for non-receipt of a parental contribution to a grant or loan.

Grants are not normally more than £3,500, although institutions have some discretion in exceptional circumstances. Individual institutions have different application processes and different pressures on the funds, and no sum is guaranteed. However, there is an appeals process if you want to challenge a decision.

Notes

1. Full-time undergraduates
1 Sch 1 E(SS)(NI) Regs
2 Reg 5 and Sch 2 E(SS)(NI) Regs
3 Regs 14 and 15 E(SS)(NI) Regs
4 Regs 20, 57, 59 and 63 E(SS)(NI) Regs
5 Reg 63(2) E(SS)(NI) Regs
6 Reg 23 E(SS)(NI) Regs
7 Reg 20(10) E(SS)(NI) Regs
8 Regs 20-25 E(SS)(NI) Regs
9 Reg 25(1) E(SS)(NI) Regs
10 Reg 25A E(SS)(NI) Regs
11 Reg 58 E(SS)(NI) Regs
12 Reg 66 E(SS)(NI) Regs
13 Regs 59 and 60 E(SS)(NI) Regs
14 Reg 68 E(SS)(NI) Regs
15 Regs 41-56 E(SS)(NI) Regs

2. Part-time undergraduates
16 Regs 122-24 E(SS)(NI) Regs
17 Reg 126 E(SS)(NI) Regs
18 Reg 127A E(SS)(NI) Regs
19 Reg 126(5A) E(SS)(NI) Regs
20 Reg 126(1)(b) E(SS)(NI) Regs
21 Reg 130 E(SS)(NI) Regs

3. How income affects student support
22 Regs 58(5) and 60(5) E(SS)(NI) Regs
23 Sch 5 para 9 E(SS)(NI) Regs
24 Regs 88 and 90 E(SS)(NI) Regs
25 Reg 127 E(SS)(NI) Regs
26 Reg 128 E(SS)(NI) Regs

5

Chapter 5

Postgraduate student support

This chapter covers:

1. Studentships (below)
2. Postgraduate loans for master's degrees (p75)
3. Postgraduate loans for doctoral courses (p77)
4. Disabled students' allowance (p79)
5. Postgraduate support in Northern Ireland (p79)

Basic facts

– Students on postgraduate courses of initial teacher training (eg, a Postgraduate Certificate in Education) can apply for financial support in the same way as undergraduates.

– English and Welsh students may be able to receive a bursary for postgraduate study in social work, but this is not available to Northern Irish students studying in England or Wales.

– Individual scholarships or 'studentships' are available from seven research councils, but the demand far outstrips supply and funding is not guaranteed.

– Non-means-tested loans are available for students normally resident in England, Wales or another European Union country to assist with the cost of certain master's courses and, from 2018/19, certain doctoral courses.

– Disabled postgraduates may be able to receive help to meet their additional costs of learning through the disabled students' allowance.

– A non-means-tested postgraduate loan for tuition fees is available for students from Northern Ireland.

1. Studentships

Research councils fund a number of research and master's studentships (scholarships), covering fees and living costs. The indicative rate for a maintenance stipend in 2018/19 is £14,777. A grant for tuition fees is usually paid in addition to maintenance (£4,260 in 2018/19). Other schemes may be available, and eligibility and residence conditions apply. Additional allowances may also be available if you have dependants, and some research councils fund part-time study.

Research council funding is currently awarded directly to research organisations, and these organisations are responsible for selecting students. Opportunities/studentships are usually advertised on university websites and students should contact the university directly rather than the individual research council. While research fees are not regulated by government policy, institutions should not expect students to pay a fee that is higher than the amount of grant that is available for fees available.

See UK Research and Innovation (www.ukri.org/skills/funding-for-research-training) for information on studentships. Alternatively, check the various research councils websites, which are listed on the UK Research and Innovation website.

The British Academy also offers studentships on a similar basis to research councils. See www.britac.ac.uk/funding for details.

2. Postgraduate loans for master's degrees

A non-means-tested loan is available to assist with the cost of a 'stand-alone' full-time or part-time master's course, lasting up to four years. It is only available for students who normally live in England or Wales, or in another European Union (EU) country. The amount you receive depends on where you normally live and when you started your course.

To be eligible, the course cannot be combined with another qualification – eg, an undergraduate engineering course which ends with a master's year (sometimes known as an 'integrated master's' course).

The amount of the loan in 2018/19 is:
- £10,609 if you are normally resident in England (or an EU student studying in England);
- £13,000 if you are normally resident in Wales (or an EU student studying in Wales).

Note: the above amounts are for the whole course, not for each year – if, for example, you are on a part-time course taking the qualification over three years, the loan is divided by three and then paid in instalments over the length of the course.

The loan is offered by Student Finance England and Student Finance Wales to students living in the relevant country. The regulations for each scheme are different, but the rules are essentially the same. If you are from Northern Ireland, see p79.

Who is eligible

To be eligible, you must:[1]
* be aged under 60 on the first day of the first academic year of your course;
* not already hold a master's level qualification (including an integrated master's);
* not be in breach of any obligation to repay a student loan;
* not be deemed 'unfit' to receive a loan – eg, if you have been involved in fraud;
* not be eligible for a healthcare bursary or social work bursary for the course. However, if you apply for a bursary and are unsuccessful, you can then apply for a postgraduate loan;
* meet the residency rules (see below).

To be eligible, you must be domiciled in England or Wales (as appropriate) and show that you have been ordinarily resident in the 'UK and islands'[2] for three years prior to the first day of the first academic year of the course. Your master's course can be undertaken anywhere in the UK. Migrant workers from the EU (see p23) and those with 'long residence' (see p21) can also qualify under this category.

A non-UK EU national who has been ordinarily resident anywhere in the European Economic Area or Switzerland for three years prior to the start of the course, but who does not meet the above three-year residency rule, can apply for a loan if s/he plans to study at an institution in England or Wales.

EU students undertaking a distance learning course must live in England (if studying in England) or Wales (if studying in Wales) while undertaking the course.

All applicants are asked to provide evidence of their residency.

Students who are ordinarily resident in Scotland or Northern Ireland cannot apply for this loan, even if they wish to study in England or Wales. If you moved to England or Wales for the purposes of full-time study (including an undergraduate degree), you are not regarded as ordinarily resident there.

Note: the residency rules are complex. If you are unsure about whether you are entitled, speak to an adviser in your institution or students' union.

Which courses are eligible

Only designated courses wholly or mainly provided by an institution in the UK, and which lead to a full 'stand-alone' master's qualification are eligible.[3] Postgraduate diplomas, postgraduate certificates and courses that allow students to top up from one postgraduate qualification to another are not eligible. Examples of eligible courses are:
* MA (Master of Arts);
* MSc (Master of Science);
* LLM (Master of Law);
* MBA (Master of Business Administration);

- MPhil (Master of Philosophy);
- MLitt (Master of Letters).

Students with prior experience or learning and who do not intend to enrol on a full stand-alone masters qualification are not eligible. Student Finance England or Student Finance Wales can clarify if a course is eligible.

To be eligible, the course must be at least one academic year's duration. It can be:

- a full-time course lasting one or two years; *or*
- a part-time course lasting two years which is equivalent to a one-year full-time course; *or*
- a part-time course lasting three or four years which is equivalent to a two-year full-time course; *or*
- a part-time course lasting up to three years, if no equivalent full-time course exists.

Payment and repayments

You only need make one application for a loan. Payments are then made in three equal instalments during the academic year. If your course started in 2016/17 and lasts for two or more years, your requested amount is paid over the first two years with no payments made in years three or four (if applicable). If your course started in the 2017/18 academic year or later, the payments are made over the duration of the course (up to four years if you are studying part time). The first payment is made at the start of the course, with the second and third payments made in the last week of the fourth and seventh month after the notified start of the course.

You repay the loan in broadly the same way as undergraduate student loans[4] (see p31), starting in the April after you complete the course. However, there are three significant differences:

- repayments do not start until April 2019;[5]
- repayments are collected concurrently with any existing income-contingent loans you may have with the Student Loans Company;[6]
- the repayment rate is at 6 per cent of anything you earn over £21,000.[7] This repayment threshold is frozen until at least 2021.

3. Postgraduate loans for doctoral courses

From the 2018/19 academic year, a new non-means-tested loan of up to £25,000 per course is available to assist students with the cost of a postgraduate doctoral qualification.[8]

There are two loan schemes available, one in England and the other in Wales, although the rules are essentially identical. If you are ordinarily resident in

England, or a student from a European Union (EU) country studying in England, apply to Student Finance England. If you are ordinarily resident in Wales, or a student from an EU country studying in Wales, apply to Student Finance Wales. Students ordinarily resident in Northern Ireland (or Scotland) are not eligible for a doctoral loan.

Who is eligible

To be eligible for the loan, you must:[9]
- be aged under 60 on the first day of the first academic year of your course;
- not already hold a doctoral level qualification;
- not be in breach of any obligation to repay a student loan;
- not be eligible for any research council funding for the course;
- meet the residency rules (these are the same as for master's loans – see p76).

Which courses are eligible

Your course must also be eligible. It must:[10]
- be a full, stand-alone doctoral course (not a top-up course);
- have started on or after 1 August 2018 (if you are already on a doctoral course that you started before this date, you are not eligible);
- last between three and eight academic years;
- normally be provided by a university in the UK with research degree-awarding powers.

Integrated doctoral courses (ie, those that have an integrated master's degree as part of the course) are also eligible. However, you must be registered on the full doctoral qualification and you cannot receive a postgraduate loan for a master's degree at the same time.

You can receive a doctoral loan if your course is full or part time, provided the part-time course takes no longer than eight years. The qualification can be taught or research-based, or it can be a combination of both.

Payment and repayments

To apply for the loan, you make a single application at the start of your course. Payments are made in three instalments per year, for each year of the course. The first payment is made at the start of the course once your university confirm you are attending; then you will receive the second and third payments at the end of the fourth and seventh month in the year.

The maximum annual amount of the loan is £10,609.[11] If you do not take out a loan until later in your course (eg, only in your last year), this may mean receiving less than the £25,000 maximum loan overall.

You repay the loan in the same way as a postgraduate loan for a master's degree (see p77). If you have both a master's loan and a doctoral loan, you make one monthly repayment for both. However, repayments of your doctoral loan can start in the April after you complete the course or the April four years after you commence your course (whichever comes first) should your income be over the postgraduate loan repayment threshold – currently £21,000.

4. Disabled students' allowance

Both full-time and part-time postgraduate students studying 'recognised' taught and research courses can apply for a disabled students' allowance.

A 'recognised course' is one which normally requires a first degree to gain entry, is at least one academic year long, is provided by a publicly funded institution and is not a course of initial teacher training. Your course must be eligible for an award from a research council or be equivalent to a course that is eligible for an award. However, if the course you are undertaking allows you to apply for its own equivalent allowance, you must apply for this.

Part-time courses must last for longer than one year. If you started the course in 2012/13 or later, it must be possible to complete it in no more than four times the time of an equivalent full-time course. If you started your course before 2012/13, it must be possible to complete it in no more than twice the time of an equivalent full-time course.

There is no age limit for a disabled students' allowance, but the same personal eligibility and residency conditions as for undergraduates apply (see p21).

There is one single allowance available of up to £10,993 a year in 2018/19 in England, £10,590 in Wales and £10,469 in Northern Ireland for specialist equipment, non-medical personal helpers and/or additional travel costs, subject to a needs assessment.[12]

Contact Student Finance England, Student Finance Wales or Student Finance NI for more details.

Note: students may be expected to pay the first £200 towards any IT equipment, although some institutions have hardship funds or bursaries to help with this cost. Some non-medical help and other support may be provided by the institution. Speak to an adviser in your institution for more information.

Students funded through one of the main studentship programmes (see p74) are eligible for more generous disabled students' allowance funding through the research council. Contact the disability support office at your institution about an application.

5. Postgraduate support in Northern Ireland

In Northern Ireland, postgraduate support is in the form of a limited number of postgraduate studentships and a loan for tuition fees.

Studentships

The Department for the Economy and the Department of Agriculture, Environment and Rural Affairs in Northern Ireland award funds to Ulster University and Queen's University Belfast for research and for certain approved courses of full-time study leading to higher degrees. The universities are responsible for administering these awards and the application process is very competitive.

Grants may be awarded for postgraduate research degrees (eg, MPhils and PhDs) and for approved courses of advanced study – eg, master's degrees. You can obtain a list of approved courses from the universities. Most students benefiting from these awards have degrees awarded at 2:1 or above, although you may be accepted for a taught master's degree in science and technology if you have a lower second class honours degree.

Studentship awards are for fixed amounts and are not means tested. Approved fees and maintenance costs are included. The basic rate of the maintenance grant payable in 2018/19 is £14,777 for research studentships, and £7,386 for taught studentships. Additional allowances may also be paid for dependants and students with special needs.

If you are a science and technology student working on a research project, you may also be able to apply for a Co-operative Award in Science and Technology (CAST) that involves sponsorship from industry. Details on this and other studentships are available from www.nidirect.gov.uk/articles/postgraduate-awards.

The Department of Agriculture, Environment and Rural Affairs runs a separate scheme, providing postgraduate studentships in its priority research areas. Applications for these scholarships normally open in the December before term starts and close around February before term starts, so it is important to apply early. See www.daera-ni.gov.uk/articles/postgraduate-study for more details.

Closing dates for the different awards vary, but are strictly observed. Check the closing date with the postgraduate office at the university you will be attending.

Loan for tuition fees

From the 2017/18 academic year onwards, postgraduate tuition fee loans for students from Northern Ireland wanting to study in the UK (or European Union students wanting to study in Northern Ireland) are available. The loan is non-means tested and is paid for tuition fees only – there is no loan for living costs.

A maximum of £5,500 per course can be borrowed,[13] which is paid directly to the university. The maximum loan may not cover the tuition fees you are charged – you must cover any remaining fee yourself, as well as funding for your living costs.

Residency rules are the same as for undergraduate courses (see p64). Courses can be full time, part time or distance learning, but must be no more than three years in duration.[14] The qualifications covered are as for England and Wales (see p76), but a loan can also be made for postgraduate certificate or diploma courses.[15]

If you already hold a master's qualification, you can still take out this loan for a further course. However, you are only allowed one postgraduate tuition fee loan in total.

The rules on repayments are the same as for undergraduate funding (see p68), with the postgraduate tuition fee loan being added to the undergraduate loan balance (if applicable).

Studying in Northern Ireland

If you are seeking research funding and want to study in Northern Ireland, you must apply directly to the university for a place on a course and an award. Being offered a place does not automatically mean that you will obtain funding. Closing dates for applications are at the discretion of the institution (and are generally around April/May), but late applications may be accepted subject to availability of places.

Studying elsewhere in the UK

If you plan to study elsewhere in the UK, you may be able to receive funding through various research councils (see p74). You must approach the university where you want to study, not the research council, but it is always worth checking with the research council to which universities it has allocated funding. Closing dates vary, but are normally well before the start of term.

Disabled students' allowance

A postgraduate disabled students' allowance is available to eligible postgraduate students in Northern Ireland on a similar basis as for postgraduate students in England and Wales (see p79). You should apply to Student Finance NI.

Notes

2. Postgraduate loans for master's degrees
1 Reg 3 E(PMDL) Regs; reg 3 E(PMDL)(W) Regs
2 'Islands' in this context means the Channel Islands and the Isle of Man.
3 Reg 4 E(PMDL) Regs; reg 3 E(PMDL)(W) Regs
4 E(SL)(R) Regs (as amended)
5 Reg 26(3) E(PMDL) Regs
6 Reg 39(3) E(PMDL) Regs
7 Reg 39(2) E(PMDL) Regs

5

Chapter 5: Postgraduate student support
Notes
• •

**3. Postgraduate loans for doctoral
courses**
   8 Reg 12 E(PDDL) Regs; reg 12
      E(PDDL)(W) Regs
   9 Reg 3 E(PDDL) Regs; reg 3 E(PDDL)(W)
      Regs
  10 Reg 4 E(PDDL) Regs; reg 4 E(PDDL)(W)
      Regs
  11 Reg 14 E(PDDL) Regs; reg 13
      E(PDDL)(W) Regs

4. Disabled students' allowance
  12 Reg 158 E(SS) Regs; reg 117 E(SS)(W)
      Regs; reg 146 E(SS)NI Regs

**5. Postgraduate support in Northern
Ireland**
  13 Reg 156 E(SS)(NI) Regs
  14 Reg 152(2) E(SS)(NI) Regs
  15 Reg 152 and Sch 3B E(SS)(NI) Regs

Chapter 6

. . . .

Vocational courses and other sources of student support

This chapter covers:
1. Healthcare students in England and Wales (below)
2. Healthcare students in Northern Ireland (p92)
3. Initial teacher training in England (p94)
4. Initial teacher training in Wales (p97)
5. Initial teacher training in Northern Ireland (p99)
6. Social work students (p99)
7. Dance and drama awards (p103)
8. Alternative sources of finance (p104)

. . . .

Basic facts
– Specific funding is provided for certain vocational courses, sometimes in addition to the standard student support available.
– The NHS in England and Wales, and the Northern Ireland Executive, provide support for healthcare students, including medicine, dentistry and social work students. However, there is only limited support from the NHS for most new healthcare students in England.
– Incentives are provided for teacher training in England and Wales.
– Dance and drama students in private colleges may qualify for support.
– Certain other sources of funding, including charitable support, are available.

. . . .

1. Healthcare students in England and Wales

Healthcare students who meet certain personal and residency criteria, and who are undertaking an eligible course (see p84) in England and Wales are funded by the NHS bursary scheme.

The personal and residency criteria for NHS bursaries are similar to those for other undergraduate study (see p21), although support for NHS courses is usually available even if you already hold a degree.

Healthcare courses
- Allied health professions: chiropody, dietetics, occupational therapy, orthoptics, physiotherapy, prosthetics and orthotics, radiography, operating department practice, speech and language therapy
- Professions complementary to dentistry: dental hygiene, dental therapy
- Nursing and midwifery
- Medicine and dentistry (the latter stages of pre-registration training only)

The funding that is available depends on when you started your course.
- If you started a course in England on or after 1 August 2017, see below.
- If you started your course on or after 1 September 2012 and, in England, before 1 August 2017, see p86.
- If you started your course between 1 September 2007 and 31 August 2012, see p90.

Note: medicine and dentistry students in their initial years of training are funded by Student Finance England or Student Finance Wales. When you move onto the NHS bursary scheme, you are funded under the rules that were in place when you started your course. So, a medical student who started in the 2011/12 academic year and who moved onto the NHS bursary scheme in 2015/16 is funded under the 2007 rules.

Employed students (sometimes known as seconded students) do not usually qualify for bursaries, but may qualify for student support payable by the Department for Education or the Welsh government (see Chapters 2 and 3).

Students who started their course in England on or after 1 August 2017

The NHS bursary scheme was abolished for most new healthcare students in England from 1 August 2017. It is still available for those taking medical or dental courses (see p85) and some courses in dental hygiene and dental therapy (see p85). All other healthcare students who would previously have been eligible for an NHS bursary must now apply for the standard support package from Student Finance England (see Chapter 2) or the equivalent funding body in Northern Ireland, Scotland or Wales. The NHS continues to offer some limited help to healthcare students with children, as well as placement and some limited hardship funding (see p86).

The abolition of the bursary means that affected students are charged fees for their courses. Loans for these are available, as for other students (see p27 and p49).

If you started your course before 1 August 2017 in England, or you are studying in Wales, you continue to be funded by the NHS bursary until you complete your course.

Medical and dental students

Medical and dental students studying in England continue to be eligible for NHS bursaries in the later stages of their course – usually from year five on a standard undergraduate course (see p28). Those starting in 2018/19 are funded under the 2012 bursary arrangements (see p86). As the point at which you are eligible for NHS bursary funding can be several years into your course, you should confirm the details of the NHS funding package nearer the time you are due to be entitled.

Nursing students

If you are studying for a nursing qualification in England through a nursing apprenticeship, there are no tuition fees and so you cannot apply for the usual student support for your living costs. Instead, you are paid a wage (see p13 for more details on apprenticeship pay). **Note:** there are currently only a limited number of apprenticeship places available. You can search for available places at www.gov.uk/apply-apprenticeship.

The Department of Health and Social Care is also piloting a new 'nursing associate' role in England. You follow an apprenticeship route (which does not have tuition fees) and are paid a salary, but the programme does not lead to a qualification as a registered nurse unless you undertake further study on completion. For more information, contact Health Careers (www.healthcareers.nhs.uk).

Dental therapy and dental hygiene students

You remain eligible for an NHS bursary if your course starts in the 2018/19 academic year and you are undertaking a dental hygiene or dental therapy course at one of the following schools:

- Birmingham Dental Hospital and School of Dentistry;
- Bristol Dental School;
- Eastman Dental Hospital;
- Greater Manchester School for Dental Care Professionals;
- King's College Hospital Foundation Trust.

Note: if you are studying on one of these courses, you are not eligible for payments from the Learning Support Fund (see p86). If your dental hygiene or dental therapy course is at another institution, you should apply for the standard undergraduate support package and you are also eligible for the Learning Support Fund.

Postgraduate diploma and part-time undergraduate students

From 2018/19, students on postgraduate, pre-registration diploma courses in England previously funded by the NHS bursary scheme should apply for the standard undergraduate package from Student Finance England (see Chapter 2). Part-time undergraduates should apply for the part-time student support package (see p35).

Learning Support Fund

Healthcare students who are domiciled in England can apply for limited additional funding from the NHS Learning Support Fund, provided they meet certain criteria. Students domiciled elsewhere in the UK and studying in England are also eligible for this support.

Help with travel and accommodation

In recognition that healthcare students undertaking placements have additional costs associated with travel and accommodation, further support is available from the NHS to meet these. The Learning Support Fund can cover the costs of travel over and above your normal travel costs to your institution. Apply via NHS Student Bursaries. **Note:** this funding is available in 2018/19, but may change in future years.

Exceptional Support Fund

The NHS offers additional support of up to £3,000 for healthcare students in 'extreme' hardship and who have exhausted other avenues of support (including your university hardship fund if applicable). You must complete an online application at www.nhsbsa.nhs.uk/learning-support-fund. You are assessed on your household income and expenditure and must provide evidence to support your application. Applications for one-off emergency costs are not considered – you are expected to apply to your institution's hardship fund first.

Child dependants allowance

Students with responsibility for at least one child up to the age of 15 (17 if the child is registered with special educational needs) can apply for an additional non-means-tested grant of £1,000 to meet the costs associated with her/him. You do not receive more than £1,000 if you have more than one child. The grant does not affect other funding sources, and is paid in three instalments throughout the year – £250 in the first two terms and £500 in the third term.

The 2012 bursary scheme

The 2012 bursary scheme is available to all eligible healthcare students in England and Wales, including medicine and dentistry students who started their course on or after 1 September 2012. **Note:** most healthcare students who start their course on or after 1 August 2017 in England are not eligible (see p84).

Students who started their course in Wales on or after 1 September 2017

If you start a healthcare course in Wales on or after 1 September 2017, in order to receive a bursary you must commit to working in the Welsh NHS or in a related public health role (eg, in HM Prison Service, or for a charitable healthcare provider such as a hospice) in Wales for at least two years following graduation. **Note:** medical and dental students studying in Wales move onto the Welsh NHS bursary arrangements at the appropriate point in their course and are not required to make this commitment.

If you want to study a course in Wales but are unable to commit to working in the Welsh NHS or a related public health role, you can apply for standard undergraduate support from Student Finance Wales or the equivalent funding body instead (see Chapter 3). However, this means that your institution charges you tuition fees.

If you accept a bursary place but leave your course before it is completed or do not complete two years' service in the Welsh NHS or a related public health role in Wales following graduation, you are liable to repay some, or all, of the cost of the course (although most supplementary allowances, such as childcare support, are excluded). How much depends on the number of years of the course you have completed, or the length of time remaining in the two-year commitment. If, for example, you do not work in Wales following the course, you are liable to repay £25,500. If you leave with between 18 months' and two years' service, you are liable to repay £8,500. No student loans are available to cover this cost.

You can change your mind within 10 weeks of the starting date of the course and leave without any obligation to repay. The requirement to repay is waived if you are asked to leave your course because of academic or practice failure, or ill health. You are strongly advised to speak to an adviser in your students' union or university if you are considering leaving to discuss your options and avoid unnecessary repayment. Ill health may also be taken into consideration if this is the reason why you cannot complete two years' service following graduation, but each case is considered individually and this is not guaranteed.

You are asked to provide written and electronic confirmation that you accept the commitment when you accept a bursary place at a Welsh institution. For more information on the commitment, including what counts as employment in the Welsh NHS or a related public health role in Wales, see www.nwsspstudentfinance.wales.nhs.uk/new-students.

Tuition fees

Most healthcare students funded by the NHS do not pay tuition fees. Medicine and dentistry students on standard five-year undergraduate courses have their fees paid in the years they are funded by the NHS.

Medicine and dentistry students on four-year graduate-entry courses funded under the 2012 scheme are charged a fee element (see p28).

Non-means-tested grant

All eligible students receive a non-means-tested bursary of £1,000. This is paid in monthly instalments over the year. The rate does not increase even if your course lasts longer than 30 weeks in the year.

Means-tested bursary

Depending on your household income, in addition to a non-means-tested bursary you may be eligible for a means-tested bursary. If you receive support, it is paid monthly.

Maximum amount of means-tested bursary 2018/19

	Courses lasting 30 weeks in the year	Courses lasting 45 weeks or more in the year
London	£3,191	£5,567
Elsewhere	£2,643	£4,491
Parental home	£2,207	£3,439

Extra weeks allowance

The bursary is paid for a notional academic year of 30 weeks and three days. If your course requires additional attendance, a further allowance is paid.

Extra weeks allowance 2018/19

	Weekly amount
London	£108
Elsewhere	£84
Parental home	£56

If your required attendance in an academic year is 45 weeks or more, an allowance for all 52 weeks is paid.

Reduced-rate student loan

If you get a bursary, you may also be eligible for a reduced-rate undergraduate student loan. This is not subject to a means test. You should apply through Student Finance England or Student Finance Wales. **Note:** the rates in England and Wales are different, and new amounts have been introduced for students starting their courses on or after 1 September 2018 in Wales (2018 cohort students).

Reduced-rate student loan 2018/19

England	Full year	Final year
London	£3,263	£2,498
Elsewhere	£2,324	£1,811
Parental home	£1,744	£1,324
Wales (2018 cohort)		
London	£5,125	£5,125
Elsewhere	£4,000	£4,000

Parental home	£3,325	£3,325
Wales (pre-2018 cohort)		
London	£4,920	£3,763
Elsewhere	£3,500	£2,727
Parental home	£2,625	£1,996

The loan must be repaid after graduation, with the same repayment conditions as for other undergraduate students who started new courses in the 2012/13 academic year or later (see p31).

Dependants' allowance

If you have adults or children wholly or mainly financially dependent on you, you may be eligible for an extra dependants' allowance. Eligibility is means tested and depends on the income of your dependant(s).

Amount of dependants' allowance 2018/19

Spouse or civil partner (or other adult dependant, or first child if there is no spouse or any adult dependants)	£2,448
Each additional dependant	£549

Parents' learning allowance

If you have a dependent child, you can claim an additional £1,204 to support the costs associated with her/him. This is available to all student parents, including those with partners, but is means tested.

Childcare allowance

If you have responsibility for a child under the age of 15 (or 17 if s/he has special educational needs) and you use registered or approved childcare (see p33), you can apply for a means-tested childcare allowance. You cannot receive this if you receive the childcare element in universal credit (see p212) or working tax credit (see p226).

The grant can cover up to 85 per cent of your actual costs of childcare, with a maximum payment of £128.78 a week for one child or £191.45 a week for two or more children. In Wales, the maximum payment for two or more children is £209.95 a week.

Practice placement expenses

The cost of travel between your home and a practice placement site that is not part of the college, and additional residential costs where appropriate, may be reimbursed to you. Only the amount that exceeds the cost of travel between your term-time residence and the normal place of study is reimbursed.

Disabled students' allowance

If you have a disability, you can claim a disabled students' allowance from the NHS on the same basis as higher education students in England, except that the equipment allowance is slightly higher, at £5,214 for the course (see p34 – the same rates apply to NHS students in Wales).

Students who started their course before 2012

Students who started their course before 2012/13 will almost always be studying for medicine and dentistry degrees. The rules for this version of the bursary scheme were set in 2007 and so we refer to '2007 system' system students in this section. If you started your course before 2007, speak to an adviser. This 2007 system also supported 'diploma-level' study in nursing and midwifery under different rules, but as there should be no remaining students at this level, this section describes the support for degree-level study only.

Degree-level students are eligible for a means-tested award (see below), as well as additional allowances, depending on their circumstances. To be eligible, you must also meet the personal residency conditions for higher education students in England (see p21). The NHS pays your tuition fees.

Bursaries are funded in England by NHS Student Bursaries and in Wales by NHS Wales Student Awards Services.

Institutional hardship funds may also be available.

Means-tested bursary

A means-tested bursary is available if you are a student studying for a degree-level qualification in any of the healthcare disciplines outlined on p84. If you meet the personal eligibility criteria, your tuition fees are also paid. The amount you receive for living costs depends on your (and your partner's) income or, if you are a 'dependent student' (see p40), your parents' income.

If you are eligible for a means-tested bursary, you may also be eligible for a reduced-rate undergraduate student loan, as for students eligible for the 2012 bursary scheme (see p88). This loan is not subject to a means test. Apply to Student Finance England or Student Finance Wales. The repayment conditions are the same as for other undergraduate students who started their course before 1 September 2012 (see p31).

Maximum amount of means-tested bursary 2018/19

	2007 system students
London	£3,571
Elsewhere	£2,958
Parental home	£2,470

There is a range of additional allowances available.

Extra weeks allowance

The extra weeks allowance for 2007 system students is the same as for students eligible for the 2012 bursary scheme (see p88).

Dependants' allowance

If you have adults or children wholly or mainly financially dependent on you, you may be eligible for extra dependants' allowances. However, the income of your dependants is taken into account and so eligibility for this allowance is means tested.

Amount of dependants' allowance 2018/19

Spouse or civil partner (or other adult dependant, or first child   £2,693
if there is no spouse or any adult dependants)
Each additional dependant   £549

Parents' learning allowance

If you are a 2007 system student and have a dependent child(ren), you can claim an additional £1,329. This is available to all student parents, including those with partners, but is means tested.

Childcare allowance

This is paid on the same basis as for students eligible for the 2012 bursary scheme (see p89).

Practice placement expenses

The cost of travel between your home and a practice placement site that is not part of the college, and additional residential costs where appropriate, may be reimbursed to you. Only the amount that exceeds the cost of travel between your term-time residence and place of study is reimbursed.

Disabled students' allowance

If you have a disability, you can claim a disabled students' allowance from the NHS on the same basis as students in other forms of higher education (see p34 – the same rates apply to NHS students in Wales).

NHS hardship grant

In addition to institutional hardship funds (see p44), the NHS operates a limited hardship fund for medicine and dentistry students eligible for the means-tested bursary. Contact NHS Student Bursaries or NHS Wales Student Awards Services to apply (see Appendix 2).

European Union nationals

If you are a national of a European Union (EU) member state, you may be eligible for NHS bursary support. **Note:** in England, EU students who started their courses after 1 August 2017 are not eligible for bursaries and should apply to the Student Loans Company for support.

If you or your parent(s) are non-UK EU nationals who satisfy the three-year (in Wales) or five-year (in England) residence criteria in the 'UK and islands' (see p21), you are treated as if you are a UK student and are eligible for support for both maintenance and fees. You are not required to have settled status. If your residence in the UK was mainly for the purpose of full-time higher education, you may still be eligible for an NHS bursary (maintenance grant and tuition fees) if you can show that you were ordinarily resident in a European Economic Area country or Switzerland immediately prior to your period of ordinary residence in the UK.

EU students who are not ordinarily resident in the UK may be able to get an 'EU fees only' award, under which they have the cost of their tuition fees met, but are not eligible for a student loan, hardship funds or the maintenance element of the NHS bursary.

You may also qualify for support as a migrant worker. The rules are complex, so get advice from the advice centre in your university or students' union if you think this may apply to you.

Part-time students

Part-time students on NHS-funded degree courses are eligible for support, which is paid pro rata, depending on the length of the part-time course. In England, if you are a part-time student who started your course after 1 August 2018, you should apply to the Student Loans Company for the part-time support package (see p35).

The full rate is paid if you have additional costs resulting from a disability and for reimbursing the costs of attending a clinical placement.

Students who are pregnant or who have recently given birth

If you are an NHS-funded student, have enrolled on your course and require maternity leave, you can be paid your bursary for a period of up to 45 weeks (known as a 'maternity allowance'). Seconded students and EU nationals on fees-only awards cannot receive this.

For more information, see www.nhsbsa.nhs.uk/students or contact NHS Wales Student Awards Services at www.nwssp.wales.nhs.uk/student-awards (search for NHS bursaries).

---

2. Healthcare students in Northern Ireland

If you are planning to study an allied health professions degree course in Northern Ireland, you can apply for funding from the Department of Health in Northern Ireland (DoH). Under these arrangements, you do not pay tuition fees and can apply for an income-assessed bursary to cover your living costs and a reduced-rate, non-income-assessed student loan. Medical and dental students in their final year of study are also funded through this system. Students from European Union countries who are studying in Northern Ireland are also exempt from paying tuition fees, but cannot get a bursary or loan to cover their living costs.

The amount of bursary you receive depends on your household income. Additional allowances may be available if you have dependants or a disability. **Note:** the bursaries are under review and changes may be made in future years.

Bursary rates 2018/19

Full year	Bursary	Loan
Living away from parental home	£2,355	£2,370
Living in parental home	£1,920	£1,780
Final year		
Living away from parental home	£2,355	£1,850
Living in parental home	£1,920	£1,350

Regional Education Authority offices administer the bursary arrangements on behalf of the DoH by Student Finance NI. If you are a Northern Irish student, you should, therefore, apply to your local Student Finance NI regional office. If you live in England, Scotland or Wales, apply to Student Finance NI at the address for the North Eastern Region Education Authority office. For more information, see www.nidirect.gov.uk/articles/health-professional-courses.

Nursing and midwifery students

Full-time pre-registration nursing and direct-entry midwifery students taking up a commissioned DoH place on a course leading to entry on the Nursing and Midwifery Council register can receive a bursary while undertaking the course. Students receiving a bursary do not pay tuition fees, but are not eligible for support from Student Finance NI. They can apply for discretionary help from their institution's support funds. Contact your students' union or advice centre for more details. You apply for a bursary via the Bursary Administration Unit, part of the Business Services Organisation at the DoH (see Appendix 2).

Both schemes comprise a non-means-tested basic rate, additional means-tested allowances, and travel expenses for costs incurred while on clinical placements. Disabled students' allowances are also payable, where appropriate, at the same rate as for other higher education students (see p70). The rates are set annually.

Bursary rates 2018/19

Basic award	£5,165
Partner or other adult dependant (or first child if no other dependant)	£2,389
Each subsequent child	£567
Parents' learning allowance (you must receive a dependants' addition to qualify for this)	£1,125
Contribution to childcare	Up to £1,250

3. Initial teacher training in England

There are three main routes for initial teacher training in England that lead to qualified teacher status, each with different funding arrangements.

- Bachelor of Education (BEd): an undergraduate degree, usually for four years' full-time study or equivalent, with qualified teacher status gained after a year's successful teaching, although there are now some two-year and three-year undergraduate courses that lead to qualified teacher status.
- Postgraduate Certificate in Education (PGCE) or Postgraduate Diploma in Education (PGDE): a postgraduate qualification, delivered either by a higher education institution or through a 'school-centred initial teacher training' provider, including the School Direct (non-salaried) programme, usually for one year (or the part-time equivalent), with qualified teacher status gained after a year's successful teaching.
- Employment-based initial teacher training: this can be undertaken through the School Direct (salaried) programme.

Bachelor of Education and Bachelor of Arts/Science with qualified teacher status

The main financial assistance available if you are studying for a BEd, BA or BSc qualification is the basic undergraduate student support package outlined in Chapter 2. This includes all supplementary grants and access to any hardship funds.

There are no further incentives for BEd, BA or BSc with qualified teacher status study in 2018/19.

Postgraduate Certificate/Diploma in Education

If you are on a full- or part-time PGCE/PGDE course at a higher education institution or through a 'school-centred initial teacher training' provider, including the School Direct (non-salaried) programme, and meet the personal and residential eligibility criteria for undergraduate student support (see p21), you are entitled to the same support package as undergraduate students (see

Chapter 2). You may also be able to apply for assistance from your university's or college's hardship fund. There are also incentive packages for which you may be eligible.

Tuition fees

PGCE/PGDE students are liable for variable fees of up to £9,250 in 2018/19. Eligible students can take out a non-means-tested loan to cover the cost of these.[1] See p27 for more information.

Teacher training bursary

The teacher training bursary aims to encourage 'high-quality' entrants to the teaching profession in England, as determined by the degree classification they receive at undergraduate level, or if they hold a postgraduate qualification. Those with the highest undergraduate classifications or who hold doctorate-level qualifications receive the highest bursary. The exact rates for different subject and classification combinations vary from year to year, depending on the Department for Education's priorities. For the current rates, see https://getintoteaching. education.gov.uk/funding-and-salary/overview.

If you are on a one-year course, you are paid in monthly instalments between October and June. If your course is part time, you are paid in instalments in accordance with the length of your training.

If you are a full-time trainee, the salary is not taxable and you do not have to pay national insurance contributions. If you are a part-time trainee, the salary may be taxable, depending on your total income for the year. It is included in any calculation for means-tested benefits.

Students from the European Union (EU) are also eligible for these incentives, plus a loan for tuition fees (although not for the standard maintenance support from Student Finance England). **Note:** there is no change to funding arising as a result of the UK's leaving the EU in 2018/19 or 2019/20, but arrangements for future years are uncertain.

Some subjects attract bursaries from 'subject association groups'. Where relevant, you should apply for these first. If you receive such a bursary, you are not eligible for the standard bursary. The details are as follows.

- Physics graduates with at least a first-class degree or PhD may qualify for an Institute of Physics scholarship of £28,000 to teach secondary physics.
- Chemistry graduates with at least a 2:1 may qualify for a Royal Society of Chemistry scholarship of £28,000 to teach secondary chemistry.
- Computer science graduates with at least a 2:1 may qualify for a BCS, the Chartered Institute for IT scholarship of £28,000 to teach secondary computing.
- Languages graduates with at least a 2:1 may qualify for a British Council scholarship of £28,000 to teach secondary French, German or Spanish.
- Maths graduates with at least a 2:1 may qualify for an Institute of Mathematics and its Applications scholarship of £22,000 to teach secondary mathematics.

If you then teach maths in state-funded schools in England you may be eligible for additional payments totalling £10,000 or £15,000 in the early part of your career. See www.gov.uk/guidance/mathematics-early-career-payments-guidance -for-teachers-and-schools for details of these incentives.

The exact nature of the scholarships may vary from year to year. Check with the relevant subject association group.

Full details of all scholarship programmes and bursary incentives are available on the Department for Education website at: https://getintoteaching. education.gov.uk/funding-my-teacher-training/bursaries-and-scholarships-for-teacher-training.

Employment-based initial teacher training

School Direct and Teach First

The School Direct and Teach First teacher training programmes allow you to train as a teacher in academies or local authority-maintained schools while earning a salary. Trainees on the schemes do not qualify for student support or bursaries, but are paid a salary. The salary rate depends on the type of school and, potentially, the subject you are teaching. If you are studying on a School Direct non-salaried scheme, you are funded in the same way as those on PGCE or PGDE courses.

More details are available at https://getintoteaching.education.gov.uk.

Reimbursement of loan repayments

In 2018/19 a new pilot scheme is available which reimburses the student loan repayments of newly qualified teachers in state-funded schools in participating local authorities in England. To qualify, you must:

• be employed in a maintained secondary school, maintained special school, secondary academy or secondary free school in one of 25 participating local authorities;

• spend at least 50 per cent of your time teaching a priority subject: languages, physics, chemistry, biology or computer science;

• have received qualified teacher status in 2013/14 or later. Reimbursement is available for 10 years following the year you received qualified teacher status so, for those who received this in 2013/14, the reimbursement will end by 2023/24 at the latest.

Although the reimbursement is subject to income tax and national insurance, this is covered by the Department for Education. For more information, including a list of participating local authorities, see www.gov.uk/guidance/teachers-student-loan-reimbursement-guidance-for-teachers-and-schools.

A similar pilot scheme is available for newly qualified teachers who took teaching posts in the academic years 2002/03, 2003/04 and 2004/05. If you are eligible and you work in a shortage subject, your student loan is repaid for you.

The scheme only applies if you spend at least half of your teaching time teaching the shortage subjects. To be eligible you must:
- be employed in England or Wales in a teaching post at a maintained school, a non-maintained special school, a city technology college, a city college for the technology of arts or a city academy;
- have begun employment between 1 July 2002 and 30 June 2005;
- be employed to teach one or more of the shortage subjects for at least half of your teaching time within a normal school week.

More information is available at www.studentloanrepayment.co.uk. This scheme is not available to teachers who started employment after 30 June 2005.

4. Initial teacher training in Wales

In Wales, there are three main routes for initial teacher training that lead to qualified teacher status.
- Bachelor of Education (BEd): an undergraduate degree, usually for four years' full-time study or equivalent, with qualified teacher status gained after a year's successful teaching.
- Postgraduate Certificate in Education (PGCE): a postgraduate qualification, usually for one year (or the part-time equivalent), with qualified teacher status gained after a year's successful teaching.
- School-centred initial teacher training, through a graduate teacher programme.

Bachelor of Education

The main financial assistance available if you are studying a BEd qualification is the basic undergraduate student support package for Welsh students, outlined in Chapter 3. This includes all supplementary grants and access to the hardship funds. There are no further incentives for undergraduate study.

Postgraduate Certificate in Education

If you are on a full- or part-time PGCE course and meet the personal and residential eligibility criteria for undergraduate student support (see p47), you are entitled to the same support package as new undergraduate students in the relevant cohort (see p48), including support for fees. You can apply for assistance from the local hardship funds. There are also incentive packages for which you may be eligible.

Teacher training grant

If you undertake a PGCE initial teacher training course in Wales, you may be eligible for a teacher training grant if you are studying a priority subject. How much you receive depends on your undergraduate degree classification, with bursaries of up to £20,000 available in 2018/19. The bursary rates for different subject and degree combinations vary each year, depending on the Welsh government's priorities. **Note:** students with lower classifications, particularly third-class degrees, may not be entitled to a bursary at all. For the latest rates, see http://discoverteaching.wales/teacher-training-incentives.

Students from the European Union (EU) are also eligible for these incentives. There are currently no changes as a result of the UK's leaving the EU in 2018/19 or 2019/20, but arrangements in future years are uncertain.

The incentives are paid by the Welsh government to the provider, which then pays the relevant amount to eligible students on a monthly basis once they have enrolled and started their training.

Welsh Medium Improvement Scheme

To help those students who need additional assistance to raise their competence and confidence, a £2,000 grant is available to undergraduate or postgraduate students undertaking secondary initial teacher training in Wales using the Welsh language.[2] Once qualified, you are expected to take up a secondary school teaching post using the Welsh language. Your institution assesses your eligibility and advises you on the application process. For more details, see http://discoverteaching.wales/teacher-training-incentives.

Iaith Athrawon Yfory Incentive Scheme

An additional scheme to support teaching in Welsh has been established in 2018/19. Eligible recipients can recieve £3,000 in two instalments: £2,500 on receiving qualified teacher status and a further £500 on completion of an induction in either a Welsh-medium or bilingual school, or of teaching Welsh in any secondary setting. Together with the Welsh Medium Improvement Scheme funding above, this means that up to £5,000 is available. Claims must be submitted to the Welsh government. For more details, see http://discoverteaching.wales/teacher-training-incentives.

Graduate teacher programme

If you are a graduate aged 24 or over, the graduate teacher programme allows you to train as a teacher in maintained schools while still earning a living.

You receive a salary from the school in which you are based. The level of salary to be paid by the school is agreed by the governing body and may be at a rate based on the scales for either qualified or unqualified teachers, but must be no lower than the minimum salary grade for unqualified teachers. If you are on this scheme, you are not eligible for the training bursary, outlined above. In addition, the school receives a grant for the cost of your training. This can be used to cover the cost of an initial training needs assessment, tuition fees, supply cover, mentoring training, learning resources and materials. This funding cannot be used as a wage supplement.

Repayment of teachers' loans

Some Welsh teacher training students qualified for a pilot repayment of teachers' loans scheme, available in England and Wales in the early 2000s. This has closed to new applicants, but existing teachers on this scheme can still benefit (see p96).

5. Initial teacher training in Northern Ireland

Students accepted on a course of initial teacher training in Northern Ireland in the 2018/19 academic year, including Postgraduate Certificate in Education (PGCE) courses, receive the same funding as undergraduate students (see pp65–68). This means that PGCE students are liable for tuition fees, but can take out a loan to cover these.

You can make an application for funding through Student Finance NI.

The additional financial incentives available for undergraduate and PGCE study in England and Wales are not available in Northern Ireland, but Northern Irish students studying in England or Wales can claim these.

6. Social work students

England

Undergraduate support

Bursaries

Students studying an undergraduate diploma or degree in social work in England may be eligible for a non-means-tested bursary from the Department of Health and Social Care. The NHS Business Services Authority (BSA) administers these bursaries on its behalf.

If you are a full-time undergraduate studying at an institution in England, you may be eligible to receive this bursary in addition to the standard student support package (see Chapter 2), which includes a tuition fee loan, as the bursary is not intended to cover tuition fees for undergraduates.

New undergraduate students do not receive a social work bursary in their first year of study. Once students move into their second and third years of study, bursaries are payable. These are limited in number and, therefore, not all students receive one. Higher education institutions are expected to allocate bursaries in a way that produces 'high-quality' graduates, so while the exact allocation criteria varies, factors such as assessments and previous experience before the course are expected to be used in making decisions. You should ask what criteria your institution uses to allocate bursaries, ideally before you start your course. In 2018/19 around 2,500 bursaries were available for students who started their courses in the 2017/18 academic year.

If you are allocated a bursary, the amount you receive depends on where you study. The bursary paid includes a contribution of £862.50 to cover the costs of travel to placements.

If you are awarded a bursary, you can get £3,362.50 if you are studying at an institution outside London, or £3,762.50 if you are studying at a university or college in London or at the University of London. Essentially, if Student Finance England deems you eligible for the London rate of loan, you are eligible for the London rate of bursary. The bursary is paid for 52 weeks and is taken into account as income for benefit purposes, except for the element paid for travelling expenses, which is disregarded.[3] However, this is not usually specifically identified and can be taken into account by mistake. Check your calculation if this might apply to you.

Part-time students

If you are a part-time undergraduate student, you can receive the above bursary pro rata over the length of your course. As with full-time undergraduates, new part-time undergraduates do not receive a bursary in the first year of the course, and numbers are capped thereafter. All students are also eligible for help with placement costs. You are not entitled to any other forms of support.

Placement expenses

If you do not receive a bursary but incur placement expenses, you can claim a contribution towards your placement costs of £862.50 (pro rata if you are a part-time student) from the BSA.

Postgraduate support

Bursaries

The BSA administers support for students studying a postgraduate-level course, such as a master's degree in social work, or for students studying an undergraduate degree or diploma who already have a first degree.

The number of bursaries is limited, although it is expected that most postgraduate students will receive support. There are around 1,500 bursaries available across England. Bursaries are allocated to support 'high-quality' applicants (eg, those with relevant previous experience), with the institution making the final decision. You should ask your institution what criteria it intends to use to allocate bursaries. If you do not receive a bursary, you can still get help with your placement costs (see p101).

If you qualify for a bursary, it helps with your extra study and living costs, and there is additional money available if you have a child(ren) or a disability.

If you receive a postgraduate social work bursary, you cannot also apply for a postgraduate master's loan from Student Finance England (see p75). However, if you are unsuccessful in securing a social work bursary, you can then apply for the postgraduate loan.

Tuition fees

If you receive a bursary, you also receive a grant of up to £4,052 towards your tuition fees. This grant is paid by the BSA, directly to the institution. The grants are not means tested. You should check how much your institution intends to charge for tuition as, in some cases, it may exceed the tuition fee grant available.

Basic grant

Eligible postgraduate students who get a bursary can also receive a basic non-means-tested grant from the NHS. You can get £3,362.50 if you are studying at an institution outside London, or £3,762.50 if you are studying at a university or college in London or at the University of London. This includes a placement travel expenses allowance of £862.50. Postgraduate students who receive a bursary are not eligible for student support from Student Finance England.

Additional maintenance grant

This is a means-tested grant paid in addition to the basic grant for those who get a a bursary. Up to £4,201 is available to students studying in London or at the University of London, with up to £2,721 available to those studying elsewhere.

The grant is means tested on your unearned income and any taxable income of your partner, if you have one.

Students with dependants

If you have a child and/or an adult who is financially dependent on you, you can apply for an **adult dependants' grant**, the **parents' learning allowance** and the **childcare grant**. These broadly mirror the same grants that undergraduates can apply for from Student Finance England (see p32).

Disabled students' allowance

Postgraduate social work students can apply for a disabled students' allowance from the BSA at the same rates as for undergraduates (see p34). If you do not receive a bursary, you may still be able to claim a postgraduate disabled students' allowance from Student Finance England (see p79).

Part-time students

Part-time postgraduate students who receive a bursary have their tuition fees paid by the BSA. They receive the bursary at half the rate for full-time study, plus help with placement costs. They are not eligible for other forms of support.

Placement expenses

If you do not receive a bursary but incur placement expenses, you can still claim a contribution towards your placement costs of £862.50 (pro rata if you are a part-time student) from the BSA.

How to apply

If you are an undergraduate, you should first apply to Student Finance England for student support. When it has assessed your application and you have received notification of this (sometimes known as an 'award notification'), contact the BSA for an application form for the bursary. Postgraduates should apply directly to the BSA. There is a deadline for applications: for 2018/19 applications, this is 1 November 2018 for courses starting in autumn 2018 and 14 February 2019 for courses starting in January 2019.

Application forms are available at www.nhsbsa.nhs.uk/social-work-students.

Wales

Students in Wales studying for a qualification in social work may qualify for financial help from Social Care Wales. The number of bursaries is restricted: there are 224 available in Wales in 2018/19. Higher education institutions nominate which students should receive support, subject to their meeting the standard eligibility criteria in relation to residency and their personal circumstances.

Undergraduate support

If you are studying for an undergraduate degree or diploma in social work, first apply for student support through your local authority, as for other undergraduate students (see Chapter 3).

If you are nominated for a bursary and you meet the eligibility criteria, you receive a non-means-tested bursary to help cover your living costs of £2,500 a year in 2018/19. If you are studying part time, the bursary is calculated on a pro rata basis.

In addition, a **practice learning opportunity allowance** is paid to help cover the costs of attending placements. This is paid at £7.50 per day of placement. If your travel costs to placements are more than the initial payment, you can apply to Social Care Wales for reimbursement of these extra costs, subject to a daily maximum. Keep all receipts, as you may be asked to submit these as proof of expenditure.

To apply, contact Social Care Wales at https://socialcare.wales/careers/student-funding.

Postgraduate support

If you are on a postgraduate diploma or master's course in Wales, you may get a non-means-tested graduate bursary of £6,640 in 2018/19. This includes a contribution of £3,390 towards tuition fees. You can apply for the adult dependants' grant, the parents' learning allowance and the childcare grant at the same time as the additional graduate bursary, although these are means tested. You can also get a practice learning opportunity allowance, as for undergraduates (see above).

If you have a disability, you may be eligible for extra help through the postgraduate disabled students' allowance (see p79).

Northern Ireland

If you are studying for a degree in social work in Northern Ireland, you can apply for an additional incentive grant from the Department of Health. Non-means-tested grants of £4,000, plus a further £500 towards placement expenses, are available for each year of the course.

You must pay tuition fees, but the funding is in addition to any money to which you are entitled through Student Finance NI as part of the main undergraduate support system, including loans for fees.

Students in receipt of the incentive grant can apply to the discretionary support funds for extra help (see p72).

Note: the Northern Ireland Executive intends to review the bursary for future years, and it is possible that changes will be introduced from 2019/20.

7. **Dance and drama awards**

The Department for Education has a scholarship programme to ensure that talented dance and drama students can attend courses at the leading dance and drama institutions in England, in cases where fees and living costs would otherwise be prohibitively expensive. Dance and drama awards fund Trinity College London level five and six diploma courses in dance, drama and musical theatre. Funding is available through selected, approved specialist schools for between one and three years of study. You must be aged 16 and over for dance courses, or 18 and over for drama-related courses. There are a limited number of awards made each year and they are generally issued to those who show exceptional talent in an audition.

The residency rules for other higher education support apply (see p21). Students from England, Wales and Northern Ireland can apply for full support; European Union students can apply for support with fees only.

You cannot receive any support if your household income is more than £90,000 a year.

If you are a new student in 2018/19, you receive an award and your household income is below £33,000 (£30,000 if you live with your parents), your fees are paid in full. If your household income is between £33,000 (£30,000 if you live with your parents) and £90,000, you can receive a contribution towards your fees on a sliding scale, with a higher contribution expected the higher your family's income.

The award may also provide support for your living costs, depending on your circumstances. The maximum available is £5,185 if you live in London, and £4,550 if you live elsewhere. If you live at home with your parents, the maximum is £1,417. If your household income is more than £30,000, you are not eligible for maintenance support.

Dance and drama award recipients cannot access student loans and grants through Student Finance England.

Other allowances may be available if you have extra costs associated with a disability or childcare expenses.

More information on the awards is available through the participating dance and drama schools or from www.dadainfo.org.uk (where a list of the participating schools can also be found).

8. **Alternative sources of finance**

Professional and career development loan

The Department for Education, in participation with the Co-operative Bank, offers professional and career development loans with deferred repayment arrangements.[4] You can borrow between £300 and £10,000 towards your fees and other expenses if you are on a vocational full-time, part-time or distance learning course lasting up to two years (and including up to one year's practical work experience if it is part of your course). Degree and postgraduate courses are included, and the loans are available across the UK. **Note:** the scheme is closing from 25 January 2019, although loans obtained before this date are not affected.

The interest charged varies, depending on when you apply and the length of the repayment period, but currently is around 9.9 per cent a year. You should, however, check with the bank. Throughout your period of study and up to one month after completing or leaving the course, the Education and Skills Funding Agency (which administers the scheme) pays the interest on the loan for you. Repayments are fixed and can be spread between one and five years. If you are registered unemployed at the end of the first month of completing your course, you can apply to the bank to have your repayments deferred for up to five months initially, and for two further extensions of six months each.

Students undertaking master's qualifications in England, Wales or Northern Ireland may be eligible for a postgraduate loan (see Chapter 5). If you get a postgraduate loan, this does not prevent you from also applying for a professional and career development loan, but you should consider carefully whether you can afford the repayments.

More information on professional and career development loans is at www.gov.uk/career-development-loans.

Armed forces bereavement scholarship scheme

The armed forces bereavement scholarship scheme provides additional support for children of servicemen/women killed on active duty since 1990. The scheme offers support of up to £9,000 a year to help pay for fees if you are liable and a maintenance grant of £4,950 for the length of the course (2016/17 rates).

To qualify, your parent must have died while in service with the UK armed forces and her/his death must be attributable to that service.

Parent

A person counts as your '**parent**' if s/he was your biological or adoptive parent, or you were the subject of a special guardianship order, or if s/he was your step-parent and had financial responsibility for you. A foster parent does not count.

If your parent dies while you are in higher education, support can be backdated to the start of the current term, or it starts from the next term if s/he dies during a vacation.

Support is not means tested. You must study at an institution in the UK, although you do not have to be resident in the UK.

If you are on a further education course, you can also receive help from the scheme (see p6).

You can download an application form and get further information at www.gov.uk/support-military-bereaved-children.

Charities

It is unlikely that a course lasting more than one year could be financed entirely by trust fund help. Educational charities and trusts can, however, provide supplementary help to students who may be without funding for part of their course or who, for various reasons, need help over and above that provided by public funds.

Educational charities and trusts often have specific, even unusual, terms of reference. For example, thay may be restricted to helping only students:
- on certain courses of study; *or*
- above or below a certain age (often 21 or 25); *or*
- from particular parts of Britain or the world; *or*
- in defined occupations, professions or industries, or who have a parent working in one of these.

A student does not usually receive more than a few hundred pounds from any one charity, although higher amounts are not unknown. Charities usually make single, rather than ongoing, payments. Payments tend to be:
- for particular items – eg, tools or equipment; *or*
- for a specific purpose – eg, childcare; *or*
- those which the charity or trust believes might make the difference between completion and non-completion of the course.

Charities are more sympathetic to students whose need for assistance is as a result of sickness or unforeseen circumstances than to students who have mismanaged their money or who have started a course knowing they had insufficient funds.

Many charities only give assistance to first-time students. Assistance is more difficult to find if you are a postgraduate or taking a second undergraduate course. Applications often take some time to process, so it is wise to apply for support well in advance of the course start date.

Further information

There are a number of publications that contain details of charities and trusts. See Appendix 1 for details.

Students in financial need should also consult their local authority, students' union, careers service, local Citizens Advice office, town hall and local religious leaders as they may know of other trusts. In addition to awarding scholarships and prizes in specific subjects, colleges may have funds available for students in financial difficulties and unable to apply to the discretionary hardship/support funds, so it may be useful to consult your institution's student services.

Notes

3. Initial teacher training in England
1 Reg 4 and Sch 2 E(SS) Regs

4. Initial teacher training in Wales
2 E(WMTTIS) Regs

6. Social work students
3 **UC** Reg 70 UC Regs
IS Reg 62(2)(h) IS Regs
HB Reg 59(2)(g) HB Regs
See also para 30122 DMG

8. Alternative sources of finance
4 s2 ETA 1973

Part 2

Benefits and tax credits

Chapter 7

. . . .

Carer's allowance

This chapter covers:
1. What is carer's allowance (below)
2. Who is eligible (p110)
3. Amount of benefit (p111)
4. Claiming carer's allowance (p111)
5. Challenging a decision (p111)
6. Other benefits and tax credits (p111)

. . . .

Basic facts
– Carer's allowance (CA) is paid to people who care for someone with a severe disability.
– Part-time students are eligible to claim.
– Full-time students cannot claim.
– CA is not means tested, but you cannot get it if you work and earn more than £120 a week.
– Getting CA qualifies you for a carer element in universal credit or a carer premium in your income support, income-based jobseeker's allowance, income-related employment and support allowance and housing benefit.

. . . .

1. **What is carer's allowance**

Carer's allowance (CA) is for people who spend at least 35 hours a week looking after a disabled person (an adult or child). The disabled person must be getting attendance allowance, the middle or highest rate of disability living allowance care component or the daily living component of personal independence payment. The amount of CA you get is not means tested and your student loan, grant or other income does not affect it. Part-time students can get CA, but full-time students are not eligible.

2. **Who is eligible**

You are eligible if you are a part-time student and you satisfy the basic rules below. You are not eligible if you are in full-time education.

Full-time education

You are in full-time education if an overall consideration of your course requirements and your performance against these suggests this. If you are on a full-time course of education, you are normally taken to be in full-time education for the purpose of carer's allowance (CA).[1] If you think that, given your circumstances, you are not in full-time education, you may be able to argue that you are a part-time student.[2]

You are also treated as being in full-time education if you 'attend a course' (see below) at a university, college or other educational establishment for 21 hours or more a week.[3] These 21 hours include not just classes, lectures and seminars, but also individual study for course work. Meal breaks and unsupervised study are ignored. However, you are regarded as studying under supervision if you are doing course work, whether at home or at college, alone or in the presence of a supervisor.[4] Unsupervised study is work beyond the requirements of the course.

If your college or university says that it expects students to spend 21 hours or more a week in supervised study and classes, the Department for Work and Pensions usually assumes that you are in full-time education.

In practice, if you want to show that you spend fewer hours on course work than the college or university expects, you need to provide detailed evidence and be prepared to appeal. If your particular circumstances mean that you are not expected to satisfy the normal requirements of the course (eg, because you are exempt from certain subjects), you may be able to argue that your hours of study are fewer than those expected of other students on the course.[5]

Time out from a course

'**Attending**' a course means being enrolled on and pursuing a course.[6] You are treated as still being in full-time education during short and long vacations, and until the course ends or you abandon it or are dismissed from it. You are still regarded as being in full-time education during temporary interruptions.[7] If you have taken time out to care for someone and the interruption is not temporary (eg, if you have agreed with your institution to take a whole year out of your course), you may be able to claim CA.[8]

Basic rules

As well as being a student who is eligible to claim, to qualify for CA you must satisfy all of the following conditions.[9]

- You are aged 16 or over.
- You spend at least 35 hours a week caring for someone.
- The person for whom you care gets the middle or highest rate of disability living allowance care component, the daily living component of personal independence payment, attendance allowance or constant attendance allowance.
- You are not working and earning more than £120 a week.
- You satisfy certain rules on residence and presence in the UK and are not a 'person subject to immigration control'. See CPAG's *Welfare Benefits and Tax Credits Handbook* for details.

3. Amount of benefit

The amount of carer's allowance (CA) is £64.60 a week (April 2018 rate).

4. Claiming carer's allowance

You claim carer's allowance on Form DS700, available from local Jobcentre Plus offices or by phoning the Carer's Allowance Unit on 0800 731 0297. You can also claim online at www.gov.uk/carers-allowance/how-to-claim. Your claim can be backdated for up to three months if you qualified during that earlier period.
    Benefit is usually paid directly into a bank account.

5. Challenging a decision

If you think a decision about your carer's allowance is wrong, you can ask the Department for Work and Pensions (DWP) to look at it again. This process is known as a 'reconsideration' (the law refers to it as a 'revision'). Provided you ask within the time limit (usually one month), the DWP notifies you of the decision in a 'mandatory reconsideration notice'. If you are still not happy when you get this notice, you can appeal to the independent First-tier Tribunal. If it was not possible to ask the DWP to reconsider the decision within a month, you can ask for a late revision (within 13 months), explaining why it is late. You can also ask the DWP to look at a decision again at any time if certain grounds are met – eg, if there has been an official error.

6. Other benefits and tax credits

The benefit cap does not apply if you get carer's allowance (CA).

The disabled person's benefit

Your entitlement to CA depends on the person for whom you care continuing to get her/his disability benefit. If her/his benefit stops, your benefit should also stop. To avoid being overpaid, make sure you tell the Carer's Allowance Unit if the disabled person's attendance allowance, disability living allowance or personal independence payment stops being paid.

It is not always financially prudent to claim CA. Although it may mean more money for you, it may result in the person for whom you care losing some income support (IS), income-related employment and support allowance (ESA), pension credit or housing benefit (HB). If s/he lives alone, s/he may be getting a severe disability premium included in the assessment of these benefits. S/he cannot continue to get this premium if you get CA for her/him. See CPAG's *Welfare Benefits and Tax Credits Handbook* for details.

Overlapping benefits

Although CA is not means tested, you cannot receive it at the same time as incapacity benefit, maternity allowance, severe disablement allowance, bereavement benefits, retirement pension, contribution-based jobseeker's allowance (JSA) or contributory ESA. If you are eligible for more than one benefit, you get whichever is worth the most.

Getting a carer premium or element

If you are a part-time student, getting CA may mean you become eligible for IS. Carers are not expected to look for work and are eligible for IS instead of JSA. If you are getting CA and claiming universal credit (UC), you are eligible for a carer element in your UC and you are not expected to look for work. An extra carer premium is included in IS, income-based JSA, income-related ESA and HB, even if your CA is not being paid because you are getting another benefit that overlaps with it.

Working tax credit

If you have a child(ren) and a partner and you get CA, you are eligible for working tax credit if your partner works at least 16 hours a week, rather than the usual 24.

Notes

2. Who is eligible
1 *SSWP v Deane* [2010] EWCA Civ 699
2 CG/1154/2010
3 Reg 5 SS(ICA) Regs
4 *Flemming v SSWP* [2002] EWCA Civ 641;
   *Wright-Turner v Department for Social
   Development* [2002] NICA 2
5 CG/3189/2004
6 *Flemming v SSWP* [2002] EWCA Civ 641
7 Reg 5(3) SS(ICA) Regs
8 *SM v SSWP* [2016] UKUT 406 (AAC);
   Memo DMG 2/17
9 s70 SSCBA 1992

Chapter 8

Child benefit

This chapter covers:
1. What is child benefit (below)
2. Who is eligible (below)
3. Amount of benefit (p118)
4. Claiming child benefit (p118)
5. Challenging a decision (p118)
6. Other benefits and tax credits (p119)

Basic facts
- Child benefit is paid to people who are responsible for a child or a 'qualifying young person'.
- Both full-time and part-time students can claim child benefit.
- If you are under 20, someone else may be able to claim child benefit for you if you are studying.
- Child benefit is not means tested.

1. **What is child benefit**

Child benefit is paid to people who are responsible for a child or 'qualifying young person'. You do not have to have paid national insurance contributions to qualify for child benefit. It is not means tested, so the amount you get is not affected by your student loan, grant or other income. If you earn over £50,000 and you or your partner get child benefit, you may have extra income tax to pay (known as the 'high income child benefit charge').

2. **Who is eligible**

You qualify for child benefit if:[1]
- you are responsible for a child or 'qualifying young person' – ie:
  - s/he lives with you; *or*

– you contribute to the cost of supporting her/him at a rate of at least the amount of child benefit for her/him; *and*

• you have priority over other potential claimants. Only one person can get child benefit for a particular child. There is an order of priority for who receives it where two or more people would otherwise be entitled; *and*

• you are 'present and ordinarily resident' in Britain, not a 'person subject to immigration control' and have a 'right to reside'. These terms are explained in CPAG's *Welfare Benefits and Tax Credits Handbook*.

You do not have to be the child's parent to claim child benefit for her/him.

Being a student, whether full or part time, does not affect your entitlement to child benefit.

If you are a 'qualifying young person' (see below), your parent or someone else who is responsible for you may be able to claim child benefit. You cannot, however, claim child benefit for yourself.

If a qualifying young person gets universal credit, income support, income-based jobseeker's allowance, employment and support allowance, working tax credit or child tax credit in her/his own right, any child benefit paid for the young person stops.

If a young person lives with a partner, or is married or in a civil partnership, you can get child benefit for her/him if s/he lives with you or you still contribute to her/his support, but only if her/his partner is in 'relevant education' (see p163) or approved training. The young person's partner cannot be the claimant.

In some circumstances, special rules apply – eg, if your child is being looked after by a local authority or is in prison or a young offenders' institution.

Who counts as a child

Anyone aged under 16 counts as a **'child'** for child benefit purposes, whether or not s/he goes to school. Provided you meet the other qualifying conditions, child benefit can be paid for her/him.[2] Child benefit can also be paid for a child after s/he reaches 16 until at least the 31 August after her/his 16th birthday, and then for as long as s/he continues to count as a 'qualifying young person'.

Who counts as a qualifying young person

A **'qualifying young person'** is someone who:[3]

• is aged 16 and has left full-time non-advanced education (see p116) or training. This only applies up to 31 August after her/his 16th birthday (but see below); *or*

• is aged 16 or 17, has left education or training and satisfies the extension period rule (see p117); *or*

• is aged 16 or over but under 20 and is on a course of full-time non-advanced education (see p116) not provided as a result of her/his employment, or approved training not provided under a contract of employment – ie, Traineeships or Foundation Apprenticeships in Wales or United Youth Pilot (if started before 1 June 2017), PEACE IV Children or Training for Success programmes in Northern Ireland. **Note:** there is currently no 'approved training' in England, so check whether your course counts as 'full-time non-advanced education' (see below).[4] The young person must have started the course or training before reaching 19, or have been accepted or enrolled to undertake it before that age; *or*

- is aged 16 or over but under 20 and has finished a course of full-time non-advanced education not provided as a result of her/his employment, or approved training not provided under a contract of employment, but is accepted or enrolled on another such course. **Note:** if the course s/he has finished is an approved training course, this only applies if the following course is also approved training. Although someone must have started, or been accepted or enrolled on, the training or education when s/he was under 19 to be a qualifying young person once the course begins, the rules do not specify this for the gap between courses.[5] If the young person was accepted or enrolled after reaching age 19, you can argue that s/he is a qualifying young person from the end of the course until the next course begins; *or*

- is aged 16 or over but under 20 and is receiving 'appropriate full-time education' in England, which s/he started, or was enrolled or accepted on, before reaching 19. To count as 'appropriate', the course must be non-advanced and suitable for the person's age, ability and any special educational needs s/he has; *or*

- is aged 16 or over but under 20 and has left full-time non-advanced education (see below) or approved training but has not passed her/his terminal date (see p117).

Full-time non-advanced education

'**Full time**' is more than 12 hours a week of classes and supervised study during term time. '**Non-advanced education**' is anything below degree, Higher National Certificate or Higher National Diploma level, and includes school-level courses, national vocational qualifications levels 1–3, GCSEs, AS levels, A levels and traineeships in England.

If your child counts as a qualifying young person on more than one of the above grounds, s/he counts as a qualifying young person until the last day that applies.[6]

If you stop being entitled to child benefit for your child because s/he no longer counts as a qualifying young person, but s/he later satisfies one of the above conditions again and so counts as a qualifying young person once more, child benefit can again become payable for her/him. **Note:** in some cases, you can continue to claim during such an interruption – eg, if the young person is ill or the gap is less than six months. In both cases, the interruption must be accepted as being reasonable.[7]

Note: in the rest of this chapter, the term 'child' is used to mean both children under 16 and qualifying young people aged 16 or over.

The extension period

If your child is 16 or 17, s/he continues to count as a qualifying young person, and so child benefit can continue to be paid for her/him, during an 'extension period' if:[8]
- s/he has left education or training; *and*
- s/he is registered as available for work, education or training with the Careers Service in England and Northern Ireland or Careers Wales in Wales; *and*
- s/he is not in remunerative work – ie, work of 24 hours a week or more for payment or in expectation of payment; *and*
- you were entitled to child benefit for her/him immediately before the extension period started; *and*
- you apply in writing or by phone within three months of the date your child's education or training finished.

In this context, 'education' and 'training' are not defined and so may mean any kind of education or training.

The extension period starts from the Monday after your child's course of education or training ends and lasts for 20 weeks from that date. If your child reaches 18 during the extension period, unless s/he counts as a qualifying young person on another ground (see p115), your child benefit for her/him ends from the first child benefit payday on or after which s/he reaches 18.[9]

The terminal date

If your child leaves full-time non-advanced education (see p163) or approved training before reaching 20, s/he continues to count as a qualifying young person until either:[10]
- the 'terminal date' (see below); *or*
- her/his 20th birthday, if this falls before the terminal date.

The general rule means that unless s/he continues to count as a qualifying young person on another ground or is returning to sit an exam (see below), you stop receiving child benefit for her/him on that date.

The terminal date

Your child's **'terminal date'** is the first of the following dates that falls after the date her/his full-time non-advanced education or approved training finishes:
– the last day in February;
– the last day in May;
– the last day in August;
– the last day in November.

A child who returns to sit an external examination in connection with her/his course of relevant education is treated as still being in relevant education until the date of the last exam.[11]

3. **Amount of benefit**

Weekly rate from April 2018

Eldest eligible child	£20.70
Other children (each)	£13.70

Note: child benefit rates are frozen for the next two years.[12]

4. **Claiming child benefit**

Child benefit is administered by HM Revenue and Customs (HMRC). You claim child benefit on Form CH2, which you can get at www.gov.uk/child-benefit or from the Child Benefit Office on 0300 200 3100, HMRC's website (www.gov.uk/government/organisations/hm-revenue-customs) or from Jobcentre Plus offices.

You should make a claim within three months of becoming eligible. This is because your claim can usually only be backdated for up to three months. You do not have to show any reasons why your claim was late.

Getting paid

Child benefit is usually paid directly into your bank (or similar) account. Which account it goes into is up to you. If you do not want your benefit to go into an account that is overdrawn, give HMRC details of an alternative account if you have access to, or can open, one.

5. **Challenging a decision**

If you think a decision about your child benefit is wrong, you can ask HM Revenue and Customs (HMRC) to look at it again. This process is known as a 'reconsideration' (the law refers to it as a 'revision'). Provided you ask within the time limit (usually one month), HMRC notifies you of the decision in a 'mandatory reconsideration notice'. If you are still not happy when you get this notice, you can appeal to the independent First-tier Tribunal. If it was not possible to ask HMRC to reconsider the decision within a month, you can ask for a late revision (within 13 months), explaining why it is late. You can also ask HMRC to look at a decision again at any time if certain grounds are met – eg, if there has been an official error.

6. **Other benefits and tax credits**

If you get child benefit, you count as being responsible for a child for income support (IS) and income-based jobseeker's allowance (JSA), and usually for housing benefit (HB). This can help you qualify for these benefits in some circumstances while you are a full-time student (see Chapters 12, 13 and 14).

Child benefit is ignored as income for IS and income-based JSA if you are getting child tax credit. However, if you have been getting IS or income-based JSA since before 6 April 2004 which includes amounts for your child(ren), child benefit is taken into account as income. Child benefit is ignored as income for universal credit, income-related employment and support allowance and HB.

Child benefit is taken into account when calculating whether the benefit cap applies (see p160 and p214).

Notes

2. **Who is eligible**
1 ss141-47 SSCBA 1992
2 s142(1) SSCBA 1992; reg 4 CB Regs
3 s142(2) SSCBA 1992; regs 2-8 CB Regs
4 Reg 1(3) CB Regs
5 Reg 3 CB Regs
6 Reg 2(2) CB Regs
7 Reg 6 CB Regs
8 Reg 5 CB Regs
9 Reg 14 The Child Benefit and Guardian's Allowance (Administration) Regulations 2003, No.492; reg 5(3) CB Regs
10 Reg 7 CB Regs
11 Reg 7(2) case 2.1 CB Regs

3. **Amount of benefit**
12 s11(2) WRWA 2016

Chapter 9

Disability living allowance

This chapter covers:
1. What is disability living allowance (below)
2. Who is eligible (p121)
3. Amount of benefit (p124)
4. Claiming disability living allowance (p124)
5. Challenging a decision (p124)
6. Other benefits and tax credits (p124)

Basic facts
- Disability living allowance (DLA) is paid to disabled people who need personal care or who have mobility difficulties.
- You must be under 16 to make a new claim.
- Getting DLA allows you to claim income-related employment and support allowance as a full-time student. You may also be able to claim housing benefit as a full-time student and you may get a disability premium.
- Getting DLA allows you to claim universal credit as a full-time student, provided you satisfy certain other conditions.
- DLA is not means tested.

1. What is disability living allowance

Disability living allowance (DLA) is a benefit for disabled people who need help with personal care or who have mobility difficulties. Unless you are under 16, you cannot make a new claim for DLA and must claim personal independence payment (PIP) instead (see p196).

DLA has two components:
- care component, paid at either the lowest, middle or highest rate;
- mobility component, paid at either the lower or higher rate.

You can get either or both components.

Students already getting DLA can continue to do so, but will be invited to claim PIP instead. Starting college or university does not usually lead the DWP to reassess your entitlement to DLA.

The amount you get is not means tested, and so is not reduced because of student support or other income.

If you are a full-time student getting DLA and you satisfy certain other conditions, you are eligible for universal credit (see p206). If you are a full-time student and get DLA, you are eligible for income-related employment and support allowance. You may also be eligible for housing benefit.

2. Who is eligible

Full-time and part-time students can continue to get disability living allowance (DLA). You cannot make a new claim unless you are under 16, but should claim personal independence payment (PIP) instead if you think you may be entitled.

If you get DLA and your condition changes which means you should qualify for a different rate of DLA (see below), or your DLA award is due to end, or you turn 16, you must claim PIP instead. Otherwise, at some point you will be reassessed for PIP.

Care component

To get the care component, you must have a physical or mental disability that means you need the following kinds of care from another person. What is important is the help you need rather than the help you actually get.

You get paid either the lowest, middle or highest rate.

Lowest rate

You get the lowest rate if you need attention in connection with your bodily functions (see p122) for a significant portion of the day. This attention might be given all at once or be spread out. It should normally add up to about an hour or more, or be made up of several brief periods.

Middle rate

This is for people who need care either during the day or during the night, but not both. You get the middle rate if you meet one (or both) of the day care conditions *or* one (or both) of the night care conditions.

Care during the day
• You need frequent attention throughout the day in connection with your bodily functions (see p122). This means you may qualify if you need help several times, not just once or twice, spread out throughout the day. If you

need help just in the mornings and evenings, for instance, you might get the lowest rate instead.

- You need continual supervision throughout the day in order to avoid substantial danger to yourself or others. The supervision must be frequent or regular, but need not be continuous.

Care at night

- You need prolonged or repeated attention at night in connection with your bodily functions (see below). You should qualify if you need help once in the night for 20 minutes or more. You should also qualify if you need help twice in the night (or more often), however long it takes.
- In order to avoid substantial danger to yourself or others, you need another person to be awake at night for a prolonged period (20 minutes) or at frequent intervals (three times or more) to watch over you.

Highest rate

This is for people who need care both day and night. You get the highest rate if you meet one (or both) of the above day care conditions and one (or both) of the above night care conditions. You also get the highest rate if you are terminally ill – ie, you have a progressive disease and could reasonably be expected to die within six months.

Attention with bodily functions

This is help from someone else to do personal things you cannot do entirely by yourself. 'Bodily functions' are things like breathing, hearing, seeing, eating, drinking, walking, sitting, sleeping, getting in or out of bed, dressing, undressing, and using the toilet. However, any help in connection with an impaired bodily function can count if it involves personal contact (physical or verbal in your presence) and it is reasonably required.

For example, a blind student might need the help of a notetaker or reader, or a guide around campus or around town. A deaf student might need an interpreter. A student with arthritis might need help getting in and out of chairs.

You must need the help of another person to qualify for DLA. If you only need artificial aids, you cannot get DLA.

You cannot count help with domestic chores, unless someone is helping you to do them for yourself.

If you have dyslexia, you could argue that you qualify for DLA, but only if you need someone to be with you to help you read and write – ie, someone sitting beside you reading to you or helping you develop reading skills.[1] This could count as attention with the bodily function of seeing or of the brain.[2]

Having a social life

The kind of help you need must be reasonably required. This means that you need it to enable you as far as reasonably possible to live a normal life. You can include help needed to take part in social activities, sport, recreation, cultural or political activities, provided the help required is in connection with a bodily function.

Mobility component

There are two rates of the mobility component.

Lower rate

This is for people who can walk, but need guidance or supervision. You qualify if you are able to walk but, because of your disability, you cannot walk outdoors without guidance or supervision from someone else most of the time.

You can still qualify if you are able to manage on familiar routes. If you cannot manage without guidance or supervision on unfamiliar routes or you cannot manage anywhere, you should qualify. For example, someone with learning disabilities may qualify even if s/he has learned the route to and from home and college if s/he still needs guidance in other places.

Higher rate

This is for people who cannot walk or have great difficulty walking because of a physical disability. You qualify if:
- you are unable to walk; *or*
- you have no legs or feet; *or*
- you are virtually unable to walk. This takes account of the distance you can walk before you experience severe discomfort. There is no set distance at which you pass or fail the test. Some people have passed who can walk 100 metres. Others have failed who can walk only 50 metres. The speed at which you walk and how you walk also count; *or*
- the exertion required to walk would be dangerous or could cause a serious deterioration in your health; *or*
- you are deaf and blind; *or*
- you have a severe visual impairment.

Someone who is severely mentally impaired may also qualify if s/he gets the highest rate care component and meets other conditions.

Claiming for children

You can claim DLA for a disabled child. There is no lower age limit for the care component. You can claim the higher rate mobility component for your child from age three and the lower rate mobility component from age five.

Because all children need care or supervision to some extent, there is an extra test. As well as passing the disability test, children must have needs substantially in excess of the normal requirements of other children their age to qualify for the care component. For the lower rate mobility component, children must need substantially more guidance or supervision than other children of their age.

3. **Amount of benefit**

Weekly rate from April 2018
Care component

Lowest rate	£22.65
Middle rate	£57.30
Highest rate	£85.60

Mobility component

Lower rate	£22.65
Higher rate	£59.75

4. **Claiming disability living allowance**

You cannot make a new claim for disability living allowance (DLA) unless you are under 16; you must claim personal independence payment (PIP) instead (see p196).

If you still get DLA, you will be reassessed for PIP at some point.

DLA is usually paid directly into your bank account, and usually paid every four weeks in arrears.

5. **Challenging a decision**

If you think a decision about your disability living allowance is wrong, you can ask the Department for Work and Pensions (DWP) to look at it again. This process is known as a 'reconsideration' (the law refers to it as a 'revision'). Provided you ask within the time limit (usually one month), the DWP notifies you of the decision in a 'mandatory reconsideration notice'. If you are still not happy when you get this notice, you can appeal to the independent First-tier Tribunal. If it was not possible to ask the DWP to reconsider the decision within a month, you can ask for a late revision (within 13 months), explaining why it is late. You can also ask the DWP to look at a decision again at any time if certain grounds are met – eg, if there has been an official error.

6. **Other benefits and tax credits**

If you meet certain other conditions and are a full-time student getting disability living allowance (DLA), you are eligible for universal credit (UC – see p204).

If you are a full-time student and get DLA, you are eligible for income-related employment and support allowance (ESA). You may also be eligible for housing benefit (HB).

DLA is paid in addition to UC, income support (IS) and HB, and may qualify you for an additional premium in IS and HB.

If you claim other benefits or tax credits, make sure the office dealing with your claim knows you get DLA. Similarly, inform the local authority office dealing with your HB. Also notify the local authority or Tax Credit Office if your child gets DLA (or the Department for Work and Pensions if you are getting UC).

If you, your partner or a child for whom you are responsible get DLA, you are exempt from the benefit cap (see p160 and p214).

Notes

2. **Who is eligible**
  1 CDLA/1983/2006; CDLA/3204/2006
  2 *KM v SSWP (DLA)* [2013] UKUT 159
      (AAC), reported as [2014] AACR 2

Chapter 10

· ·

Employment and support allowance

This chapter covers:
1. What is employment and support allowance (below)
2. Who is eligible (p127)
3. Limited capability for work (p129)
4. Amount of benefit (p130)
5. Claiming employment and support allowance (p135)
6. Challenging a decision (p135)
7. Other benefits and tax credits (p135)

· ·

Basic facts

– Employment and support allowance (ESA) is for people who are assessed as having limited capability for work because of their health or disability.
– There is an income-related and a contributory ESA.
– Part-time students who have limited capability for work and full-time students who get disability living allowance or personal independence payment are eligible for income-related ESA.
– Part-time and full-time students can claim contributory ESA if they have paid sufficient national insurance contributions.

· ·

1. What is employment and support allowance

Employment and support allowance (ESA) is for people who have limited capability for work because of illness or disability.[1]

There is a contributory and an income-related ESA. **Contributory ESA** is for people who have paid national insurance contributions. **Income-related ESA** is means tested and is for people whose income and capital are low enough. It is possible to receive one or both types of ESA.

Note: you cannot usually make a new claim for income-related ESA if you are in a universal credit 'full service' area (see p204), unless you have three or more children (**Note:** this exception may end from February 2019). All areas are expected to be full service by the end of 2018. An exception may also be introduced if you get a severe disability premium (see p133). See CPAG's *Welfare Rights Bulletin* for updates.

2. Who is eligible

To qualify for employment and support allowance (ESA), you must meet all the basic conditions.[2]

* You have limited capability for work (see p129).
* You are aged 16 or over and under pension age.
* You are in Great Britain (although some absences are allowed – see CPAG's *Welfare Benefits and Tax Credits Handbook* for more details).
* You satisfy the rules for contributory ESA (see below) or income-related ESA (see below).
* You are not working, although some 'permitted work' is allowed. See CPAG's *Welfare Benefits and Tax Credits Handbook* for more details.

Contributory employment and support allowance

Contributory ESA is not means tested. To qualify, you must meet the basic conditions on p above and have paid sufficient national insurance contributions.[3] See CPAG's *Welfare Benefits and Tax Credits Handbook* for details on this. There are no special rules for students. The same rules apply if you are taking time out from your course because of ill health (see p298).

Income-related employment and support allowance

Income-related ESA is means tested. You are eligible if you are a part-time student and have limited capability for work. If you are a full-time student, you are only eligible if you get disability living allowance (DLA) or personal independence payment (PIP). The same rules apply if you are taking time out from your course because of ill health (see p298).

To qualify for income-related ESA while studying, you must satisfy the basic conditions above and all the following conditions.[4]

* You are either a full-time student (see p128) who is entitled to DLA (either component, paid at any rate – see p120) or PIP (either component paid at any rate – see p196), or you are a part-time student.[5]
* Your income is less than the set amount the law says you need to live on (known as your 'applicable amount') – see p132.
* You have no more than £16,000 capital.
* Your partner (if you have one) is not working 24 hours or more a week.

• You are in Great Britain, satisfy the 'habitual residence' and the 'right to reside' tests, and are not a 'person subject to immigration control'. These terms are explained in CPAG's *Welfare Benefits and Tax Credits Handbook*. Further advice is available from UKCISA (see Appendix 2).

Full-time student

You are a full-time student if you are:[6]
• under 20 and a 'qualifying young person' (see below); *or*
• 19 or over and a full-time student, unless you are aged 19 and count as being a qualifying young person (see below); *or*
• under 19 in full-time advanced education (see p129).

Under 20 and a qualifying young person

You are a 'qualifying young person' if you are 19 or under and attending a full-time course of non-advanced education which you were accepted on, enrolled on or started when you were under 19. If you are accepted on, enrol on or start the course on or after your 19th birthday, you are not a qualifying young person (see below). 'Non-advanced education' is anything below degree, Higher National Certificate or Higher National Diploma level and includes school-level courses. Your course is classed as 'full time' for income-related ESA if it is for more than 12 hours a week during term time. These 12 hours include classes and supervised study, but not meal breaks or unsupervised study either at home or at college. You may count as a qualifying young person in a gap between courses or for a period after you have finished a course (see p115).

19 or over and a full-time student

You count as a full-time student if you are undertaking a full-time course of study at an educational establishment. There are two definitions of 'full time' that apply: the first covers mostly courses of advanced education; the second covers most courses of non-advanced education.
• Your course is full time if it is classed as full time by the institution. If the institution describes the course as full time, you need convincing evidence to persuade the Department for Work and Pensions otherwise, bearing in mind that what matters is the course itself rather than the hours you attend. This definition covers all courses of advanced education and any courses of non-advanced education not funded in whole or in part by the government at a further education (FE) college.
• Your course is full time if it involves more than 16 hours a week. What matters is the number of hours specified in a document signed by the college. This is often called a 'learning agreement', but your college may refer to it by some other name – eg, Passport to Employment. This definition applies if you are at an FE college, not undertaking a higher education course, and your course is fully or partly funded by the government. In Northern Ireland, whether or not

your course is full time depends on the institution's definition. When applying for ESA, a letter from the institution stating that your course is part time should be sufficient.

Under 19 in full-time advanced education

If you are under 19 and in full-time advanced education rather than in non-advanced education, the rules on when you count as full time are the same as for those aged 19 or over (see p128).

3. Limited capability for work

One of the basic rules of entitlement to employment and support allowance (ESA) is that you must be assessed as having 'limited capability for work'. This means that your mental or physical condition makes it unreasonable to require you to work. You are normally assessed at a medical, known as the 'work capability assessment'. This also assesses whether you have 'limited capability for work-related activity'. If you are assessed as having both limited capability for work and limited capability for work-related activity, you are in the 'support group' and your ESA includes an amount called a 'support component'.

If you are assessed as only having limited capability for work, you are in the 'work-related activity group'. You are expected to attend work-focused interviews and may be required to undertake work-related activity. If you do not do so, your benefit may be reduced. If your claim began before 3 April 2017, your ESA includes a 'work-related activity component'. If it began on or after this date, it does not.

If you are assessed as not having limited capability for work, you are not entitled to ESA. However, you can appeal (see p135).

Full-time students who get disability living allowance (DLA) or personal independence payment (PIP) and who are claiming income-related ESA are treated as having limited capability for work and do not have to satisfy this part of the test.[7] However, this does not apply to all full-time students. You must still satisfy the test if:

- you are a qualifying young person under 20; *or*
- you are claiming contributory ESA.

All students, unless they are in the support group, must take part in work-focused interviews and may have to undertake work-related activity as a condition of getting full benefit.[8]

If you are required to undertake full-time study as part of your work-related activity, you can continue to get ESA, whether or not you get DLA or PIP.[9]

Starting to study may prompt the Department for Work and Pensions to call you for a reassessment, although this should not happen routinely. At the next assessment, your ability to perform the set activities is considered in the context of what you can do in a typical day, including your college or university routines. For example, you may be asked questions about your ability to get around campus, your ability to get to and from lectures, how long you can sit comfortably to study, or your ability to hold a pen to take notes or write essays.

The questions you are asked depend on which of the set activities (such as standing and sitting, manual dexterity and understanding communication) are relevant to your condition.

See CPAG's *Welfare Benefits and Tax Credits Handbook* for advice on medical examinations and what to do if you do not pass the assessment.

Example

Rachel is 29 and getting contributory ESA that includes a support component. She starts a full-time course of study in August 2018. She continues to be eligible for contributory ESA, but is called for a medical reassessment. Her condition is still the same, she passes the assessment and her contributory ESA continues.

4. **Amount of benefit**

Employment and support allowance (ESA) is payable after seven 'waiting days'. You are paid a limited amount of ESA during an initial 'assessment phase'. In most cases, this is expected to last 13 weeks. After this, you are then paid more in the 'main phase' that follows.

The exact amount of ESA you are paid depends on:
- whether you are claiming contributory ESA or income-related ESA;
- whether you are in the assessment or the main phase;
- whether you are in the support group or the work-related activity group after the assessment phase. If you are in the support group, you get a support component of £37.65 a week. If you are in the work-related activity group and you claimed before 3 April 2017, you get a work-related activity component of £29.05 a week.

ESA is worked out as follows.

In the assessment phase, you get a basic allowance of contributory ESA. The amount of income-related ESA you get depends on your needs (your applicable amount) and how much income you have.

In the main phase, if you claimed before 3 April 2017, either the work-related activity component or the support component is added. If you claimed on or after 3 April 2017, a support component can be added but no work-related activity component can be added. For income-related ESA, the component is added to your applicable amount and your income is then subtracted from your applicable amount. For contributory ESA, it is added to the basic allowance.

Contributory employment and support allowance

Weekly rate from April 2018[10]

Assessment phase, basic allowance (under 25)	£57.90
Assessment phase, basic allowance (25 or over)	£73.10
Main phase, basic allowance (16–24)	£73.10
Main phase, basic allowance (25 or over)	£73.10
Main phase, support component	£37.65
Main phase, work-related activity component	£29.05
(claims before 3 April 2017 only)	

Contributory ESA is paid for up to a year if you are in the work-related activity group, or indefinitely if you are in the support group.

Income-related employment and support allowance

The amount of income-related ESA you get depends on your circumstances and the circumstances of your partner.[11] The amount also depends on your income and capital. Go through the following steps to work out the amount of ESA to which you are entitled.

Step one: capital

If your capital is over £16,000, you cannot get income-related ESA (see p127). Some kinds of capital are ignored. For details, see CPAG's *Welfare Benefits and Tax Credits Handbook*.

Step two: work out your applicable amount

This is an amount for basic weekly needs. It is made up of:[12]
- personal allowances (see p133);
- premiums (see p133);
- a support component or, for claims before 3 April 2017, a work-related activity component (see p134);
- housing costs (see p134).

Step three: work out your weekly income

Chapter 22 explains how your loan, grant or other income is taken into account for ESA and how to work out your weekly income.

Step four: deduct weekly income from applicable amount

If your income is *less* than your applicable amount, your ESA equals the difference between the two.

If your income is *the same as or more than* your applicable amount, you cannot get ESA. You can claim again if your income decreases – eg, during the long vacation.

Income-related ESA tops up contributory ESA if you are entitled to both and the income-related amount is higher.

Example

Doreen is 19 and has cerebral palsy. She gets the standard rate daily living component of personal independence payment (PIP) and lives with her parents. In August 2018 she starts a full-time National Certificate course. She claims ESA. She is eligible for income-related ESA.

Assessment phase:

Step one	Doreen has no savings or capital.
Step two	Her applicable amount is:
	Basic allowance for herself = £57.90
Step three	Her weekly income is:
	£0 (PIP is disregarded).
Step four	She gets income-related ESA of £57.90.

Main phase:

Doreen is assessed as having limited capability for work and work-related activity and as being in the support group.

Step two	Her applicable amount is:
	Basic allowance for herself (£73.10) and support component (£37.65) and enhanced disability premium (£16.40) = £127.15
Step three	Her weekly income is:
	£0 (PIP is disregarded).
Step four	She gets income-related ESA of £127.15.

Applicable amount

Your applicable amount is worked out by adding together your personal allowances, premiums, the component that applies to you in the main phase and any eligible housing costs. **Note:** benefit rates are usually uprated in April each year, although many amounts are frozen for the next three years.[13] It is usually possible to find out what the new rates will be from the beginning of December. Check the Department for Work and Pensions (DWP) website at www.gov.uk/government/organisations/department-for-work-pensions for a press release on social security uprating. The rates on pp133–34 are from April 2018.

Personal allowance

Your personal allowance is paid at either the single, lone parent or couple rate depending on your situation. The amount depends on your age and whether you are in the assessment phase or the main phase (see p130).

	Assessment phase £	Main phase £
Single		
Under 25	57.90	73.10
25 or over	73.10	73.10
Lone parent		
Under 18	57.90	73.10
18 or over	73.10	73.10
Couple		
Both under 18 (higher rate)	87.50	114.85
Both under 18 (not eligible for higher rate)	57.90	73.10
One under 18, one 18 or over (higher rate)	114.85	114.85
One under 18, one 18–24 (not eligible for higher rate)	57.90	73.10
One under 18, one 25 or over (not eligible for higher rate)	73.10	73.10
Both 18 or over	114.85	114.85

If you are both under 18, you get the higher rate if:
- one of you is responsible for a child; or
- you and your partner would both be eligible to claim income-related ESA if you were single; or
- your partner would qualify for income support (IS) if s/he were single; or
- your partner would qualify for income-based jobseeker's allowance (JSA) or severe hardship payments of JSA.

If one of you is under 18 and the other is 18 or over, you get the higher rate if the younger partner would:
- qualify for IS or income-related ESA if s/he were single; or
- qualify for income-based JSA or severe hardship payments of JSA.

Premiums

Qualifying for premiums depends on your circumstances. You can qualify for the following.
- **Pensioner premium.** You or your partner must have reached the qualifying age for pension credit (see p170). If you are single, you get £89.90; if you are a couple, you get £133.95. In the main phase, these amounts are reduced by the

amount of the work-related activity component (if applicable) or support component for which you qualify.

- **Carer premium** of £36. The qualifying conditions are the same as for IS (see p174).
- **Enhanced disability premium.** You qualify for this if you or your partner get the highest rate of the disability living allowance (DLA) care component, the enhanced rate of the daily living component of PIP or if you get the support component of ESA. You get £16.40, or £23.55 if you are a couple.
- **Severe disability premium.** This is for severely disabled people who live alone, or can be treated as living alone. You qualify if you get the middle or highest rate of the DLA care component or the daily living component of PIP paid at either rate, and no one gets carer's allowance for looking after you. You do not get the premium if you live with another person aged 18 or over (eg, a friend or parent), unless s/he is separately liable for rent, you only share a bathroom or hallway, or in some other circumstances. See CPAG's *Welfare Benefits and Tax Credits Handbook* for details. If you have a partner, you do not qualify unless s/he also qualifies in her/his own right or is certified as severely sight impaired or blind. If you both qualify, you get two premiums. The rate of the premium is £64.30.

Components

In the main phase (see p130), you receive either the support component or, if your claim began before 3 April 2017, the work-related activity component (see p131). The work-related activity component is £29.05. The support component is £37.65.

Housing costs

ESA can include help with certain service charges and some other housing payments, after a waiting period.

If you own your own home, the DWP may offer you a loan to help with the cost of your mortgage interest payments. Usually help only starts once you have been getting ESA for 39 weeks, although there are some exceptions to this.

Normally you have to live in the home you own to get a loan, but there are exceptions for full-time students (and some others). You can still get a loan for mortgage interest if you have moved elsewhere to study but are not paying rent or a mortgage at the term-time address. If you pay for both places, you can get a loan for both if you are a couple and it is unavoidable that you live in two separate homes. Otherwise, you can get a loan if you are away from your home temporarily and have not let it out and are not likely to be away for more than 52 weeks.[14]

You must claim housing benefit for help with your rent (see Chapter 12). For full details, see CPAG's *Welfare Benefits and Tax Credits Handbook*.

5. Claiming employment and support allowance

You start your claim by phoning a Jobcentre Plus contact centre on 0800 055 6688 (textphone 0800 023 4888). You can also claim on Form ESA1 which you can download from www.gov.uk/employment-support-allowance.

Either member of a couple can make a claim for income-related employment and support allowance (ESA) for both, but whoever claims must be eligible in her/his own right. You claim contributory ESA for yourself only.

You are usually interviewed after you claim. You must provide medical certificates from your GP until you are assessed under the work capability assessment.

Claims for ESA can be backdated for up to three months.

6. Challenging a decision

If you think a decision about your employment and support allowance is wrong, you can ask the Department for Work and Pensions (DWP) to look at it again. This process is known as a 'reconsideration' (the law refers to it as a 'revision'). Provided you ask within the time limit (usually one month), the DWP notifies you of the decision in a 'mandatory reconsideration notice'. If you are still not happy when you get this notice, you can appeal to the independent First-tier Tribunal. If it was not possible to ask the DWP to reconsider the decision within a month, you can ask for a late revision (within 13 months), explaining why it is late. You can also ask the DWP to look at a decision again at any time if certain grounds are met – eg, if there has been an official error.

7. Other benefits and tax credits

You cannot get employment and support allowance (ESA) if you are getting statutory sick pay (SSP) from an employer.[15] SSP runs out after 28 weeks, after which you can claim ESA.

You cannot get ESA if you are getting income support (IS) or jobseeker's allowance (JSA). You can claim contributory ESA if your partner is getting IS or JSA. You are excluded if you get joint-claim JSA.[16] You cannot get income-related ESA if your partner gets universal credit, IS, income-based JSA or pension credit.

Income-related ESA passports you to maximum housing benefit, free school lunches and social fund payments. It also passports you to free prescriptions, free dental treatment, vouchers for glasses, and to Healthy Start vouchers and free vitamins if you are pregnant (see Chapter 11).

If you have a child(ren) and a partner and you get contributory ESA, you may be eligible for working tax credit if your partner works 16 hours or more a week, rather than the usual 24 hours.

ESA is taken into account when calculating whether the benefit cap applies, unless you or your partner get a support component in your ESA. If this is the case, you are exempt from the benefit cap (see p160 and p214).

Notes

1. What is employment and support allowance
1   Reg 1 ESA Regs

2. Who is eligible
2   s1 WRA 2007
3   s1 WRA 2007
4   Sch 1 para 6 WRA 2007
5   Reg 18 ESA Regs
6   Regs 14-16 ESA Regs

3. Limited capability for work
7   Reg 33(2) ESA Regs
8   Regs 54 and 63(1) ESA Regs
9   Reg 14(2A) ESA Regs

4. Amount of benefit
10 s2 WRA 2007; reg 67(2) and (3) ESA Regs
11 s4 WRA 2007; reg 67(1) and (3) ESA Regs
12 Reg 67 and Sch 4 ESA Regs
13 s11 WRWA 2016
14 Sch 3 para 4 LMI Regs

7. Other benefits and tax credits
15 s20 WRA 2007
16 s1(3)(f) WRA 2007

Chapter 11

Health benefits

This chapter covers:
1. What are health benefits (below)
2. Who is eligible (p138)
3. Claiming health benefits and refunds (p144)
4. Challenging a decision (p145)
5. Overseas students (p145)

Basic facts
- People under 19 and in full-time education can get free prescriptions, sight tests, vouchers for glasses and dental treatment.
- Prescriptions are free in Wales. In addition, you can get a free dental examination if you are under 25, or are 60 or over. Prescriptions in Northern Ireland are also free.
- Other students can get help if they are on a low income or in certain other circumstances.

1. **What are health benefits**

This chapter gives an outline of the rules on health benefits and focuses on issues relevant to students. For more detailed information, see CPAG's *Welfare Benefits and Tax Credits Handbook*.

Although most health treatment is free under the NHS for UK residents, there are fixed charges for some NHS services and treatments. These include:
- prescriptions;
- sight tests;
- glasses or contact lenses;
- dental treatment; *and*
- wigs and fabric supports.

You may also have fares to pay to get to hospital. You are exempt from the charges in specified circumstances, or if your income is sufficiently low, and may get help with the fares. As a student, you are not automatically exempt from paying these charges unless you come into one of the categories listed on p138. Otherwise, you can apply for a 'remission certificate' under the low income scheme (see p141). If you get a remission certificate, part or all of the charges are waived, depending on how much income you have. For information about claims, see p144.

Note: you may also qualify for vouchers for Healthy Start food and for free vitamins. See p141 for further information.

2. Who is eligible

You are exempt from NHS charges if:[1]

- you or a member of your family receive income support (IS), income-based jobseeker's allowance (JSA), income-related employment and support allowance (ESA) or the guarantee credit of pension credit (PC);
- in England and Wales, you or a member of your family receive universal credit (UC) and either have no earnings or your earnings are no more than £435 a month (£935 if you have a child or a limited capability for work or limited capability for work-related activity element included in your UC);
- you or a member of your family receive:
  - child tax credit (CTC); or
  - CTC and working tax credit (WTC); or
  - WTC including a disabled worker or severe disability element.
  To be exempt because you receive tax credits, your gross annual income must be £15,276 or less a year.

There are other categories of people who are exempt from NHS charges – eg, if you are a permanent resident in a care home, a hospital inpatient, an asylum seeker (see p145), aged 16 or 17 and being financially maintained by a local authority, a war disablement pensioner and you need the item or service because of your war disability, or if you are in prison or a young offenders' institution.

You may also be exempt from some charges because of your age or a specific health condition – see the individual types of charges on pp139–41.

If you are not exempt on any of the grounds listed above or below, you may be entitled to a full or partial remission of charges on grounds of low income – this includes if you are claiming UC in Northern Ireland (see p141).

If you are exempt because you receive tax credits

If you are exempt from NHS charges because you receive tax credits, you should automatically be sent an NHS tax credit exemption certificate. This could be up to six weeks after you are awarded tax credits. If you have a tax credits award, but have not yet been sent your certificate, you can sign the relevant treatment forms to say you do not have to pay. You can use your award letter as evidence of this. If this is not accepted and you are charged, keep your receipts so you can claim a refund (see p144). Get advice if there is a delay in getting your exemption certificate.

If you are getting CTC but are exempt from charges because you are getting IS, income-based JSA, income-related ESA or the guarantee credit of PC, you do not get an NHS tax credit exemption certificate. However, if you stop getting IS, income-based JSA, income-related ESA or the guarantee credit of PC because of, for example, your student income, you need a certificate. You should let HM Revenue and Customs know about your change in circumstances as soon as possible. It notifies the NHS Business Services Authority (BSA) in Newcastle upon Tyne, which issues you with a certificate.

Free prescriptions

The cost of a prescription in England is £8.80 (April 2018). Prescriptions are free if you live in Wales or Northern Ireland.

In England, you qualify for free prescriptions if:[2]
- you are in one of the exempt groups listed on p138; *or*
- you are aged under 16, or under 19 and in full-time education (see below); *or*
- you are aged 60 or over; *or*
- you are pregnant or have given birth within the last 12 months; *or*
- you are undergoing treatment for cancer, the effects of cancer or the effects of cancer treatment;
- you have one or more of the following specific medical conditions:
  - a continuing physical disability which prevents you from leaving home except with the help of another person;
  - epilepsy requiring continuous anticonvulsive therapy;
  - a permanent fistula, including caecostomy, ileostomy, laryngostomy or colostomy, needing continuous surgical dressing or an appliance;
  - one of the following conditions: diabetes mellitus (except where treatment is by diet alone), myxoedema, hypoparathyroidism, diabetes insipidus and other forms of hypopituitarism, forms of hypoadrenalism (including Addison's disease) for which specific substitution therapy is essential, or myasthenia gravis;
  - a sexually transmitted disease; *or*
- your income is low enough (see p141).

Full-time education
'Full-time education' is full-time instruction at a recognised educational establishment – eg, a school, college or university. If you are studying elsewhere, or you have finished your A levels and are waiting to start college or university, check whether you are exempt because you are on a low income.

Prepayment certificates

Prepayment certificates are available in England and can save you money if you are likely to need a lot of prescriptions, but are not exempt from paying for them. You do not have to pay any further charges for prescriptions for the duration of the certificate, regardless of how many are required.[3]

A three-month certificate saves money if you need four or more items in the three-month period, while a 12-month certificate saves money if you require more than 12 prescriptions in a year. Apply by post on Form FP95, available from chemists, some doctors' surgeries and relevant health bodies. Applications can also be made by telephone on 0300 330 1341 or online at www.nhsbsa.nhs.uk and at registered pharmacies. The cost of 12-month certificates can be split over 10 direct debit instalments.

Free sight tests

You qualify for a free NHS sight test if:[4]
- you are in one of the exempt groups listed on p138; *or*
- you are under 16, or under 19 and in full-time education (see p139); *or*
- you are aged 60 or over; *or*
- you are registered as blind or partially sighted; *or*
- you have been prescribed complex or powerful lenses; *or*
- you have diabetes or glaucoma or are at risk of getting glaucoma; *or*
- you are 40 or over and are the parent, sibling or child of someone who has glaucoma; *or*
- you are a patient of the Hospital Eye Service; *or*
- in England, if you are on leave from prison or a young offenders' institution; *or*
- your income is low enough (see p141).

Note: you may also qualify for a voucher towards the cost of buying or repairing glasses or contact lenses.[5]

Free dental treatment and dentures

If you live in Wales and are under 25 or are 60 or over, you qualify for free dental examinations.[6] Otherwise, you qualify for free dental treatment (including check-ups) and appliances (including dentures) if:[7]
- you are in one of the exempt groups listed on p138; *or*
- you are aged under 18, or are under 19 and in full-time education (see p139); *or*
- you are pregnant or have given birth within the last 12 months; *or*
- you are a patient of the community dental service; *or*
- your income is low enough (see p141).

Free wigs and fabric supports

In Wales and Northern Ireland, wigs and fabric supports are free. In England, you qualify for free wigs and fabric supports if:[8]
- you are in one of the exempt groups listed on p138; *or*
- you are under 16, or under 19 and in full-time education (see p139); *or*
- you are a hospital inpatient when the wig or fabric support is provided; *or*
- your income is low enough (see below).

Fares to hospital

You qualify for help with the costs of travel to hospital or any other establishment for NHS treatment or services if:[9]
- you are in one of the exempt groups listed on p138; *or*
- you live on the Isles of Scilly; *or*
- your income is low enough (see below).

Note: in some cases, you can get help with the costs of travel to obtain NHS treatment abroad.

Healthy Start food and vitamins

You can get free Healthy Start food vouchers and vitamins if:[10]
- you are aged 18 or over and pregnant and you or your partner get IS, income-based JSA or income-related ESA, or get CTC (but not WTC, except during the four-week run-on) and have an income for tax credit purposes of £16,190 or less; *or*
- you are aged under 18 and pregnant, whether or not you get any of the above benefits; *or*
- you have a child under four and get IS or income-based JSA, or get CTC (but not WTC, except during the four-week run-on) and have an income for tax credit purposes of £16,190 or less; *or*
- you are 18 or over and pregnant or have a child under four, and get UC with an earned income of £408 or less per assessment period.

The low income scheme

You may be entitled for help with NHS charges if you have a low income. The NHS BSA has a means test to determine whether you qualify for either full or partial remission. The means test is roughly based on the applicable amounts for IS (see Chapter 13), but there are some differences.

See p144 for how to apply.

Calculating your entitlement

To qualify for help, you must have less than £16,000 capital (£23,250 if you are in a care home in England, or £24,000 if you are in a care home in Wales).[11]

If your weekly income (see below) does not exceed your requirements (see below) by more than 50 per cent of the cost of an English prescription (currently 50 per cent of £8.80, so £4.40), you receive a full remission certificate (an HC2 in England and Northern Ireland; HC2W in Wales).[12] If your income exceeds your requirements by more than this amount, you receive a partial remission certificate (an HC3 in England and Northern Ireland; HC3W in Wales). Depending on the level of excess, you may get:[13]

- a remission of dental charges and charges for wigs and fabric supports which are higher than three times your excess income;
- a voucher for glasses or lenses, reduced by an amount equal to twice your excess income;
- a reduction in the cost of a sight test to the amount of your excess income, if lower, plus the amount by which the cost exceeds the NHS sight test fee;
- a reduction by the amount of your excess income in the amount you can get for hospital fares.

If you qualify for a remission certificate, it is normally valid for 12 months. If you are a full-time student, your certificate is normally valid until the end of your course or the start of the next academic year. You should make a repeat claim shortly before the expiry date. Remember that if you qualify for IS or income-based JSA over the summer vacation, you are automatically exempt from NHS charges during that period.

Calculating your income

Income is calculated in the same way as for IS, with some modifications.[14] Your and your partner's income is taken into account. Your parents' income is not taken into account. However, any money given to you by your parents may be taken into account when assessing your eligibility. See Chapter 24 for how your income is calculated and how student income is treated.

Calculating your requirements

Your requirements are based on those used for calculating the applicable amount for IS.[15] This is an amount for your basic weekly needs. See Chapter 13 for more details.

Your requirements are made up of:

- **personal allowance**
  - single person aged under 25, £57.90;
  - single person aged under 25 entitled to an ESA component, or incapable of work for 28 weeks since 27 October 2008, £73.10;
  - single person aged 25–59, £73.10;
  - single person aged 60 or over, £163.00;
  - lone parent aged under 60, £73.10;
  - lone parent aged 60 or over, £163.00;
  - couple aged under 60, £114.85;
  - couple aged 60 or over, £237.55;

- **premiums**
  - carer premium (as for IS);
  - disability premium (as for IS, except that you can include a disability premium after 28 weeks of incapacity for work, rather than 52 weeks). You can also get a disability premium if you or your partner are under 60 and get ESA with a work-related activity or support component or you or your partner have been getting ESA for at least 28 weeks, or have been incapable of work for at least 28 weeks and have had the incapacity since 27 October 2008. The amount of the disability premium increases to £37.65 if you are single or a lone parent and *either* get ESA with the support component *or* get the disability living allowance middle or highest rate care component or personal independence payment and have been getting ESA or have been incapable of work, for 28 weeks since 27 October 2008 and your incapacity did not start before that date;
  - enhanced disability premium for an adult (as for IS);
  - severe disability premium (as for IS);
- **weekly rent** less any housing benefit (HB) and non-dependant deductions;
- **weekly council tax;**
- **mortgage interest**, endowment payments and capital repayments on your home, as well as on loans to adapt a home for a disabled person, deducting any non-dependant deductions.

If your income is £4.40 or less (half the cost of a prescription in England) higher than your needs, you are entitled to health benefits. If your income is more than £4.40 higher than your needs, you do not get free prescriptions, but you might get partial help with other charges.

Examples
Oliver is 21, and a second-year full-time undergraduate in Wales. His income is assessed to be £144.04 a week.
His requirements are calculated as his personal allowance (£57.90) plus his weekly rent (£110). This gives a total of £167.90. This is more than his income, so he receives full help with health costs. As a Welsh-domiciled student, however, Oliver already qualifies for free prescriptions and, as he is under 25, free dental examinations.

Louisa is 24, and a second-year full-time undergraduate in London. Her income is assessed to be £198.25 a week.
Her requirements are calculated as her personal allowance (£57.90) plus her weekly rent (£150). This gives a total of £207.90. This is more than her income, so she receives full help with health costs.

3. **Claiming health benefits and refunds**

How and where you claim help with NHS charges depends on your circumstances.

Under 19 and in full-time education

- To claim an exemption from NHS prescription charges, you must sign the declaration form on the back of the prescription.
- To claim a free sight test, you must sign the optician's form before your test.
- To claim free dental treatment, you must tell the receptionist before your treatment that you think you are exempt from charges and complete a form at this point. Remember, in Wales, if you are under 25 you qualify for free dental examinations.

Pregnant women and women who have recently given birth

- To claim free dental treatment and prescriptions, you must apply for a maternity exemption certificate on Form MATB1, available from your midwife, health visitor or doctor.
- You must claim Healthy Start food and vitamins in writing. Complete Form HS01 in the Healthy Start application leaflet, available from maternity clinics and some doctors' surgeries or from 0345 607 6823. A downloadable claim form is also available at www.healthystart.nhs.uk. Your claim form must be countersigned by a health professional (eg, a midwife or health visitor), certifying that you have been given appropriate advice about healthy eating and breastfeeding.

Prescribed medical condition

To claim free prescriptions because you have a prescribed medical condition, you must apply for an exemption certificate on a form available from your doctor, hospital or pharmacist.

The low income scheme

Applications for help under the low income scheme should be made to the NHS Business Services Authority on Form HC1 (HC1W in Wales), available from Jobcentre Plus offices, NHS hospitals, some doctors' surgeries, some chemists, many students' union advice centres or at www.nhsbsa.nhs.uk.

Refunds

If you pay for an item or service that you could have got free of charge or at a reduced cost, you can apply for a refund. You must apply within three months of payment, although the time limit can be extended if you can show a good cause for applying late – eg, you were ill.[16]

For a refund of prescription charges, use Form FP57, which you must get when you pay for the prescription at the pharmacy or dispensing chemist.

For other items and services, use Form HC5 (HC5W in Wales), available from post offices, Jobcentre Plus offices, NHS hospitals and some doctors' surgeries.

If you wish to have your costs refunded on the basis of low income, but do not already have an HC2 or an HC3 remission certificate (see p141), send a completed Form HC1 with Form HC5.

4. Challenging a decision

If you think a decision about your health benefits is wrong, you can ask for a review. Write to the Service Improvement Team, NHS Help with Health Costs, Bridge House, 152 Pilgrim Street, Newcastle upon Tyne NE1 6SN. You can also request a review at www.nhsbsa.nhs.uk.

If you think a decision is wrong because it was based on your circumstances at the time you applied for a remission certificate and these have now changed, consider making a fresh claim, or reporting the change, if you think you would now be entitled to more help with NHS charges.

If there are delays in obtaining a certificate, you can complain to the customer services manager. If necessary, you could pay for the treatment or items you need, then apply for a refund (see p144).

5. Overseas students

Many overseas students can get certain types of treatment free from the NHS. However, since April 2015, there are charges for non-European Economic Area (EEA) students (see below).

Asylum seekers

If you are an asylum seeker or a dependant of an asylum seeker and receiving support from either the Home Office or a local authority, you are exempt from NHS charges. If you are getting asylum support, you should be sent an HC2 certificate with your first support payment. If you are not supported by the Home Office or a local authority, apply using Form HC1.

European Economic Area students and Swiss nationals

If you are a student from any part of the EEA or Switzerland, you can get NHS treatment during a temporary stay in the UK on the same basis as UK residents, provided you have a European health insurance card (EHIC). You can also get help with NHS charges on the same basis as UK residents. Following the introduction of charges for non-EEA international students, if you are an EEA or Swiss student, it is essential to have an EHIC to avoid charges. At the time of writing, it was not yet known how the results of the referendum to leave the European Union will affect entitlement to healthcare.

Other overseas students

Since April 2015, non-EEA international students are subject to charges for some types of treatment, and may have to make a payment towards health costs as part of any visa application. Whether you are required to make this payment, or whether a specific treatment is free or a charge applies, depends on several factors. These include your specific immigration status, your length of stay in the UK, your country of origin and the type of treatment. It can also depend on whether you are living in England, Wales or Northern Ireland. Detailed information is available at www.ukcisa.org.uk.

All overseas students can get emergency treatment, treatment for certain communicable diseases and compulsory psychiatric treatment free of charge through the NHS. Nevertheless, you are strongly advised to take out adequate medical insurance for the duration of your stay in the UK.

Notes

2. Who is eligible
1 Regs 3-5 NHS(TERC) Regs; regs 3-5 NHS(TERC)(W) Regs
2 Regs 3-6 NHS(CDA) Regs; regs 4 and 5 NHS(TERC) Regs; NHS(FP&CDA)(W) Regs
3 Reg 9 NHS(CDA) Regs
4 Reg 13 NHS(GOS) Regs; reg 3 NHS(OCP) Regs
5 Regs 9 and 15 NHS(OCP) Regs
6 Reg 3 NHS(DC)(W) Regs
7 Regs 4 and 5 NHS(TERC) Regs; regs 4 and 5 NHS(TERC)(W) Regs; Sch 2 and 3 NHS(DC) Regs; reg 9 and Sch 5 NHS(DC)(W) Regs
8 Regs 4 and 5 NHS(TERC) Regs; NHS(CDA) Regs; NHS(FP&CDA)(W) Regs
9 Regs 3, 5 and 9 NHS(TERC) Regs; regs 3 and 5 NHS(TERC)(W) Regs

10 Reg 3 HSS&WF(A) Regs
11 Sch 1 NHS(TERC) Regs; Sch 1 NHS(TERC)(W) Regs
12 Reg 5 NHS(TERC) Regs; reg 5 NHS(TERC)(W) Regs
13 Reg 6 NHS(TERC) Regs; reg 6 NHS(TERC)(W) Regs
14 Reg 16 and Sch 1 NHS(TERC) Regs; reg 15 and Sch 1 NHS(TERC)(W) Regs
15 Reg 17 and Sch 1 NHS(TERC) Regs; reg 16 and Sch 1 NHS(TERC)(W) Regs

3. Claiming health benefits and refunds
16 Reg 11 NHS(TERC) Regs; reg 10 NHS(TERC)(W) Regs; reg 10 NHS(CDA) Regs; Sch 1 para 1 NHS(FP&CDA)(W) Regs; regs 6 and 20 NHS(OCP) Regs; reg 10 NHS(DC) Regs; reg 10 NHS(DC)(W) Regs

Chapter 12

Housing benefit

This chapter covers:

Basic facts

- Housing benefit (HB) helps with your rent. In Northern Ireland, it also helps with your rates.
- It is administered by local authorities.
- Full-time students are eligible if they are on a non-advanced course and are under 21 (or are 21 and turned 21 on their course).
- Other full-time students can claim if they get income support, income-based jobseeker's allowance or income-related employment and support allowance, or if they are a lone parent, disabled or over the qualifying age for pension credit.
- Couples with a child can claim throughout the year, whether one or both are students.
- There are limits to the rent covered by HB.
- HB is means tested and the amount you get depends on your grant, loan and other income.

---

1. **What is housing benefit**

Housing benefit (HB) helps with your rent. In Northern Ireland, it also helps with your rates. Most full-time students cannot claim, but part-time students can. You can get help with rent in private accommodation, but not if you live with your parents. There are limits to the level of rent that HB covers. HB is means tested, so your grant, loan and other income affect the amount you get.

Note: you cannot usually make a new claim for HB if you are in a universal credit (UC) 'full service' area (see p204) (all areas are expected to be full service by the end of 2018) unless:

- you have three or more children and are not already getting UC (**Note:** this exception may end from February 2019); *or*
- you live in 'specified accommodation' or 'temporary accommodation'. This includes certain types of supported, refuge, hostel and homeless accommodation (you may still need to claim UC as well for your living costs).

2. **Who is eligible**

To qualify for housing benefit (HB), you must be a student who is eligible to claim (see below), your accommodation must be eligible for HB (see p152) and you must satisfy the basic HB rules (see p150).

Full-time students

If you are a full-time student 'attending or undertaking a full-time course of study', you cannot normally claim HB.[1] However, there are exceptions that allow some students to claim.

You start being a student from the first day you attend or undertake the course. You stop being a student after the last day of the final academic term in which you are enrolled, or from the day you finally abandon your course or are dismissed from it.[2]

Who counts as a full-time student

In most cases you are treated as a full-time student if your college or university says your course is full time.

If you are at a further education (FE) college, not on a higher education course, and your course is government funded, a learning agreement from the college shows how many hours are involved in the course and a 16-hour rule determines whether it is full or part time.[3] The rules on whether or not you count as a full-time student are the same as for income support (IS), except that there is no 12-hour rule if you are claiming HB and are aged under 20 and in relevant education. In this case, the 16-hour rule applies (see p166).

Guidance states that postgraduates stop being treated as full-time students for HB purposes when their course ends. If you go on to do further research or write up a thesis, whether or not you are regarded as full time depends on how much work you are doing at the time, not on whether the course is full time.[4]

Who can claim housing benefit

You can claim HB as a full-time student if you are in one of the following groups.[5]

- You are under 21 on a full-time course of non-advanced education (see p163) (benefit can continue if you turn 21 on your course, but stops once you turn 22), or you are a child or qualifying young person for child benefit purposes (see Chapter 8), even if no one gets child benefit for you.[6] If HB stops because you are no longer in this group, check below to see whether you are in one of the other groups of people who can claim HB. If not, ask your college if there is discretionary financial assistance available. **Note:** if you are a care leaver and are aged 16 or 17, you cannot get HB, even if you come into one of the groups below, because the local authority should be supporting you.

- You are on IS, income-based jobseeker's allowance (JSA) or income-related employment and support allowance (ESA).

- You are a lone parent of a child under 16, or under 20 if s/he is still a qualifying young person (see p115). Lone parents can only usually get IS until their youngest child's fifth birthday (see p167). If your IS stops, make sure you tell the local authority that pays your HB.

- You or your partner have reached the qualifying age for pension credit (PC). Entitlement to PC for both men and women is linked to the minimum age at which a woman can receive state retirement pension. From April 2010, this has been rising gradually from age 60 and reached 65 in November 2018. For more details, see CPAG's *Welfare Benefits and Tax Credits Handbook*.

- You qualify for a disability premium or severe disability premium with your HB – eg, you get disability living allowance (DLA), personal independence payment or long-term incapacity benefit (IB), or are certified as severely sight impaired or blind. See pp173–75 for details. **Note:** you cannot qualify for a disability premium if you have limited capability for work.[7]

- You have been incapable of work for the last 28 weeks. Since 27 October 2008, new claimants are assessed under the limited capability for work test (see below). However, the previous incapacity for work test may still apply to you if you are already getting IB, or IS on the basis of disability.

- You have had limited capability for work for the last 28 weeks and you continue to have limited capability for work. You should claim ESA to have your limited capability for work acknowledged (although you do not have to get any ESA to qualify). You can add together weeks of limited capability for work on either side of a gap of up to 12 weeks.

- You get a disabled students' allowance because of deafness. You are eligible for HB from the date you apply for the allowance.[8] However, if you are still waiting to hear about the allowance, the local authority may put off making a decision on your HB claim, but should then fully backdate your benefit.[9]

- You are in a couple, your partner is also a full-time student and you have a dependent child under 16, or under 20 if s/he is a qualifying young person (see p115). Unlike IS and JSA, which you can only claim in the summer vacation,

you can claim HB throughout the academic year. If you are claiming IS or income-based JSA, remember that if these benefits stop at the end of the summer vacation, you must tell the local authority so it can reassess your HB. If your partner is not a student, s/he can claim HB for both of you, whether or not you have a child.
- You are single and caring for a child boarded out with you by the social services department.

Studying part time

You can claim HB throughout your studies. You must meet all the basic rules below, including being liable for rent and being in eligible accommodation. You are a part-time student if you do not count as a full-time student under the definition on p166. The rules on who counts as full time are the same as those for IS, with one exception. If you are under 20 and in 'relevant education', there is no 12-hour rule. The 16-hour rule applies to you if you are on a non-advanced course, whatever your age.

3. Basic rules

As well as being a student who is eligible to claim housing benefit (HB – see p149), you must also meet all the following conditions to qualify.
- You are liable to pay rent (see below).
- You pay rent for the home in which you normally live (see p151).
- Your accommodation is eligible for HB (see p152).
- You satisfy the 'habitual residence' and 'right to reside' tests, and are not a 'person subject to immigration control'. These terms are explained in CPAG's *Welfare Benefits and Tax Credits Handbook*. Overseas students can get further advice from UKCISA (see Appendix 2).
- You have no more than £16,000 capital. There is no capital limit if you are getting pension credit (PC) guarantee credit.
- Your income is sufficiently low (see Chapter 22).

What follows is a brief outline of the basic HB rules, including those that refer specifically to students. For more details, see CPAG's *Welfare Benefits and Tax Credits Handbook*.

Liable for rent

You must be liable for rent. If you are jointly liable for the rent with others (eg, you have each signed the tenancy agreement), the amount of HB you get is based on your share of the rent (although, less commonly, it may not be an equal share if that seems reasonable to the local authority).

If you are part of a couple, it does not matter whose name is on the rent agreement; either of you can claim. So if you are a student who is eligible for HB, you can claim for both of you, or if you are not eligible for HB, your non-student partner can claim for both of you.

There are some circumstances in which a local authority has the discretion to treat you as liable for the rent even when you are not legally liable – eg, if you have taken over paying the rent from someone else.

Your normal home

Usually, you can only get HB for one home and that is the place where you normally live. If you are away from your normal home, in some cases your HB may stop. In other cases, you can get HB for two homes at the same time.

You are away from your term-time home

In the summer vacation, you cannot get HB for any weeks you are away from your term-time home, unless you would live there even if you were not studying. To continue to get HB for weeks of absence, you need to argue that your main purpose for living there is not simply to make it easier to attend the course – eg, you were settled there before the course or you are independent of, or estranged from, your parents.[10] However, if your grant or loan covers the summer vacation, your HB does not stop during any weeks of absence.[11] HB does not stop if you have to go into hospital.

If you leave your home during the academic year (or at any time if you live there not just to facilitate attending your course), your HB does not stop, provided you intend to return, you do not sublet, and you are not likely to be away for more than 52 weeks.[12] You cannot use this provision if you can get HB under the 'two homes rule' described below. The two homes rule is, however, more generous because it does not have a time limit.

Examples
John flatshares in Sheffield while attending university. He gets HB as a disabled student. During the summer vacation he goes home to his parents in Leicester for seven weeks. His HB stops for these seven weeks. He should give the local authority the dates he intends to be away.

Donna has always lived in Cardiff and is attending her local college. She is a lone parent and gets HB. She regularly visits her family in Aberystwyth during vacations. Her HB continues during her absence.

You have two homes

If you live in one home so that you can attend your course and in another home at other times, but you are only liable for rent on one, you can get HB for that place even while you are not there. This rule applies to lone parents and single students eligible for HB. It does not help you if you pay rent at one place and a mortgage on the other.[13]

Example

Emily's normal home is in Bristol, where she lives with her 18-year-old daughter who is at college. She has to pay rent for her Bristol home. Emily is studying at Leeds University and lives with a cousin rent free while in Leeds. Emily is eligible to claim HB for her Bristol home throughout the year. Whether any HB is payable, and at what times, depends on the amount of her grant and loan.

A couple (one of whom is a student eligible for HB) who have to live in two separate homes can get HB on both if the local authority decides that this is reasonable.[14]

Eligible accommodation

You can get HB to help pay the rent – eg, to a private landlord, local authority, housing association or co-operative. It is not essential for you to have a written tenancy agreement; it could be verbal. In some circumstances you cannot get HB – eg, if:[15]

- you live with and pay rent to your parents, a sister or brother, or a son or daughter (including in-laws, partners and step-relatives);
- you pay rent to someone (who might be a relative or friend), but your tenancy is not on a commercial basis. This rule often prevents people getting HB if they live in a property owned by their parents. It is possible, however, to get HB in these circumstances if the tenancy is a commercial one. If this applies to you, get advice;
- your tenancy was contrived in order to try to get HB;
- you pay rent to an ex-partner with whom you used to share the home in which you now live.

Halls of residence

You can get HB for rent in a student hall of residence.[16] You must be a full-time student who is eligible to claim HB (see p149). You cannot get HB in a hall if you are claiming while waiting to return to your course after taking time out because of disability, illness or caring responsibilities.

Part-time students can also get HB in a hall of residence if, had they been full time, they would have been eligible to claim HB as:

- an under-22-year-old in non-advanced education;
- a lone parent;
- a disabled student;
- someone with a child and a full-time student partner; *or*
- someone who has reached the qualifying age for PC (see p149).

If you get income support (IS), income-based jobseeker's allowance (JSA) or income-related employment and support allowance (ESA) as a part-time student, you can only get HB in a hall of residence if you are also one of the above. Although you can claim HB, it might not cover the whole cost (see below).

Full-time students waiting to return to their course after a period of illness or caring, and part-time students on IS, income-based JSA or income-related ESA, and not in another category cannot get HB in a hall of residence during term time or short vacations unless the educational establishment does not own the hall, does not have a long-term lease on the building or does not rent it from the education authority.[17] For example, if the university leases flats on a short-term lease from a private landlord and rents these to students, you can get HB. During the summer vacation, you can get HB if you remain in the hall, unless your student support covers the summer vacation.

4. **Amount of benefit**

The amount of housing benefit (HB) you get depends on the maximum rent the local authority is prepared to pay, and on your income compared with the amount the law says you need to live on. The amount you get may be reduced if your total income from benefits and tax credits is above a certain level (see p160). To work out your HB, go through the following steps.

Step one: capital
If your capital is over £16,000, you cannot get HB unless you are over 60 and get pension credit (PC) guarantee credit (see p258). Some kinds of capital are ignored. For details, see CPAG's *Welfare Benefits and Tax Credits Handbook*.

Step two: maximum rent
This is the maximum rent the local authority is prepared to pay. This might be less than the actual amount of rent you pay – eg, if you pay service charges that are not covered by HB (see below), or if your rent for HB purposes is reduced because you have a spare bedroom (see p154).

HB does not cover some items included in rent, such as charges for:
- water or sewerage;
- fuel. Either the actual charge specified in the rental agreement or a fixed rate is deducted;
- meals. If these are included in your rent, the local authority may deduct a fixed rate;
- services. Some are included (eg, cleaning communal areas, provision of a laundry room and TV signal relay, including free-to-view TV but not an individual satellite dish or set-top box) and others are not – eg, sports facilities and TV rental.

See CPAG's *Welfare Benefits and Tax Credits Handbook* for details of the deductions.

If you rent from a private landlord (including a hall of residence) and you claimed HB or moved home on or after 7 April 2008, the 'local housing allowance' rules apply. If this is the case, HB is based on the standard local housing allowance for the size of property that applies to you, even if your rent is higher than this amount. If your rent is lower, HB is based on the amount of your actual rent. Each local authority has its own rates for properties of different sizes. Check your local authority's rates at http://lha-direct.voa.gov.uk/search.aspx.

Generally, unless you are a single person aged under 35, you are allowed one bedroom for:

- an adult couple;
- another single adult aged 16 or over;
- two children under 16 of the same sex;
- two children under 10;
- any other child.

You are allowed a maximum of four bedrooms. If you are a single person under 35, you usually only get the lower, shared-accommodation rate. If you are disabled and need overnight care, you may qualify for an additional bedroom for a carer. See CPAG's *Welfare Benefits and Tax Credits Handbook* for details.

If the local housing allowance rules do not apply, your case is usually referred to a rent officer to decide how much help with rent you should get, based on other local rents. For details of these 'local reference rent' rules, see CPAG's *Welfare Benefits and Tax Credits Handbook*.

If you rent from a local authority or housing association, your maximum rent is usually the same as the weekly rent due less any of the above ineligible charges. However, your HB is reduced if you are considered to have a spare bedroom (known as the 'bedroom tax'). The rules about how many bedrooms you can have are similar to the local housing allowance rules, but see CPAG's *Welfare Benefits and Tax Credits Handbook* for more information. If you are considered to have one spare bedroom, your maximum rent is reduced by 14 per cent and by 25 per cent if you have two spare bedrooms. If your HB is reduced in this way, you should apply for a discretionary housing payment from the local authority (see below).

Discretionary housing payments

If your HB does not cover your rent, you may be able to get a discretionary housing payment from your local authority. These can be paid if you get HB and need additional help with your housing costs – eg, to make up the shortfall in rent due to HB being reduced because you have a spare bedroom. They are usually awarded for a temporary period, beyond which you have to reapply.

Step three: deductions for non-dependants

An amount is deducted from your maximum rent if you have a 'non-dependant' living with you.

A 'non-dependant' is someone, usually a friend or adult relative, who lives with you but not on a commercial basis. A deduction is made to reflect an assumed contribution from her/him to the household, whether or not s/he pays anything. There is no deduction for:[18]

- a full-time student during the academic year (whether or not s/he works);
- a full-time student during the summer vacation (but there is a deduction if s/he starts working 16 hours or more a week unless her/his student support covers the summer vacation);
- a full-time student at any time if you or your partner are 65 or over;
- a joint occupier or joint tenant;
- a resident landlord;
- a sub-tenant;
- your partner or dependent child;
- anyone under 18;
- anyone under 25 if s/he gets universal credit (UC), provided s/he does not have any earned income for UC purposes, income support (IS), income-based jobseeker's allowance (JSA), income-related employment and support allowance (ESA) without a work-related activity component (or who is not in the 'work-related activity group') or support component (this usually only applies in the first 13 weeks of an ESA claim);
- someone who gets a youth training allowance;
- someone who normally lives elsewhere;
- someone in hospital for more than 52 weeks or in prison;
- a live-in paid carer from a voluntary organisation;
- someone on PC.

No deductions are made for your non-dependants if you or your partner are registered blind, get disability living allowance care component, personal independence payment daily living component or attendance allowance.

For anyone else, fixed deductions are made based on the non-dependant's income. See CPAG's *Welfare Benefits and Tax Credits Handbook* for details and amounts. **Note:** if your non-dependant is working, you should provide the local authority with evidence of her/his gross income. If you do not, the local authority may make the highest deduction.

If you or your partner are aged 65 or over, the deduction is not made until 26 weeks after the non-dependant moves in with you or her/his income goes up, increasing the deduction.

Step four: getting a means-tested benefit
If you get IS, income-based JSA, income-related ESA or PC, HB is the amount worked out at Step three – ie, your maximum rent less any amount for non-dependants. In this case, you do not need to continue with the rest of these steps.

Step five: not getting a means-tested benefit

If you do not get IS, income-based JSA, income-related ESA or PC, you must compare your income with your weekly needs.

Step six: work out your applicable amount

This is an amount for your basic weekly needs. It is made up of:

- personal allowances;
- premiums;
- a work-related activity or support component if you have limited capability for work.

The applicable amount includes amounts for yourself and for your partner, if you have one. It also includes amounts for any dependent children. The amounts for HB are the same as for IS (see p172), but with the following differences.

- **Personal allowance:**
  - the child allowance is included in HB;
  - single people aged under 25 and lone parents under 18 who are entitled to main phase ESA get £73.10;
  - young couples get £114.85, unless both are under 18 and the claimant is not entitled to main phase ESA (see p130), in which case they get £87.50;
  - single people have a personal allowance of £163 if they are under 65 but have reached the qualifying age for PC (see p149) or £176.40 if aged 65 or over;
  - couples get £248.80 if at least one is under 65 but has reached the qualifying age for PC (see p149), and £263.80 if one or both are 65 or over.
- **Premiums:**
  - a family premium is included in your HB if you already have an existing claim which includes a child. It is not included in existing claims where you later have a child, or in new claims from 1 May 2016;
  - disabled child premium and enhanced disability premium for a child are included in HB;
  - you do not get a disability premium if you have been assessed as having limited capability for work for ESA and you (ie, not your partner) are the HB claimant.
- **Components:**
  - instead of a disability premium, add a work-related activity component of £29.05 if you have claimed ESA before 3 April 2017 and have limited capability for work, or a support component of £37.65 if you have limited capability for work-related activity (see p134).

Step seven: work out your weekly income

Chapter 22 explains how your loan, grant or other income is taken into account and how to work out your weekly income.

Step eight: calculate your housing benefit

If your income is *less than or the same as* your applicable amount, HB is the amount worked out at Step three – ie, your maximum rent less any amounts for non-dependants.

If your income is *more than* your applicable amount, work out 65 per cent of the difference. Your HB is the amount worked out at Step three (ie, your maximum rent less any amounts for non-dependants) minus 65 per cent of the difference between your income and applicable amount.

Examples

Maria is 18 and studying full time for a National Diploma in animal care. Her course lasts for one year (40 weeks in total). She shares a private-rented flat with a friend. They each pay £70 a week rent. She has payments from the 16–19 bursary fund, totalling £500. The local housing allowance amount for a single-room rent in her area is £60 a week (her maximum rent for HB).

	£
Maximum rent	60.00
Applicable amount	57.90
Income (16–19 bursary fund payments disregarded)	0
Weekly HB	**60.00**

Craig is a lone parent with two children, aged three and six. He is a first-year student, and his course commences on 1 October 2018. He is also a joint tenant with his friend Karl, who is not a student. Craig's share of the rent is £95. His income is his student support (including a loan with a maintenance element and a special support element, plus a parents' learning allowance), child tax credit (CTC) and child benefit. He makes a claim for HB at the start of the academic year.

Craig's HB entitlement from September 2018 is calculated as follows:

	£
Eligible rent	95.00
Applicable amount:	
Personal allowance	73.10
Allowances for two children	133.80
Family premium	17.45
Total applicable amount	**224.35**
Income:	
Student loan	6,236.00
Less travel	303.00
Less books and equipment (£390) =	5,543.00
Divided by 43 weeks =	128.91
(3 September 2018 to 30 June 2019)	
Less £10 disregard =	118.91

(Special support element of the loan and parents' learning allowance disregarded in full)

CTC	117.40
Total income	**236.31**

Craig's HB is worked out as follows:

Craig's income (£236.31) is more than his applicable amount (£224.35) by £11.96. He must contribute 65 per cent of this (£7.77) to his rent, with the remaining **£87.23 met by HB**. However, as his course does not start until 1 October, his student income is not taken into account for the first four weeks. If he were a second-year student, it would be.

Summer 2019:

Craig's student loan is only treated as income between 3 September 2018 and 30 June 2019. If Craig has no other income at this point, he is entitled to claim UC.

Northern Ireland:

If Craig were living in Northern Ireland, his HB for rent would be calculated using the rules set out above (although he would receive different rates of student support). If, in addition to his rent, he were liable to pay rates of £15 a week, he would receive this in full if his income is below his applicable amount. If, however, he had, for example, £26 more weekly income than his applicable amount, his HB for rates would be calculated as follows:

	£
Income less applicable amount	26.00
20% x £26 =	5.20
12% x £26 =	3.12
HB for rates:	
Maximum rates (£15) – £5.20 =	9.80
Rate relief:	
Maximum rates (£15) – £9.80 =	5.20
Remaining rate liability (£5.20) – £3.12 =	2.08

Craig would be entitled to **£78.10 HB** for rent (his rent less 65% of his excess income) and **£9.80** for rates, plus rate relief of **£2.08**.

5. **Claiming housing benefit**

You can get a claim form from your local authority housing benefit (HB) office. When you return it, ask for a receipt. If you return it by post, keep a copy, as claim forms are often lost. If you need to fill in another form, the local authority can backdate it if you can show the date of your original claim.

If you are also claiming income support (IS), income-based jobseeker's allowance (JSA), employment and support allowance (ESA) or pension credit (PC), you can claim HB at the same time. The Department for Work and Pensions should either take your claim over the phone or give you a form, usually Form HCTB1.

When your housing benefit starts

Your HB starts from when you make your claim. It can be backdated for up to one month if you ask for this and you have continuous 'good cause' for not claiming throughout the whole period. When deciding whether there is good cause to backdate a claim, a local authority must take into account how a reasonable person of your age, experience and state of health would have acted or failed to act in the same circumstances.[19] If you have reached the qualifying age for PC (see p149) and are not on IS, income-based JSA or income-related ESA, HB can be backdated for up to three months whatever the reason for the delay.

HB is usually paid directly into your rent account if you are a council tenant, otherwise it is either paid to you or directly to your landlord.

By law, local authorities are supposed to pay you within 14 days of receiving your completed claim form or as soon as possible after that. However, in many areas there are long delays. If you are a private tenant, ask for a **'payment on account'** until your claim can be properly assessed. Local authorities are legally obliged to give you an interim payment of a reasonable amount, unless it is obvious that you will not be entitled to HB or you have not supplied information that has been requested.

6. Challenging a decision

If you think a decision about your housing benefit is wrong (eg, because the decision maker got the facts or law wrong), there are a number of ways you can try to get the decision changed.

- You can ask for a revision or a supersession of the decision. In some cases, you must show specific grounds. In others, you must apply within a strict time limit, usually one month.
- You can appeal to the independent First-tier Tribunal. There are strict time limits for appealing – usually one month from the date you are sent the decision. You can make a late appeal in limited circumstances.

If you are considering challenging a decision, get advice as soon as possible.

7. Other benefits and tax credits

Child tax credit (CTC) counts in full as income when housing benefit (HB) is worked out. It is the actual amount you are paid that counts. If your CTC award is reduced because an overpayment of tax credit is being recovered, it is the reduced amount that counts for HB. If you are underpaid CTC and get a lump-sum repayment, this is treated as capital for HB, so it only affects your HB if it takes your savings above the capital limit. The rules are the same for working tax credit (WTC).

Child benefit is disregarded as income for HB.

Bear in mind that you should tell the local authority about any changes in income when they occur, including benefit and tax credit changes. Do not assume that the Department for Work and Pensions or HM Revenue and Customs passes on the information for you.

The benefit cap

Your HB is reduced if your total income from benefits is over the maximum amount that you or your partner can receive. The amount is £384.62 a week if you are a lone parent or member of a couple, and £257.69 if you are a single person.

Most benefits count towards the cap, including income support, jobseeker's allowance, employment and support allowance (ESA), child benefit, CTC and HB. The cap also applies to universal credit (see p214).

You are exempt from the cap if you or your partner are working, or if you are disabled, a carer or a war widow/er. To count as working, you must get WTC. You are exempt from the cap because of disability if you or your partner get certain disability benefits, including disability living allowance (DLA), personal independence payment (PIP) and ESA with a support component. You are also exempt if a child or young person for whom you are responsible gets DLA or PIP. You are exempt if you or your partner get carer's allowance.

There is protection for nine months before the cap applies if you are no longer working but were working at least 16 hours a week for the last year.

Notes

2. Who is eligible
1 Regs 53(1), definition of 'full-time student', and 56(1) HB Regs
2 Reg 53(1), definition of 'last day of the course', and (2)(b) HB Regs
3 Reg 53(1), definition of 'full-time course of study', HB Regs
4 para 2.354 C2 GM
5 Reg 56(2) HB Regs

6 Reg 56(2)(h) HB Regs
7 Sch 3 paras 12 and 13(9) HB Regs
8 Reg 56(2)(i) HB Regs
9 para 2.30 C2 GM

3. Basic rules
10 Reg 55 HB Regs
11 Regs 53(1), definition of 'period of study', and 55 HB Regs

12 Reg 7(16)(c)(viii) HB Regs
13 Reg 7(3) HB Regs
14 Reg 7(6)(b) HB Regs
15 Reg 9 HB Regs
16 Reg 57(4) HB Regs
17 Reg 57(2) HB Regs

4. Amount of benefit
18 Regs 3 and 74 HB Regs

5. Claiming housing benefit
19 Reg 83(12) HB Regs; R(S) 2/63(T)

Chapter 13

Income support

This chapter covers:
1. What is income support (below)
2. Who is eligible (p163)
3. Basic rules (p170)
4. Amount of benefit (p171)
5. Claiming income support (p175)
6. Challenging a decision (p176)
7. Other benefits and tax credits (p176)

Basic facts

- Income support provides basic financial support for people who are not expected to 'sign on' for work.
- Part-time students can claim if they are a lone parent with a child under five, a carer, pregnant (and sick or nearly due), and in some other circumstances.
- Full-time students aged under 19 or 20 (sometimes 22) on non-advanced courses can claim if they are a parent, an orphan or estranged or separated from their parents, and in some other circumstances.
- Other full-time students can claim if they are a lone parent with a child under five, and in some other circumstances.
- The amount is usually affected by any grant, loan or other income you may have.

1. What is income support

Income support (IS) provides basic financial support for people under the qualifying age for pension credit (see p170) who are not expected to 'sign on' as available for work. Students who are lone parents with a child under five may be able to claim IS, as may some younger students on non-advanced courses who are estranged from their parents or who are parents themselves. Most other full-time students are not eligible. See p163 for which students can claim IS.

Note: you cannot make a new claim for IS if you are in a universal credit 'full service' area (see p204), unless you have three or more children (**Note:** this exception may end from February 2019). All areas are expected to be full service by the end of 2018.

The amount you get is based on your circumstances – eg, whether you have a partner or whether you (or your partner) have a disability or care for someone with a disability. The amount you get is usually affected by any grant, loan or other income you have.

2. **Who is eligible**

To qualify for income support (IS), you must be in one of the groups eligible to claim and you must satisfy all the basic rules described on p170.

Only certain groups of students are eligible for IS, depending on your age and your course. Check which category you are in (see below), and then check who in that category can get IS:

- under 20 and in 'relevant education' (see below); *or*
- 19 or over and a full-time student, unless you are aged 19 and count as being in relevant education (see p166); *or*
- under 19 in full-time advanced education (see p169); *or*
- studying part time (see p169).

Under 20 in relevant education

Generally, you cannot claim IS if you are under 20 and in 'relevant education', but there are exceptions.[1]

What is relevant education

You count as being in relevant education if you are a 'qualifying young person' for child benefit purposes (see p115) – ie, you are aged 19 or under and attending a full-time course of non-advanced education or an approved training course (see p115) which you were accepted on, enrolled on or started when you were under 19.[2] If you are accepted on, enrol on or start a full-time course of non-advanced education on or after your 19th birthday, you are not in relevant education. The rules on p166 apply to you instead.

Full-time non-advanced education

Your course is classed as **'full time'** for IS purposes if it is for more than 12 hours a week during term time. These 12 hours include classes and supervised study, but not meal breaks or unsupervised study either at home or at college.[3]

'Non-advanced education' is anything below degree, Higher National Certificate (HNC) or Higher National Diploma (HND) level, and includes school-level courses.

Non-advanced courses	Advanced courses
National vocational qualifications (NVQ) levels 1–3	BTEC HNC or HND
GCSEs	Diploma of higher education
AS and A levels	Degree level
	Postgraduate degree

You may still count as being in relevant education for a period after your course ends (see p165).

Who can claim income support

If you are aged 16, 17, 18 (or, in some cases, 19 – see p163), and in relevant education, you are eligible for IS if you are in one of the following groups.[4]

- You are an orphan and no one is acting in place of your parent. You do not qualify if, for example, you are living with a foster parent or being looked after by the local authority.
- You must live away from your parents or anyone acting in their place because you are estranged from them. Decision makers should believe you if you say you are estranged unless there is valid evidence that this may not be the case.[5] If a decision maker questions what you say, s/he may, with your permission, seek further evidence.[6] It is possible to be estranged from a parent even if you do not both feel the same way about it.[7]
- You must live away from your parents because there is a serious risk to your physical or mental health, or because you are in physical or moral danger. Decision makers are advised to accept your own evidence of physical or moral danger unless there is stronger evidence to the contrary.[8]
- You are living away from your parents and anyone acting in their place, they cannot support you financially, and:
  - they are chronically sick or physically or mentally disabled; *or*
  - they are in prison; *or*
  - they are not allowed to enter Britain.
- You are a parent and your child lives with you.
- You are a refugee learning English in certain circumstances (see p168).
- You have left local authority care and you have to live away from your parents or anyone acting in their place. However, 16/17-year-old care leavers normally get financial support from the local authority social services department, and you cannot get IS in relevant education unless you are a lone parent.[9]

Examples
Pete is 17 and studying cookery full time leading to an NVQ level 2. His father is in prison and his mother is chronically ill. Neither of them can support him financially and he does not live with them. He is eligible for IS.

Ginny is 18 and studying information technology for a BTEC. She is the mother of a two-year-old child and they both live with Ginny's parents. She is eligible for IS.

Ahmed is 18 and studying full time for his A levels. He is a refugee whose parents live in Somalia. It would be dangerous for him to return home. Ahmed is eligible for IS.

Kelly is 16 and studying full time for A levels. She has lived on her own since her father told her to leave home. She is estranged from both her parents. She is eligible for IS.

Laurie is 17 and has left local authority care. She is undertaking a full-time NVQ in beauty therapy. She is a lone parent and so is not excluded from IS as a 16/17-year-old care leaver.

Once you reach your 20th birthday, you are no longer classed as being in 'relevant education' and cannot get IS under these rules. You may be able to continue to get IS as a full-time or part-time student, but only if you are in one of those groups who can claim (see p167 and p169).

In particular, your claim for IS may be able to continue if you are under 22 on a non-advanced course and without parental support – ie, you are in one of the first four groups in the list above.

Alternatively, you may be able to 'sign on' for jobseeker's allowance (JSA) as a part-time student (see p182). Otherwise, you may need to contact your college for discretionary financial assistance.

Parents claiming for you

If you are in relevant education but are not in any of the above groups, you cannot get IS. Your parents may be able to claim child benefit and child tax credit (CTC) for you (see Chapters 8 and 19).

If you get IS for yourself, the amount of your parents' benefit may reduce, as:
- any child benefit or CTC they get for you stops;
- any IS or income-based JSA they get for you stops;[10]
- any working tax credit they get stops, unless there are other dependent children in the family or they qualify in another way.

When a course ends

You count as being in relevant education if you have finished a course of non-advanced education and are enrolled or accepted on another such course.[11] This means you are still in relevant education during the summer vacation between courses. Otherwise, you still count as being in relevant education when you finish a course until the latest of the following dates, or until you turn 20 if that is earlier:
- 31 August after your 16th birthday;[12]
- for 16/17-year-olds, 20 weeks after your course ends if you are registered with the Careers Service (in England and Northern Ireland) or Careers Wales in Wales. This is the 'extension period' rule in child benefit (see p117). **Note:** if you are an orphan, estranged from your parents, living away from your parents

because of a risk to your health or because they cannot support you financially, or a care leaver, the requirement that someone must have received child benefit for you immediately before the period started does not apply;[13]

- the last day in February, May, August or November following the date the course ends.[14]

19 or over and a full-time student

If you are a full-time student aged 19 or over, whether in non-advanced or advanced education, you cannot usually claim IS during your 'period of study', but there are exceptions.[15] If you are aged 19 and in relevant education, you come under the rules on pp164–65.

Period of study

The **'period of study'** starts on the first day of the course and ends on the last day of the course – ie, the last day of the final academic year.[16] It only ends earlier than this if you abandon your course or are dismissed from it, in which case it ends on the day that happens. You are within your period of study during all vacations and, for sandwich courses, during periods of work placements. In your first year, you do not count as a student at all until you first start attending or undertaking the course.[17] So if the course has already begun, you are not excluded from IS as a student until the day you actually start.

Who counts as a full-time student

You count as a **'full-time student'** if you are 'attending or undertaking a full-time course of study at an educational establishment'.[18] There are two definitions of 'full time' that apply: the first covers mostly courses of advanced education; the second covers most courses of non-advanced education.

- **Advanced education.** Your course is full time if it is classed as full time by the institution. If the institution describes the course as full time, you need convincing evidence to persuade the Department for Work and Pensions (DWP) otherwise, bearing in mind that what matters is the course itself rather than the hours you attend.[19] This definition covers all courses of advanced education funded, in whole or in part, by the government, and any courses of non-advanced education that are not wholly or partly funded by the government at a further education (FE) college.
- **Non-advanced education.** Your course is full time if it involves more than 16 hours a week of classroom or workshop learning under the direct guidance of teaching staff.[20] What matters is the number of hours specified in a document signed by the college. This is often called a 'learning agreement', but your college may refer to it by some other name. This definition applies if you are at an FE college, not undertaking a higher education course and your course is fully or partly funded by the government.

Sandwich courses

You count as a full-time student if you are on a sandwich course. A 'sandwich course' is made up of alternate periods of work experience and full-time study at college or university, where the study periods add up to at least 18 weeks in the year.[21]

Work experience includes periods of employment abroad for modern language students whose course is at least half composed of modern language study.

Initial teacher training courses are not treated as sandwich courses.

Modular courses

A 'modular course' is one that is made up of two or more modules and you are required to do a certain number to complete the course.[22] If you are attending or undertaking part of a modular course that is full time according to the rules described above, you are regarded as being a full-time student for the duration of that module, from the day it begins until the last day of registration on the module (or earlier if you abandon the course or are dismissed from it). This includes all vacations during the module on which you are registered and, except for the final module, the vacation immediately following it. It also includes periods when you are attending the course to do re-sits. If the modular course allows you to undertake some modules on a part-time basis, you are not excluded from IS while you are studying part time.

Postgraduates

If you are a postgraduate, the law is not clear on whether you still count as a student during the period at the end of your course when you are writing up your thesis. DWP guidance says someone is 'not a full-time student during the period after the end of the course when they are expected to complete any course work'.[23] If you are refused IS, consider appealing. You could try arguing that you are no longer attending or undertaking a course.

Who can claim income support

You can claim IS if you are:[24]

- a lone parent (see below);
- a single foster parent (see p168);
- in a couple, your partner is also a full-time student and you have a child (but you can only get IS in the long vacation – see p168);
- a refugee learning English (see p168);
- on a non-advanced course, under 22 and without parental support (see p168).

Lone parents

To qualify as a lone parent, your youngest child must normally be under age five (you can also qualify if you are under 18, regardless of your youngest child's age).[25] Once your youngest child reaches her/his fifth birthday, you no longer count as a lone parent and your IS stops.

You may be required to attend work-focused interviews if your youngest child is aged one to four, and to undertake work-related activity if your youngest child is aged three or four.

If you are a lone parent and your child is above the age at which you count as a lone parent for IS, but is under 20 and a qualifying young person (see p115), in certain circumstances you can get IS during the summer vacation. You must be in one of the other groups of people who are eligible for IS, such as a carer (see p169). If you are not in one of these groups, you can claim JSA in the summer vacation instead (see p181).

Single foster parents

You are eligible if you are a single foster parent with a child under 16. This includes kinship carers who are caring for a 'looked-after' child (sometimes referred to as 'approved kinship carers').

Couples

If you have a child and your partner is also a full-time student, you are not excluded from IS in the summer vacation.[26] To be eligible, you must be in one of the groups of people who can get IS (eg, a carer), listed under 'studying part time' on p169. Your child must be under 16, or under 20 and still a qualifying young person (see p115). During term time and short vacations, you are not eligible for IS.

If your partner is not a full-time student or is a part-time student, s/he is not excluded from IS and can claim for you as well as for her/himself whether or not you have a child. S/he can claim IS throughout the year, not just in the long vacation. To be eligible, s/he must be in one of the groups of people who can get IS listed on p169. If s/he is not in one of these groups, s/he cannot get IS but may be able to claim JSA for both of you.

Refugees

Your English course must be more than 15 hours a week and aimed at helping you get work. You must have refugee status and you must have been in Britain for a year or less when your course starts. Payment of IS is limited to nine months.[27]

Under 22 without parental support

To qualify, you must be on a full-time course of non-advanced education on which you were accepted, enrolled or started before you turned 21.[28] If you turn 21 on your course, you continue to be eligible. In addition, you must:

- be an orphan, and no one is acting in place of your parent; *or*
- live away from your parents, or anyone acting in their place, because you are estranged from them; *or*

- live away from your parents because there is a serious risk or danger to you; *or*
- live away from your parents. They must be unable to support you financially and be sick or disabled, in prison or not allowed to enter Britain.

For more details, see the first four groups who can claim IS in relevant education listed on p164.

Examples

Julie is studying full time for a degree in chemistry. She is a lone parent with a three-year-old child. She is eligible for IS.

Emma is studying full-time for an HND in social care. She is single and fosters a 13-year-old boy. She is eligible for IS.

Anne is a lone parent with a 14-year-old daughter who has a disability. Anne is a full-time student on a four-year degree course. She is not eligible for IS as a lone parent, but is eligible as a carer in the summer vacation only.

Under 19 in full-time advanced education

If you are under 19 and in full-time advanced education rather than in non-advanced education, the rules are the same as for those aged 19 or over. You count as a full-time student if you are 'attending or undertaking a full-time course of advanced education'.[29] What is or is not a full-time course is the same as for over-19-year-olds (see p166). Only some students can claim IS. The groups who can claim are the same as for full-time students aged 19 or over (see p166).

Studying part time

Part-time students can claim IS under the usual rules without restriction. You must satisfy all the basic rules (see p170) and you must be in one of the groups of people who are eligible for IS. In brief, these are:

- lone parents under age 18 (regardless of the child's age) or lone parents with a child under five;
- some young people up to age 25 on youth training schemes;
- carers who get carer's allowance or care for someone who gets attendance allowance, the middle or highest rate of the disability living allowance care component, or the daily living component of personal independence payment;
- pregnant women from 11 weeks before to 15 weeks after the birth (or earlier if they are incapable of work because of pregnancy);
- single foster parents of children under 16 or with a child placed for adoption, or people looking after a child while their partner is abroad or if the parents are temporarily ill, or away temporarily;

- some people on unpaid paternity or parental leave;
- people caring for a family member who is temporarily ill;
- refugees on English courses in their first year in Britain;
- people entitled to statutory sick pay;
- people appealing against a decision that they are not incapable of work;
- people who are incapable of work, but only if they already get incapacity benefit (IB);[30]
- people who are registered or certified as blind, but only if they already get IB.

For more details of all the groups of people who are eligible for IS, see CPAG's *Welfare Benefits and Tax Credits Handbook*.

What counts as part time

You are regarded as a part-time student if you are not a full-time student. If you are under 20 and in relevant education, see p163 for who counts as full time. If you are in advanced education at any age or you are 19 or over and in non-advanced education (and not a 19-year-old in relevant education), see p166 for who counts as full time.

If you are at an FE college studying a non-advanced course (see Chapter 1), the DWP may ask you for a learning agreement to show that the course is part time – ie, no more than 16 classroom hours. Your college can provide you with this.

Example
Betty is a carer for her disabled mother and has been getting IS on this basis for two years. She starts studying at college 12 hours a week towards an NVQ. She continues to be eligible for IS.

3. **Basic rules**

As well as being a student who is eligible to claim, to qualify for income support (IS) you must satisfy all the following conditions.[31]
- You are aged 16 or over.
- You have not reached the qualifying age for pension credit (PC). If you have reached this age, you may be eligible for PC instead. Entitlement to PC for both men and women is linked to the minimum age at which a woman can receive state retirement pension. This has been rising gradually from age 60 from April 2010 and reached 65 in November 2018. See CPAG's *Welfare Benefits and Tax Credits Handbook* for more details.
- You are not working 16 hours or more a week. If you are working 16 hours or more, you may be eligible for working tax credit instead (see p224).
- Your partner is not working 24 hours or more a week.

- You are present in Great Britain, satisfy the 'habitual residence' and 'right to reside' tests, and are not a 'person subject to immigration control'. (You can sometimes be paid IS for the first four or eight weeks you are outside Britain.) These terms are explained in CPAG's *Welfare Benefits and Tax Credits Handbook*. Further advice is available from UKCISA (see Appendix 2).
- You have no more than £16,000 capital.
- Your income is less than the set amount the law says you need to live on (known as your 'applicable amount' – see p172).

4. **Amount of benefit**

The amount of income support (IS) you get depends on your and your partner's circumstances. The amount also depends on your income and capital. Go through the following steps to work out the amount of IS to which you are entitled.

Step one: capital

If your capital is over £16,000, you cannot get IS (see p258). Some kinds of capital are ignored. For details, see CPAG's *Welfare Benefits and Tax Credits Handbook*.

Step two: work out your applicable amount

This is an amount for basic weekly needs. It is made up of:
- personal allowances (see p172);
- premiums (see p173);
- housing costs (see p175).

Step three: work out your weekly income

Chapter 22 explains how your loan, grant or other income is taken into account and how to work out your weekly income.

Step four: deduct weekly income from applicable amount

If your income is *less* than your applicable amount, IS equals the difference between the two.

If your income is *the same as or more than* your applicable amount, you cannot get IS. You can claim again if your income goes down – eg, during the long vacation.

Example
Karen is 23 and a full-time, second-year undergraduate student in England and a lone parent of Penny, aged two. She gets a tuition fee loan of £9,250, plus a loan for living costs of £6,236, a special support loan of £3,680, a parents' learning allowance of £1,669 and a childcare grant of £80 per week. Her only other income is child benefit of £20.70 a week and child tax credit (CTC) of £64.52 a week.

During the academic year September 2018 to June 2019:
Step one   Karen has no savings or capital.
Step two   Her applicable amount is:
                Personal allowance for herself   £73.10
Step three   Her weekly income is:
                Loan   £121.98
                The tuition fee loan, special support loan, parents' learning allowance
                and childcare grant are all disregarded, as well as her child benefit
                and CTC. See Chapter 21 for details of how the student loan for living
                costs is taken into account.
Step four   Her income is above her applicable amount, so she cannot get IS.

During the long vacation from June 2019 to September 2019:
It is likely that Karen would have to claim universal credit if she wants help with her living
costs.

Applicable amount

Work out your applicable amount by adding together your personal allowances, premiums and eligible housing costs. Benefit rates are uprated in April each year, although the government has frozen most rates for the next three years.[32] It is usually possible to find out the new rates from the beginning of December. Check the Department for Work and Pensions (DWP) website at www.gov.uk/government/organisations/department-for-work-pensions for a press release on social security uprating. The amounts in this *Handbook* are from April 2018.

Claiming for children

From 6 April 2004, IS personal allowances for children and premiums for children were abolished for all new claims and for anyone claiming CTC. Amounts for children are paid through CTC and child benefit instead. If you were already getting IS with amounts for children included before 6 April 2004 and have not claimed CTC, your IS continues to include amounts for children. You can claim CTC earlier than this if you think you will be better off. If you have a grant or loan, you may be better off claiming CTC. Ask your local Jobcentre Plus for a better-off calculation.

Personal allowance

Your personal allowance is made up of the following.[33]
- One personal allowance at either the single, lone parent or couple rate depending on your situation. The amount depends on your age.
- If you still get IS with amounts for children but do not yet have an award of CTC, add one personal allowance of £66.90 for each dependent child under 16, or under 20 if s/he is still a qualifying young person. For new claims from 6 April 2004, do not include any personal allowance for children.

Circumstances	£ per week	Conditions
Single		
Under 25	57.90	No special conditions.
25 or over	73.10	No special conditions.
Lone parent		
Under 18	57.90	No special conditions.
18 or over	73.10	No special conditions.
Couple		
Both aged 16–17 (certain cases)	87.50	You get this rate if: – you or your partner are responsible for a child; *or* – you and your partner would be eligible to claim IS or income-related employment and support allowance (ESA) if you were single; *or* – your partner is eligible for income-based jobseeker's allowance (JSA) or severe hardship payments of JSA.
Both aged 16–17 (everyone else)	57.90	For everyone else who cannot get the higher rate.
One aged 16–17, one 18 or over	114.85	The younger partner: – is eligible to claim IS or income-related ESA, or would be if s/he were single; *or* – is eligible for income-based JSA; *or* – is entitled to severe hardship payments of JSA.
One aged 16–17, one 18–24	57.90	For those who are not eligible for the rate above.
One aged 16–17, one 25 or over	73.10	For those who are not eligible for the rate above.
Both aged 18 or over	114.85	No special conditions.

Premiums

Qualifying for premiums depends on your circumstances.

You can qualify for either one, but not both, of the following.

- **Disability premium** of £33.55 (£47.80 for a couple). You get a disability premium if you get:[34]
  - disability living allowance (DLA);
  - personal independence payment (PIP);

- long-term incapacity benefit (IB);
- severe disablement allowance;
- working tax credit with a disabled worker or severe disability element;
- war pensioner's mobility supplement;
- constant attendance allowance;
- exceptionally severe disablement allowance.

You also qualify if:

- you are certified as severely sight impaired or blind, and for 28 weeks after coming off the register; *or*
- you are terminally ill and have been entitled to statutory sick pay (SSP) for at least 196 days.

Since the introduction of ESA in October 2008, it is usually no longer possible to have a disability premium added to your IS because of incapacity for work. If you already get a disability premium because of incapacity for work, you continue to get this.

If you are the IS claimant and you have a partner, you get the disability premium if s/he gets any of the qualifying benefits or is blind.

- **Pensioner premium** of £133.95 for couples. People who have reached the qualifying age for pension credit (PC – see p170) claim PC rather than IS. However, you get a pensioner premium if you are under this age and claiming IS and you have a partner who has reached this age.[35]

In addition, you can qualify for any, or all, of the following.[36]

- **Carer premium** of £36. You get a carer premium if you are entitled to carer's allowance (CA – see p110). If you are entitled to CA but not paid it because it overlaps with another benefit (eg, IB), you still qualify for a carer premium. You get two carer premiums if both you and your partner qualify.
- **Enhanced disability premium** for an adult of £16.40 (£23.55 for a couple). You get this premium if you get the highest rate of the DLA care component or the enhanced rate of the PIP daily living component.[37]
- **Severe disability premium** of £64.30. This is a premium for severely disabled people who live alone, or can be treated as living alone. You qualify for this premium if you get the middle or highest rate of the DLA care component, or the standard or enhanced rate of the PIP daily living component, and no one gets CA for looking after you. You do not get it if you live with another person aged 18 or over (eg, a friend or parent), unless s/he is separately liable for rent, or you only share a bathroom or hallway, or in some other circumstances.[38] See CPAG's *Welfare Benefits and Tax Credits Handbook* for details. If you have a partner, you do not qualify unless s/he also qualifies in her/his own right or is severely sight impaired or blind. If you both qualify, you get two premiums.

If your IS was awarded before 2004 and you do not get CTC, it may also include:

- family premium of £17.45;

- disabled child premium of £62.86 for each qualifying child;
- enhanced disability premium of £25.48 for each qualifying child.

Housing costs

IS can include amounts for certain service charges if you own your home.

If you own your own home and get IS, you may be able to get a loan from the DWP (**Note:** these loans are not part of your IS) to help with the cost of your mortgage interest payments,[39] repayable when you sell your home or on your death. Payments are usually made directly to your mortgage lender. Usually help only starts once you have been getting IS for 39 weeks, although there are some exceptions to this.

Normally you have to live in the home you own to get a loan for mortgage interest, but there are exceptions for full-time students (and some others). You can still get a loan for mortgage interest if you have moved elsewhere to study but are not paying rent or mortgage payments at the term-time address. If you pay for both places, you can get a loan for both if you are a couple and it is unavoidable that you live in two separate homes. Otherwise, you can get a loan if you are away from your home temporarily and have not let it out and are not likely to be away for more than 52 weeks.[40]

You must claim housing benefit (HB – see Chapter 12) for help with your rent. For more details, see CPAG's *Welfare Benefits and Tax Credits Handbook*.

5. **Claiming income support**

If you think you might be entitled to income support (IS), claim as soon as you can. There are only very limited situations in which backdating is allowed.

To start your claim, contact the Jobcentre Plus contact centre national number on 0800 055 6688 (textphone 0800 023 4888).

When you call, details of your claim are taken and a date for a work-focused interview is arranged (unless it is agreed that you do not need to attend one). A call-back can be arranged if a single call is not appropriate – eg, if you have language or hearing difficulties. You are sent a statement to check and sign, and you are told what evidence and information you should take to your interview or forward to the Department for Work and Pensions (DWP). The work-focused interview is intended to help you into full-time work, even if you have no intention of working until you finish your studies, but you are under no obligation to look for work.

If you cannot, or do not want to, use the telephone to start your claim, you should still be able to claim in other ways. A claim form should still be accepted, which you can get from Jobcentre Plus, or you may be able to start a claim online at www.gov.uk. It is important to let your Jobcentre Plus office know you want to claim IS, as otherwise you might lose benefit. You should return the form within one month of your initial contact.

Either member of a couple can make the claim for both, but whoever claims must be eligible in her/his own right.

Getting paid

Payment is usually made directly into your bank or building society. Which account it goes into is up to you. If you do not want your benefit to go into an account that is already overdrawn, give the DWP details of an alternative account if you have access to, or can open, one. If you do not have an account, you are usually expected to open one with a bank, building society or post office.

If your claim is refused

Your claim may be unsuccessful for a variety of reasons, including if your student income is too high to qualify. However, you might find that you qualify in the long vacation because of the way your grant and loan are divided up through the year. So if you are turned down, claim again as soon as you think you might qualify.

6. **Challenging a decision**

If you think a decision about your income support is wrong, you can ask the Department for Work and Pensions (DWP) to look at it again. This process is known as a 'reconsideration' (the law refers to it as a 'revision'). Provided you ask within the time limit (usually one month), the DWP notifies you of the decision in a 'mandatory reconsideration notice'. If you are still not happy when you get this notice, you can appeal to the independent First-tier Tribunal. If it was not possible to ask the DWP to reconsider the decision within a month, you can ask for a late revision (within 13 months), explaining why it is late. You can also ask the DWP to look at a decision again at any time if certain grounds are met – eg, if there has been an official error.

7. **Other benefits and tax credits**

Income support (IS) tops up other income you have to the level of your basic requirements (your 'applicable amount'). Most other benefits you get are therefore taken into account as income when working out your IS. This means they reduce your IS pound for pound. Disability living allowance, personal independence payment and housing benefit (HB) are, however, always disregarded as income.

If you have children and get child tax credit (CTC), both CTC and child benefit are disregarded as income for IS. If you do not yet have a CTC award and have had amounts for children in your IS since before 6 April 2004, child benefit is taken into account for IS.

Even though getting another benefit may reduce your IS, it may still be worth claiming. Getting another benefit might mean you qualify for a premium with your IS (eg, getting carer's allowance means you qualify for a carer premium), so you could be better off overall (although in this case, the person you care for could get less benefit – see p112).

If you get IS and you pay rent, you are eligible as a student for HB (unless you are a care leaver aged 16 or 17).

IS is taken into account when calculating whether the benefit cap applies (see p160 and p214).

Passported benefits

Provided you meet any other conditions, getting IS entitles you to:
- free prescriptions;
- free dental treatment;
- vouchers for glasses;
- Healthy Start vouchers and free vitamins;
- social fund payments;
- free school lunches from the local authority.

See Chapters 11 and 17 for details.

Notes

2. Who is eligible
1 s124(1)(d) SSCBA 1992
2 Reg 12 IS Regs; s142 SSCBA 1992
3 Reg 1(3) CB Regs
4 Reg 13(2) and Sch 1B para 15 IS Regs
5 DWP guidance, 'Making a Severe Hardship Decision', paras 7 and 28, available at www.gov.uk. This guidance is for JSA but should equally apply for IS.
6 Vol 4, para 20686 DMG
7 CIS/4096/2005
8 Vol 4, para 20693 DMG
9 Reg 2 C(LC)SSB Regs
10 Reg 14(2) IS Regs; reg 76(2) JSA Regs
11 Reg 3(2)(b) CB Regs
12 Reg 4 CB Regs
13 Reg 13(2A)(b) IS Regs; reg 5 CB Regs
14 Reg 7 CB Regs
15 Reg 4ZA(2) IS Regs
16 Regs 2(1), definition of 'period of study', and 61(1), definition of 'last day of the course', IS Regs
17 Reg 61(2)(b) IS Regs
18 Reg 61(1), definition of 'full-time student', IS Regs
19 R(SB) 40/83; R(SB) 41/83

20 Reg 61(1)(c), definition of 'full-time
    course of study', IS Regs
21 Reg 61(1), definition of 'sandwich
    course', IS Regs
22 Reg 61(4) IS Regs
23 Vol 6, para 30238 DMG
24 Reg 4ZA(3) IS Regs
25 Sch 1B para 1 IS Regs; s137 SSCBA 1992
26 Reg 4ZA(3)(c) IS Regs
27 Sch 1B para 18 IS Regs
28 Sch 1B para 15A IS Regs
29 Reg 61(1), definition of 'full-time
    student', IS Regs
30 Regs 1(4) and 2(1) ESA(TP) Regs

3. Basic rules
31 s124 SSCBA 1992

4. Amount of benefit
32 s11 WRWA 2016
33 Sch 2 para 1 IS Regs
34 Sch 2 paras 11 and 12 IS Regs
35 Sch 2 paras 9, 9A and 10 IS Regs
36 Sch 2 para 6 IS Regs
37 Sch 2 paras 13A and 15(8) IS Regs
38 Sch 2 para 13 IS Regs
39 Reg 3 LMI Regs
40 Sch 3 para 4 LMI Regs

Chapter 14

Jobseeker's allowance

This chapter covers:

Basic facts

– Jobseeker's allowance provides basic financial support for people who are expected to 'sign on' for work.
– Full-time students cannot normally claim.
– Student couples with children can claim in the long vacation.
– Lone parents can claim in the long vacation if they are not eligible for income support.
– Part-time students can claim if they are available for work.
– You do not need to have paid national insurance contributions to qualify, but you might get more money if you have.
– The amount is usually affected by any grant, loan or other income you may have.

1. What is jobseeker's allowance

Jobseeker's allowance (JSA) provides basic financial support for people of working age who are not working full time and who are expected to 'sign on' as available for work.

Full-time students are normally excluded from JSA, but there are exceptions. Part-time students can claim if they are available for work.

If you have paid sufficient national insurance contributions, you get contribution-based JSA for the first six months. This is paid on top of any student or other income you might have. Otherwise, you may get income-based JSA. This is means tested, so most of your student income and most other income is taken into account when working out how much benefit you get. Chapter 22 explains how your income affects your benefit.

If you live in a universal credit (UC) 'full service' area, you cannot claim income-based JSA and must claim UC instead, unless you have three or more children (**Note:** this exception may end from February 2019). See Chapter 18. All areas are expected to be full service by the end of 2018.

2. **Who is eligible**

To qualify for jobseeker's allowance (JSA), you must not be excluded as a student, and you must satisfy the basic rules. See below for details of students who can claim. The basic rules are covered on p185.

Note: the following rules for full-time students and young people in relevant education do not apply to contribution-based JSA if you are in a universal credit (UC) 'full service' area (see p204). If this is the case, you can only get contribution-based JSA and study full time if you took time out of your course because of illness or caring responsibilities, you have now recovered or the caring responsibilities have ended, and you are waiting to rejoin your course.[1]

Under 20 in relevant education

You cannot get JSA while in 'relevant education'.[2]

Relevant education

You are in **'relevant education'** if:

– your course is non-advanced (ie, school level or below degree, Higher National Certificate or Higher National Diploma level) of more than 12 hours a week;[3] *and*

– you are under 19, or aged 19 and were accepted on, enrolled on or started your course before you turned 19.

This is the same definition as that used for child benefit and similar to that for child tax credit (CTC). So, although you cannot get JSA for yourself, your parents may still be able to get child benefit and CTC for you.

A special rule allows part-time students who have been on benefit for some months to study and claim JSA at the same time, even though their course is over 12 hours a week. This applies if your course is not full time according to the rules below that apply to most students over 19, and you got JSA or employment and support allowance (ESA), or you were on an apprenticeship or other similar training:

• during the last three months before the start of the course; *or*

• for three out of the last six months before the course if you were working the rest of the time.

19 or over and a full-time student

You cannot usually get JSA as a full-time student aged 19 or over (and not in relevant education – see p180), whether in advanced or non-advanced education, at any time during your 'period of study'.[4]

> ### Period of study
> Your '**period of study**' is the whole of your course from the first day you attend or undertake the course to the last day – ie, the last day of the final academic year, including short and long vacations.[5] It includes a period of study in connection with the course after you have stopped doing the course itself. It does not include freshers' week, unless your course actually starts that week.[6]

You are not a student in between courses. For example, you can claim JSA in the summer between completing an undergraduate degree and starting a postgraduate course.

Postgraduates writing up their thesis at the end of a course may be regarded by the Department for Work and Pensions (DWP) as being in 'a period of study undertaken by the student in connection with the course'. However, guidance for decision makers says someone is 'not a full-time student during the period after the end of the course when they are expected to complete any course work'.[7] If you do claim, you must show that you are available for and actively looking for work. If you say you are not prepared to fit your thesis writing around a job, should one come up, the DWP will decide that you are not available for work.

What counts as full time

In most cases, the college or university defines whether the course is full or part time. However, for some further education (FE) students, there is a 16-hour study rule. The JSA rules are the same as those for income support (IS – see p166).

Who can claim jobseeker's allowance

You can get JSA in the following circumstances. If you are claiming contribution-based JSA and are in a UC 'full service' area, see the note on p180.

- You are in a couple, both of you are full-time students and you have a dependent child aged under 16, or aged under 20 and a qualifying young person (see p115). You can get JSA during the summer vacation only. The person who claims must be available for work and meet all the other basic rules for JSA.[8]
- You are a single person with a dependent child aged under 16, or aged under 20 and a qualifying young person (see p115). You can get JSA during the summer vacation only. You must be available for work and meet all the other basic rules for JSA. Check whether you can claim IS instead. This depends on

the age of your youngest child and whether you meet the usual IS rules (see p167).[9]

- You are on a course regarded by your work coach at the Jobcentre Plus office as a qualifying course. You must be aged 25 or over and have been getting JSA for at least two years before the course starts. During term time you are not expected to sign on or look for work, although you may be required to provide evidence of your attendance and progress on the course. During vacations, you are expected to look for casual work.[10]
- You are on a full-time employment-related course approved by your work coach at the Jobcentre Plus office. You can claim JSA for just two weeks.[11]

Example

Kiera and Mike are a couple and are both studying full time on degree courses. They have a seven-year-old son. Kiera signs on for JSA during the summer, claiming benefit for herself and Mike, who is not working. They also get CTC and child benefit throughout the year.

Under 19 and in full-time advanced education

You cannot usually get JSA if you are under 19 and studying full time in advanced education. The rules are the same for you as they are for full-time students aged 19 or over (see p181).

Studying part time

You can claim JSA while studying part time. You must continue to pass all the basic rules for JSA, including being available for work and actively looking for work.

What counts as part time

Generally, your college or university determines whether you count as a part-time or full-time student, rather than the number of hours you study or attend lectures.[12] The rules are the same as for IS (see p170).

However, if you are under age 20 and in relevant education, there is a 12-hour rule (see p163). Your course is full time if it is more than 12 hours a week of classes and supervised study in term time.

If you are aged 19 or over (and not a 19-year-old in relevant education) at an FE college but not on a higher education course, there is a 16-hour rule for courses funded, or partly funded, by the government. A part-time course is up to 16 hours a week of guided learning.[13]

This is set out in a learning agreement provided by your college.

Examples
Keira is 20 and attending an FE college, studying for A levels. She has 10 hours a week of classes and 10 hours a week of timetabled independent study. She is classed as a part-time student.

Gwyneth is 24 and at an FE college on an NVQ level 2 course. She has classes for 18 hours a week and three hours of timetabled study. She is classed as a full-time student.

Russell is 18 and studying for a BTEC. He has 15 hours of classes a week. He is classed as full time.

Saleem is 19 and studying for a degree. He has 15 hours of lectures a week. The university regards his course as full time. He is classed as a full-time student for JSA.

Studying and availability for work

When you claim JSA, you may have agreed which hours of the day and which days of the week you are available for work. This 'pattern of availability' is set out in your 'claimant commitment'. You are allowed to do this provided the hours you choose still give you a reasonable chance of getting work and do not considerably reduce your prospects of getting work.

If the hours you study are completely different to the hours you have agreed to be available for work, you should have no problem. If, however, there is some overlap, or if you have agreed to be available for work at any time of day and on any day of the week, the DWP must be satisfied that you are available for work despite your course. It expects you to:

- rearrange the hours of your course to fit round a job or be prepared to give up the course if a job comes up; *and*
- be ready to take time off the course to attend a job interview; *and*
- be ready to start work immediately.

Guidance tells DWP decision makers to look at various factors when deciding whether you are genuinely available for work, such as:[14]

- what you are doing to look for work;
- whether your course will help you get work. Bear in mind that if you say the course is necessary to get the kind of job you want, the DWP may assume you are not prepared to give it up to do another kind of job and, therefore, decide you are not available for work;
- whether you can be contacted about a possible job if you are studying away from home;
- whether you gave up work or training to do the course;
- your hours of attendance on the course;
- whether it is possible to change the hours if necessary;

- whether you could still complete the course if you missed some classes;
- how much you paid for the course and whether any fees could be refunded if you gave up the course. The DWP is likely to assume that you are not prepared to give up the course to take a job if you have paid a significant amount in course fees;
- whether any grant would need to be repaid if you gave up your course.

At the Jobcentre Plus office you are given a student questionnaire, Form ES567S *Attending a Training or Education Course*, to complete.

However, the DWP does not need to know about any of the above factors if you got JSA, incapacity benefit, IS on incapacity for work grounds or ESA, or were on an apprenticeship or similar training:

- during the last three months before the start of the course; *or*
- for three out of the last six months before the course if you were working the rest of the time.

If this applies to you and your course hours overlap with your pattern of availability but you are willing and able to rearrange them in order to take up employment, no other questions about your course are relevant to your availability for work.[15] You need only complete Part 1 of the student questionnaire and sign Part 3.

Once you have qualified for JSA, you must continue to be available for work and actively look for work. When you 'sign on', you must show what steps you have taken to look for work – eg, checked job adverts or applied for jobs. If you do not look for work each week, or you turn down a job or interview, you could be given a sanction and lose some or all of your JSA , which could be for up to three years. If this happens, you can appeal. You might be able to reduce the amount of the sanction or have it overturned (get advice about this) – ask for a hardship payment in the meantime.

Open University students can attend a residential course for up to a week and keep their JSA. You are not expected to be available for, or to look for, work during that week.[16]

16/17-year-olds

Usually you can only get JSA if you are aged 18 or over. If you are under 18, you can get income-based JSA in the following circumstances, provided you meet all the other entitlement conditions.

- You are in severe hardship. All your circumstances should be considered. Payments are discretionary and usually for just eight weeks at a time.
- You come within one of the groups of people who can claim IS. These are the same groups as for part-time students who can claim IS (see p169).
- You are a couple with a child.

- You are married or in a civil partnership and your partner is aged 18 or over. JSA is paid for a limited period after you leave full-time education.
- You are married or in a civil partnership and your partner is under 18 and registered for work or training, or long-term sick or disabled, or a student who can claim IS, or a carer who can claim IS. JSA is paid for a limited period after you leave full-time education.
- You are leaving local authority care and are a lone parent.[17] JSA is usually paid for just eight weeks. **Note:** your local authority social services department may give financial support if you have been in care.

3. **Basic rules**

As well as being a student who is eligible to claim jobseeker's allowance (JSA), you must satisfy all of the basic rules.[18]

- You are available for work. You must be willing and able to take up work immediately (although some people are allowed notice). You must be prepared to work at least 40 hours a week. People with caring responsibilities and disabled people can restrict themselves to fewer than 40 hours. During your child's school holidays, you are not expected to be available for work if there is no childcare reasonable for you to arrange, but this provision does not apply if you are a full-time student.[19]
- You are actively seeking work.
- You have a claimant commitment. This sets out, for instance, the hours you have agreed to work, the type of work you are looking for and any restrictions on travel and pay.
- If you are doing any work, it is for less than 16 hours a week. You can get contribution-based JSA if your partner is working, but not income-based JSA unless s/he works less than 24 hours a week.
- You are capable of work (although you can continue to get JSA for up to 13 weeks while sick).
- You are under pension age (rising from age 60 for women from April 2010 and reached 65 in November 2018; 65 for men).
- You are in Great Britain, although JSA can be paid in other countries in some circumstances. See CPAG's *Welfare Benefits and Tax Credits Handbook* for details.
- You meet the conditions for either contribution-based JSA or income-based JSA (see below). If you meet the conditions for both, you get contribution-based JSA topped up by income-based JSA.

Contribution-based jobseeker's allowance

You must have paid sufficient national insurance contributions to qualify for contribution-based JSA, as well as meeting all the basic rules above.[20]

You must have paid class 1 contributions on earnings of at least the lower earnings limit in 26 weeks, which need not be consecutive, in one of the two complete tax years (6 April to 5 April) before the start of the benefit year (which runs from the first Sunday in January) in which you claim. You also must have paid or been credited with class 1 contributions on earnings of 50 times the lower earnings limit in these years.

For example, you qualify if you claim JSA in 2018 and you paid contributions on earnings of £5,600 in the tax year April 2015 to April 2016 and £5,650 in the tax year April 2016 to April 2017, earning in the first year £112 a week or more, or in the second year £113 a week or more, for at least 26 weeks.

Income-based jobseeker's allowance

As well as satisfying all the basic rules above, to get income-based JSA you must meet the following conditions.[21]

- You are aged 18 or over. You can still get income-based JSA if you are aged 16 or 17 but there are extra rules (see p184).
- You satisfy the 'habitual residence' and 'right to reside' tests, and are not a 'person subject to immigration control'. These terms are explained in CPAG's *Welfare Benefits and Tax Credits Handbook*. Further advice for overseas students is available from UKCISA (see Appendix 2).
- Your income is below the amount set for your basic living needs (known as your 'applicable amount').
- You have no more than £16,000 capital. See Chapter 22 for how your income and capital affect your benefits.
- You do not get pension credit.

4. **Amount of benefit**

Jobseeker's allowance (JSA) is payable after seven 'waiting days'. You may get contribution-based JSA and/or income-based JSA, depending on your circumstances.

Contribution-based jobseeker's allowance

Contribution-based JSA is paid at different weekly rates depending on your age. **Note:** the government has frozen these rates for the next three years.[22]

Weekly rate from April 2018

Under 25	£57.90
25 or over	£73.10

You may get less than this if you have part-time earnings or an occupational or personal pension, but the amount is not affected by a student loan or grant. Contribution-based JSA is only paid for up to 26 weeks. After that, you can claim income-based JSA if your income is low enough. Unlike income-based JSA, you only get amounts for yourself, not for a partner.

Income-based jobseeker's allowance

Income-based JSA is worked out in the same way as income support (IS). The amount you get is made up of:
- personal allowances;
- premiums;
- housing costs – ie, certain service charges.

The total of these is called your 'applicable amount'. If you have no other income (the student loan and some grants count as income), you are paid your full applicable amount. Otherwise, any income you have is topped up with income-based JSA to the level of your applicable amount. If your weekly income is above your applicable amount, you are not entitled to income-based JSA. See Chapter 22 for how to work out your weekly income. See Chapter 13 for how to work out your applicable amount. The rules are almost the same as for income support (IS), with the following differences.
- For couples, if only one of you is under 18, you get the higher £114.85 personal allowance if the younger partner is responsible for a child or is eligible for income-based JSA, severe hardship payments, IS (or would be if not a member of a couple) or income-related employment and support allowance (ESA).
- For couples, if both of you are under 18, you get the higher £87.50 personal allowance if:
  - you or your partner are responsible for a child;
  - both of you would be eligible for income-based JSA or your partner would be eligible for IS or income-related ESA if you were both single;
  - you are both eligible for severe hardship payments, or one of you is while the other is eligible for income-based JSA, IS or income-related ESA;
  - you are married or civil partners and one of you is registered with the Careers Service (in England or Northern Ireland) or Careers Wales or both of you are eligible for income-based JSA.
- Joint-claim couples (see p188) can get a disability premium (at the couple rate) if one has had limited capability for work for 364 days (196 days if terminally ill). You must claim ESA to establish limited capability for work, even if you might not get it.

5. Claiming jobseeker's allowance

You should claim jobseeker's allowance (JSA) by phoning the Jobcentre Plus contact centre national number on 0800 055 6688 (textphone 0800 023 4888). You are given an appointment for an interview. Claim as soon as you can, as JSA can only be backdated in very limited circumstances. If you are under 18, you should register with the Careers Service in England, Careers Wales or your local Jobs and Benefits office in Northern Ireland first.

At the interview, you are asked to complete Form ES2, *Helping You Back to Work,* which has questions about looking for work. When filling in this form, remember that even though you are a student, you are expected to be available for work and actively looking for work. Make sure your answers do not cast doubt on your willingness to work. If you are a part-time student, you are also given the student questionnaire to complete and are asked for a learning agreement from your college to show that you are studying part time.

Couples

If you are a full-time student or in relevant education but your partner is not, s/he can get JSA for both of you if s/he is eligible for JSA.[23] You both need to claim, but only your partner must continue to sign on and look for work. Similarly, your partner can get JSA for both of you, if you are not yet a full-time student but you have applied for or been accepted on a course.

Most other couples, including if one or both of you are part-time students, need to claim income-based JSA jointly. This means that both of you must make the claim, be eligible for JSA, sign on and look for work.

Some people need not claim jointly. Only the person who makes the claim for the couple must be eligible and sign on if:
- you have dependent children; *or*
- you are both under 18.

6. Challenging a decision

If you think a decision about your jobseeker's allowance is wrong, you can ask the Department for Work and Pensions (DWP) to look at it again. This process is known as a 'reconsideration' (the law refers to it as a 'revision'). Provided you ask within the time limit (usually one month), the DWP notifies you of the decision in a 'mandatory reconsideration notice'. If you are still not happy when you get this notice, you can appeal to the independent First-tier Tribunal. If it was not possible to ask the DWP to reconsider the decision within a month, you can ask for a late revision (within 13 months), explaining why it is late. You can also ask the DWP to look at a decision again at any time if certain grounds are met – eg, if there has been an official error.

7. **Other benefits and tax credits**

You cannot get income support (IS) and jobseeker's allowance (JSA) at the same time, so if you are eligible for both, you must choose which to claim. In general, the amounts of income-based JSA and IS are the same, but you are not expected to sign on for work for IS.

Child tax credit (CTC) and, except for some existing claimants, child benefit are ignored as income when JSA is assessed. If you have been getting income-based JSA since before 6 April 2004 and still have amounts for children included in JSA, child benefit is taken into account as income.

If you get income-based JSA, you are also eligible as a student for housing benefit provided you meet the other rules of entitlement.

JSA is taken into account when calculating whether the benefit cap applies (see p160 and p214).

Passported benefits

Provided you meet any other conditions, getting income-based JSA entitles you to:
- free prescriptions;
- free dental treatment;
- vouchers for glasses;
- Healthy Start vouchers and free vitamins;
- social fund payments;
- free school lunches from the local authority.

Contribution-based JSA does not give you automatic access to these benefits, but you may qualify for health benefits on low income grounds. See Chapter 11 for details.

Notes

2. Who is eligible
1 Reg 45(6) JSA Regs 2013
2 s1(2)(g) JSA 1995
3 Reg 54 JSA Regs
4 Reg 15(1)(a) JSA Regs
5 Regs 4 and 130 JSA Regs
6 Vol 6, para 30221 DMG
7 Vol 6, para 30238 DMG
8 Reg 15(2) and (3) JSA Regs
9 Reg 15(2) and (3) JSA Regs
10 Regs 17A and 21A JSA Regs
11 Reg 14(1)(a) JSA Regs

12 Reg 1(b)(i), definition of 'full-time
student', JSA Regs
13 Reg 1(b)(iii), definition of 'full-time
student', JSA Regs
14 Vol 4, para 21242 DMG
15 Reg 11 JSA Regs
16 Regs 14(1)(f) and 19(1)(f) JSA Regs
17 C(LC)SSB Regs

3. Basic rules
18 s1 JSA 1995
19 Reg 15(4) JSA Regs
20 s2 JSA 1995
21 ss3 and 13 JSA 1995

4. Amount of benefit
22 s11 WRWA 2016

5. Claiming jobseeker's allowance
23 Sch A1 JSA Regs; Vol 6, para 30245
DMG

Chapter 15

Maternity, paternity and adoption benefits

This chapter covers:

Basic facts
– Women having a baby can claim statutory maternity pay if they have an employer, or maternity allowance if they have recently worked.
– The mother's partner can claim statutory paternity pay.
– Parents adopting a child can claim statutory adoption pay and statutory paternity pay.
– Either partner can claim statutory shared parental pay instead of statutory maternity, paternity or adoption pay.
– Part-time and full-time students are eligible for these benefits.

1. What are maternity, paternity and adoption benefits

Statutory maternity pay

You can get statutory maternity pay (SMP) for 39 weeks if you are pregnant or have just had a baby, have an employer and earn at least £116 a week (April 2018 rate).

Maternity allowance

If you cannot get SMP but you have recently worked, either employed or self-employed, you may be able to get maternity allowance (MA) for 39 weeks. You may also qualify if you have helped your partner with her/his self-employment. See CPAG's *Welfare Benefits and Tax Credits Handbook* for details.

Statutory paternity pay

You can get statutory paternity pay (SPP) for two weeks if your partner is having a baby and you are taking leave from work to care for her or for the child. You can also get statutory shared parental pay (SSPP) in some circumstances. See CPAG's *Welfare Benefits and Tax Credits Handbook* for details. Unmarried partners, including same-sex partners, can claim SPP.

Statutory adoption pay

You can get statutory adoption pay (SAP) for 39 weeks if you are adopting a child and are earning at least £116 a week from employment (April 2018 rate). If a couple (including same-sex couples) are adopting a child, one can claim SAP and the other can claim SPP for two weeks (or SSPP, in some circumstances).

Statutory shared parental pay

You or your partner can get SSPP instead of SMP, MA or SAP in certain circumstances.

2. Who is eligible

Students are eligible for maternity, paternity and adoption benefits if they pass the basic rules for these. See CPAG's *Welfare Benefits and Tax Credits Handbook* for details. What follows is a brief outline of the qualifying conditions.

Statutory maternity pay

You can get statutory maternity pay (SMP) if:
- you are pregnant or have recently had a baby;
- you have worked for the same employer for 26 weeks ending with the 15th week before your expected week of birth;
- your average gross earnings are at least £116 a week (April 2018 rate); *and*
- you give your employer the correct notice.

Maternity allowance

You can get maternity allowance (MA) if you cannot get SMP and:
- you are pregnant or have recently had a baby;
- you have worked, either as an employee or self-employed, for at least 26 weeks out of the 66 weeks before the expected week of birth; *and*
- your average earnings are at least £30 a week.

Statutory paternity pay

You can get statutory paternity pay (SPP) if:
- you are the child's father or partner of the child's mother and you will be caring for the child or supporting the mother;
- you have worked for the same employer for 41 weeks before the baby is born;
- your average gross earnings are at least £116 a week (April 2018 rate); *and*
- you give your employer the correct notice.

You can also get SPP if you are adopting a child. You cannot get both SPP (adoption) and statutory adoption pay (SAP) at the same time, although one member of a couple can claim SAP while the other claims SPP (adoption).

Statutory adoption pay

You can get SAP if:
- you are adopting a child;
- you have worked for the same employer for 26 weeks ending with the week in which you are told you have been matched with a child for adoption;
- your average gross earnings are at least £116 a week (April 2018 rate); *and*
- you give your employer the correct notice.

Statutory shared parental pay

You can get SSPP if:
- you are caring for a child; *and either*
- you are the mother of the child or have adopted the child, and you have reduced your MA, SMP or SAP period; *or*
- you are the father of the child or the partner of the mother/adopter and your partner has reduced her/his MA, SMP or SAP period.

Your partner must also meet employment and earnings tests. See CPAG's *Welfare Benefits and Tax Credits Handbook* for more details.

3. **Amount of benefit**

Weekly rate from April 2018

Statutory maternity pay	for the first six weeks	90% of average weekly earnings
	for the following 33 weeks	£145.18 (or 90% of earnings if less)
Statutory paternity pay	for two weeks	£145.18 (or 90% of earnings if less)
Statutory adoption pay	for 39 weeks	£145.18 (or 90% of earnings if less)
Statutory shared parental pay	for 37 weeks	£145.18 (or 90% of earnings if less)
Maternity allowance	for 39 weeks	£145.18 (or 90% of earnings if less)

You can end your statutory maternity pay (SMP), statutory adoption pay (SAP) or maternity allowance (NM) early and your partner can take parental leave instead of you and be paid statutory shared parental pay (SSPP). Or you can end your SMP, SAP or MA early and get SSPP yourself, as it gives you more flexibility in when you take your paid leave. See CPAG's *Welfare Benefits and Tax Credits Handbook* for more details.

4. **Claiming maternity, paternity and adoption benefits**

You claim statutory maternity, adoption, paternity and shared parental pay from your employer. You claim maternity allowance from your local Jobcentre Plus office.

5. **Challenging a decision**

If you think a decision about your maternity allowance is wrong, you can ask the Department for Work and Pensions (DWP) to look at it again. This process is known as a 'reconsideration' (the law refers to it as a 'revision'). Provided you ask within the time limit (usually one month), the DWP notifies you of the decision in a 'mandatory reconsideration notice'. If you are still not happy when you get this notice, you can appeal to the independent First-tier Tribunal. If it was not possible to ask the DWP to reconsider the decision within a month, you can ask for a late revision (within 13 months), explaining why it is late. You can also ask the DWP to look at a decision again at any time if certain grounds are met – eg, if there has been an official error.

If you disagree with your employer's decision on your entitlement to statutory maternity, adoption, paternity or shared parental pay, or your employer fails to make a decision, you can ask HM Revenue and Customs to make a formal decision on your entitlement.

6. **Other benefits and tax credits**

There are a number of other benefits you may get when you have a baby, such as:
- child benefit when the baby is born;
- universal credit (UC), if you are in a UC 'full service' area (see p204) and have fewer than three children. **Note:** this may change from February 2019 to include claims from those with three or more children;
- child tax credit (CTC) or an increase in your existing award. Tell HM Revenue and Customs within three months of the birth;
- if you are 19 or under and in full-time non-advanced education or approved training on which you were accepted, enrolled or started before you turned 19, income support (IS) as a parent;
- if you are a lone parent, IS whether or not you are a full-time student;
- if there is no other child under 16 in the household, a Sure Start maternity grant within six months of the birth, provided you get a qualifying benefit (including UC, IS and CTC). If you are still waiting for a decision on your UC, IS or CTC, claim the grant anyway. If you are refused the grant, rather than your claim being held until your benefit or tax credit is awarded, make another claim within three months of being awarded the benefit or tax credit;
- Healthy Start vouchers.

Maternity allowance is taken into account when calculating whether the benefit cap applies (see p160 and p214). Statutory maternity, adoption, paternity and shared parental pay are not taken into account.

Chapter 16

Personal independence payment

This chapter covers:
1. What is personal independence payment (below)
2. Who is eligible (p197)
3. Amount of benefit (p198)
4. Claiming personal independence payment (p198)
5. Challenging a decision (p199)
6. Other benefits and tax credits (p199)

Basic facts

– Personal independence payment (PIP) is for people who need help with daily living or who have mobility difficulties.
– Part-time and full-time students can claim.
– If you are a full-time student, getting PIP allows you to claim universal credit (although you must meet a medical test). Getting PIP also allows you to claim income-related employment and support allowance and may also allow you to claim housing benefit.

---

1. What is personal independence payment

Personal independence payment (PIP) is a new benefit which replaces disability living allowance (DLA) for people of working age (aged 16 to 64).

If you are already on DLA and are of working age, you will be assessed for PIP at some point. If you were 65 or over on 8 April 2013 (20 June 2016 in Northern Ireland), you remain on DLA. If you are getting DLA and are of working age, you must claim PIP instead if you are invited to do so, or if your DLA award is due for renewal, you have a change of circumstances or you turn 16.

PIP is not means tested, so it is not reduced because of your student support or other income. It comprises two components: for daily living and mobility. Each component has two rates: a standard rate and an enhanced rate.

2. **Who is eligible**

You qualify for personal independence payment (PIP) if you meet all the following conditions.

- You are aged 16 or over and under 65.
- You satisfy certain rules on residence and presence in the UK, and are not a 'person subject to immigration control'. See CPAG's *Welfare Benefits and Tax Credits Handbook* for details.
- You satisfy the disability conditions for the daily living component and/or the mobility component.
- You have satisfied the disability conditions for the last three months (unless you are terminally ill) and are likely to continue to do so for the next nine months.

Your ability to undertake various activities is assessed, usually at a medical examination. Depending on the type and level of help you need, you score points on different activities. If you score eight points, you get the standard rate of a component; if you score 12 points, you get the enhanced rate. For example, if you cannot dress or undress yourself, you score eight points.

See CPAG's *Welfare Benefits and Tax Credits Handbook* for more information about the activities and the points awarded.

Daily living component

To get the standard rate of the daily living component, your ability to undertake certain specified day-to-day activities must be limited by your health or disability. To get the enhanced rate, your ability to undertake the activities must be severely limited.

You are assessed on your ability to carry out the following activities:
- preparing food. If you cannot prepare and cook a simple meal yourself, you can score points;
- taking nutrition;
- managing your therapy or monitoring your health condition;
- washing and bathing;
- managing your toilet needs or incontinence;
- dressing and undressing;
- communicating verbally. If you need to use an aid to help you speak or hear, you can score two points; if you need a British Sign Language interpreter to help you understand or express information, you can score four to eight points, depending on the help you need;
- reading and understanding signs, symbols and words. If you need help to read, or need to use an appliance or aid (other than glasses or contact lenses), you can score points;

- engaging face-to-face with other people;
- making budgeting decisions. You can score points if your disability means you need help with budgeting.

Mobility component

You get the standard rate of the mobility component if your ability to undertake certain mobility activities is limited by your health or disability. If your ability to undertake the activities is severely limited, you get the enhanced rate.

You are assessed on your ability to plan and follow journeys, and to move around. You can score points if you need help to follow an unfamiliar or familiar route, including if you can only do so with the help of a guide dog or orientation aid.

Students

If you are a part-time or full-time student, you can get PIP if you meet the qualifying conditions. Starting studying should not affect your award, provided you still have daily living and/or mobility needs.

3. **Amount of benefit**

Weekly rate from April 2018
Daily living component
Standard rate   £57.30
Enhanced rate   £85.60
Mobility component
Standard rate   £22.65
Enhanced rate   £59.75

4. **Claiming personal independence payment**

Phone 0800 917 2222 (textphone 0800 917 7777) (in Northern Ireland 0800 012 1573; textphone 0800 012 1574) to make a claim for personal independence payment (PIP). If you cannot claim by phone, you can ask for a claim form to be sent to you. Claims cannot be backdated, so claim as soon as you think you qualify.

When you phone, some basic information is taken from you. You are then sent a form on which to give more information about your condition and how it affects you. You must normally return this form within one month. You must then usually attend a medical assessment.

Awards of PIP are usually made for a fixed period – eg, two years or five years.

PIP is usually paid directly into your bank account, and is paid every four weeks in arrears.

5. Challenging a decision

If you think a decision about your personal independence payment is wrong, you can ask the Department for Work and Pensions (DWP) to look at it again. This process is known as a 'reconsideration' (the law refers to it as a 'revision'). Provided you ask within the time limit (usually one month), the DWP notifies you of the decision in a 'mandatory reconsideration notice'. If you are still not happy when you get this notice, you can appeal to the independent First-tier Tribunal. If it was not possible to ask the DWP to reconsider the decision within a month, you can ask for a late revision (within 13 months), explaining why it is late. You can also ask the DWP to look at a decision again at any time if certain grounds are met – eg, if there has been an official error.

6. Other benefits and tax credits

If you get personal independence payment (PIP) and are in a universal credit (UC) 'full service' area (see p204) and you have limited capability for work, you are eligible for UC (see p206). All areas are expected to be full service by the end of 2018. If you are a full-time student and get PIP, you are eligible for income-related employment and support allowance and, usually, housing benefit.

If you claim other benefits or tax credits, make sure the office dealing with your claim knows you get PIP, as it may qualify you for additional amounts in these.

If you, your partner or a young person you are responsible for get PIP, you are exempt from the benefit cap (see p160 and p214).

Chapter 17

The social fund

This chapter covers:
1. What is the social fund (below)
2. Sure Start maternity grants (p201)
3. Funeral payments (p201)
4. Budgeting loans (p202)
5. Local welfare assistance schemes (p202)
6. Challenging a decision (p203)

Basic facts

– To get help from the social fund, you must receive income support or another qualifying benefit.
– Most students do not qualify for help from the social fund because they do not get a qualifying benefit.
– Support may be available from local assistance schemes in some circumstances.

1. What is the social fund

The social fund consists of regulated payments and budgeting loans.
   Regulated social fund payments are:
- Sure Start maternity grants;
- funeral payments;
- cold weather payments;
- winter fuel payments.

You are entitled to regulated social fund payments if you satisfy the qualifying conditions. For more information on cold weather payments and winter fuel payments, see CPAG's *Welfare Benefits and Tax Credits Handbook*.

2. **Sure Start maternity grants**

A Sure Start maternity grant is a grant of £500 to help with the costs of a new baby. You are usually only eligible if there is no child under 16 in the household already. To qualify you must get:

- income support; *or*
- income-based jobseeker's allowance; *or*
- income-related employment and support allowance; *or*
- pension credit; *or*
- child tax credit; *or*
- working tax credit including a disability or severe disability element; *or*
- universal credit.

Claim at the local Jobcentre Plus office on Form SF100 up to 11 weeks before the birth or within six months of the birth. If you are waiting to hear about a claim for one of the qualifying benefits, make sure to claim the maternity grant within the deadline. Your entitlement is then protected and the grant can be awarded once the benefit decision is made, although you may need to fill in a second SF100.

3. **Funeral payments**

A funeral payment is made to help with burial or cremation costs. To qualify you must get:

- income support; *or*
- income-based jobseeker's allowance; *or*
- income-related employment and support allowance; *or*
- pension credit; *or*
- housing benefit; *or*
- child tax credit; *or*
- working tax credit including a disability or severe disability element; *or*
- universal credit.

Unless you are the partner of the person who dies, you may not get a payment if there is a close relative who does not get one of these benefits.

Claim at the local Jobcentre Plus office on Form SF200 within three months of the funeral.

4. Budgeting loans

You can get a budgeting loan to help you pay for certain items – eg, furniture, clothes, removal expenses, rent in advance, home improvements, travelling expenses, maternity expenses, funeral expenses and jobseeking expenses. If you are claiming universal credit, you must apply for a budgeting advance instead of a budgeting loan (see p213).

The amount of budgeting loan you can get depends on the size of your family and how long you have been on benefit. To qualify, you must have been getting one of the following for at least 26 weeks before your claim is decided:

- income support;
- income-based jobseeker's allowance;
- income-related employment and support allowance; *or*
- pension credit.

See CPAG's *Welfare Benefits and Tax Credits Handbook* for details of who can get a loan and how to apply.

5. Local welfare assistance schemes

The discretionary elements of the social fund (community care grants and crisis loans) have been abolished. Their replacement varies depending on where you live.

Local provision in England

Local authorities in England are now responsible for providing replacement schemes for community care grants and crisis loans. Schemes vary, so contact your local authority for details of its scheme. Although students are not excluded from applying, your local authority usually expects you to first claim assistance from your university's or college's hardship fund, if this is available. Funding is, in general, likely to be limited.

Discretionary Assistance Fund in Wales

The Welsh government has set up a national scheme to replace social fund community care grants and crisis loans in Wales, called the Discretionary Assistance Fund.

The Fund consists of 'individual assistance payments' to help people remain in or establish themselves in the community, and 'emergency assistance payments' for people without money because of a disaster or emergency. To qualify for an individual assistance payment, you must usually be getting a qualifying benefit (income support, income-based jobseeker's allowance, income-related employment and support allowance, pension credit or universal credit).

Students on a qualifying benefit are eligible for individual assistance payments if they meet the other criteria, but you are expected to apply to your college's or university's discretionary fund first.

More information on the Fund, and how to apply, is at https://beta.gov.wales/discretionary-assistance-fund-daf

Discretionary support in Northern Ireland

In Northern Ireland the discretionary scheme is called Finance Support. It offers help to people experiencing a crisis which puts their or their immediate family's health, safety or wellbeing at significant risk. Support is in the form of a loan or grant, depending on the circumstances. For more details, see www.nidirect.gov.uk/articles/introduction-finance-support.

6. **Challenging a decision**

If you think a decision about your maternity grant or funeral payment is wrong, you can ask the Department for Work and Pensions (DWP) to look at it again. This process is known as a 'reconsideration' (the law refers to it as a 'revision'). Provided you ask within the time limit (usually one month), the DWP notifies you of the decision in a 'mandatory reconsideration notice'. If you are still not happy when you get this notice, you can appeal to the independent First-tier Tribunal. If it was not possible to ask the DWP to reconsider the decision within a month, you can ask for a late revision (within 13 months), explaining why it is late. You can also ask the DWP to look at a decision again at any time if certain grounds are met – eg, if there has been an official error.

You can ask for a review of a budgeting loan decision within 28 days of the day the decision was issued to you (or sometimes later, if you have special reasons or if there is a mistake in the decision about the law or the facts of your case).

Chapter 18

Universal credit

This chapter covers:
1. What is universal credit (below)
2. Who is eligible (p206)
3. Basic rules (p209)
4. Amount of benefit (p209)
5. Claiming universal credit (p213)
6. Challenging a decision (p214)
7. Other benefits and tax credits (p214)

Basic facts

– Universal credit (UC) is a new benefit, replacing means-tested benefits and tax credits.
– It can include amounts for adults, children, illness, caring responsibilities, rent and childcare costs.
– You claim with your partner, and you are paid monthly in arrears in a single household payment.
– UC 'full service' is being rolled out to all areas by the end of 2018.
– If you already get UC when you start studying, you can only continue to do so in certain circumstances – eg, if you have a child.
– The amount you get is usually affected by any grant, loan or other income you have.

1. What is universal credit

Universal credit (UC) is a new means-tested benefit for people of working age. The 'full service' of UC has been introduced in most local authority areas, with all areas expected to become full service by the end of 2018, including in Northern Ireland.

In a UC 'full service' area, you cannot make a new claim for a benefit or tax credit that UC is replacing. There is an exception for housing benefit (HB) in some cases (see p147) and if you have not yet claimed UC and you have three or more children (this exception may end from 1 February 2019). There is also expected to be an exception if you get a severe disability premium. If none of the exceptions

204

apply, you must claim UC instead. Once you claim UC, you remain on UC (provided you are still eligible), even if your circumstances change.

UC replaces the following benefits and tax credits:

- income support;
- income-based jobseeker's allowance (JSA);
- income-related employment and support allowance (ESA);
- HB;
- child tax credit (CTC);
- working tax credit (WTC).

UC is being introduced gradually, so whether a new claim is for UC or an existing benefit depends on your circumstances and where you live. For example, if you have recently lost your job and you live in a 'full service' area, you have to claim UC rather than make a new claim for income-based JSA (unless you have three or more children). This applies even if you already get HB or tax credits. These benefits then stop, as they are replaced by UC.

If you have claimed UC and then start studying, you may be able to remain on UC in some circumstances – broadly, if you are a parent, have a disability, if you are a young student in non-advanced education and without parental support, or if you have a partner who is not a student.

If you are in a UC 'full service' area and claim contributory ESA and contribution-based JSA, slightly different rules apply concerning your ability to work and your work-related responsibilities.

The amount you get is based on your circumstances (eg, whether you have a partner or child, or care for someone with a disability) and is usually affected by any grant, loan or other income you have.

Universal credit in Northern Ireland

UC in Northern Ireland follows almost all the same rules as in Great Britain. However, there are a few differences. These include:

– paying UC twice a month, rather than monthly (although you can request monthly payments if you wish);

– the option of a split payment of UC to both partners in a couple;

– payment of the housing costs element directly to a landlord, rather than to you.

In addition, you may also be able to claim extra help for certain work-related expenses. Check with the benefits office when applying.

2. **Who is eligible**

Students

To qualify for universal credit (UC), you must satisfy all the basic rules described on p209. Most students cannot claim UC, although there are some exceptions (see below). For UC, a student is referred to as someone 'receiving education'.

If you get UC then start studying, or you are a student who starts living with a partner who gets UC, you can stay on UC if you are in one of the groups of students who can claim, and you satisfy the basic rules.

Receiving education

You are **'receiving education'** if you are:[1]

– a qualifying young person. This applies if you are in non-advanced education of at least 12 hours a week and have not yet reached 31 August after your 19th birthday;

– undertaking a full-time course of advanced education (see p163 – the rules are the same as for income support);[2]

– on another full-time course for which a loan, grant or bursary is provided for your maintenance;

– if none of the above apply, on a course that is not compatible with your 'work-related requirements' – ie, what you are expected to do in terms of looking for work.

You are 'undertaking a course' from the day you start the course until the last day of the course (or an earlier date when you abandon or are dismissed from the course).[3]

Who can claim universal credit

If you do not count as receiving education, you can claim UC in the same way as anyone else.

If you count as receiving education, you are only eligible for UC if you:[4]

- are responsible for a child or young person;
- are under 22 on a non-advanced course, you were under 21 when you started the course, and you are 'without parental support' (see p207);
- have limited capability for work and also get disability living allowance or personal independence payment. **Note:** if the Department for Work and Pensions (DWP) refuses to allow you to claim UC and be referred for a work capability assessment to assess whether you have limited capability for work, you may be able to claim contributory employment and support allowance in order to establish your limited capability for work, and then claim UC once it has been established;
- are a single foster parent;
- are a member of a student couple and one of you is a foster parent;
- are over the qualifying age for pension credit and your partner has not yet reached that age;

- have a partner who is not a student, or who is a student but would be eligible for UC her/himself while studying;
- have taken time out because of illness or caring responsibilities, you have now recovered or your caring responsibilities have ended, and you are not eligible for a grant or loan.

If you are in one of the above groups and have a partner who is also a student, you can make a joint claim for UC with her/him, even if s/he is not in one of these groups.[5]

Without parental support
'Without parental support' means you:[6]
– are an orphan; *or*
– cannot live with your parents because you are estranged from them, or because there is a serious risk to your physical or mental health, or you would face significant harm if you lived with them; *or*
– are living away from your parents, and they cannot support you financially because they are ill or disabled, in prison or not allowed to enter Great Britain.

Note: if you are aged 16 or 17 and receiving education, you can only claim UC if you are covered by one of the first three bullet points on p206 – ie, you have a child, are without parental support and in non-advanced education, or are ill or disabled. If you are a 16/17-year-old care leaver and are receiving education, you can only claim if you have a child or are ill or disabled, and you cannot get help with housing costs.[7]

Examples
Jodie is 18 and on UC. She starts a full-time course of non-advanced education. She is estranged from her parents. She is still eligible for UC.

Lewis is on UC. He moves in with his partner Liz, who is on a full-time advanced course and has a three-year-old child. They are eligible for UC.

Pauline is 23 and is on UC. She starts a full-time non-advanced course. The DWP decides that her course is not compatible with her work-related requirements, so she counts as 'receiving education'. She is single and not disabled. She is not eligible for UC while she is on her course.

Karen is on UC. She moves in with her partner, Jake, who is unemployed. Karen starts a full-time advanced course. They are still eligible for UC.

Donna is a lone parent with a nine-year-old son. She is on housing benefit (HB) and child tax credit (CTC). She lives in a UC 'full service' area. In the summer vacation she claims UC and her HB and CTC stop.

Work-related requirements

Even if you are a student who can claim UC, you may have to meet certain 'work-related requirements' in order to get UC. These are set out in a 'claimant commitment', drawn up by your work coach at the job centre. If it is not possible to do so while on your course, you may be given a sanction and your UC may be reduced. See CPAG's *Welfare Benefits and Tax Credits Handbook* for more information about work-related requirements and sanctions.

There are no work-related requirements if you are receiving education and you are:[8]

- under 22 (and were under 21 when you started your course), in non-advanced education and have no parental support; *or*
- eligible for UC as a student (unless you are eligible after having taken time out because of illness or caring responsibilities) and you are in receipt of student income which is taken into account for UC – ie, a student loan or a grant for maintenance. This only applies during the period of the year in which your student income is taken into account. Normally, this is over the academic year (see Chapter 21). Over the summer vacation you may be subject to work-related requirements.

If you are not exempt from work-related requirements under the rules above and not exempt for any other reason (eg, because you have a child under one or you are severely disabled), you must meet your work-related requirements, otherwise you can be sanctioned. This means that your UC is reduced by the level of your standard allowance (see p210). This reduction can last up to three years in some cases, even if you later meet your work-related requirements. You may be able to challenge a sanction. If you are given a sanction, get advice as soon as possible.

Examples

Sukhi is a full-time postgraduate student studying for a postgraduate diploma in Wales. She is funding her course through her savings. She has a 12-year-old daughter, Natalie. She claims UC. Because she is not in receipt of a student loan or grant for her course, work-related requirements apply. If she cannot meet these requirements, she may be given a sanction.

Sean is a lone parent with one child aged eight, studying a full-time Higher National Diploma course. He claims UC and does not have any work-related requirements applied because he gets a student loan. His long vacation starts on 14 June 2019. For the assessment period covering 15 June and the next two assessment periods, which are wholly within his summer vacation, he is subject to work-related requirements. If Sean cannot meet these requirements, he may be sanctioned and his UC reduced.

3. **Basic rules**

Universal credit (UC) is for people on a low income who are in or out of work. You can claim regardless of your circumstances, provided you meet the basic rules about age, education, residence, income and capital. So, for example, lone parents, people with a disability, carers and unemployed people can all claim UC. However, because UC is being introduced gradually, you can only claim in a 'full service' area and if you are a student who can get UC.

As well as being a student who is eligible to claim UC, you must satisfy all the following conditions.

- You are aged 18 or over. There are exceptions for some 16/17-year-olds – eg, if you are estranged from your parents, are a parent yourself, are sick or disabled or if you are caring for someone with a disability.
- You are under the qualifying age for pension credit (see p170).
- You are in Great Britain, satisfy the 'habitual residence' and the 'right to reside' tests, and are not a 'person subject to immigration control'. These terms are explained in CPAG's *Welfare Benefits and Tax Credits Handbook*.
- You have no more than £16,000 capital.
- Your income is less than your 'maximum amount' of UC (see p210).
- You have agreed a 'claimant commitment', setting out what you must do to receive your UC. If you have a partner, you must each agree a claimant commitment to get benefit.

4. **Amount of benefit**

The amount of universal credit (UC) you get depends on your circumstances and the circumstances of your partner. The amount also depends on your and your partner's income and capital. Go through the following steps to work out the amount of UC to which you are entitled.

Step one: capital

If your capital is over £16,000, you cannot get UC. Some kinds of capital are ignored. For details, see CPAG's *Welfare Benefits and Tax Credits Handbook*.

Step two: work out your maximum amount

Your maximum amount is worked out by adding together the monthly amounts of the standard allowance and any other elements for which you are eligible.

Step three: work out your monthly income

Chapter 21 explains how your loan, grant or other income is taken into account.

Step four: deduct monthly income from maximum amount

If your income is *less* than your maximum amount, UC is the difference between the two. If your income is *the same as or more than* your maximum amount, you cannot get UC.

Your maximum amount

Work out your maximum amount by adding together your standard allowance and any additional elements that apply. For the amounts, see pvi. The rates are monthly and are from April 2018. **Note:** the government has frozen most of the rates for the next two years.[9]

Standard allowance

You get one standard allowance for yourself and any partner. There are different rates depending on whether you and your partner are under 25, or 25 or over.

Child element

You get one child element for the first two dependent children who 'normally live' with you.[10] Each child must be under 16, or aged 16 to 19 and in full-time non-advanced education or approved training.[11] You can only claim for a child up to 31 August following her/his 19th birthday, and s/he must have been under 19 when s/he started her/his education or training. You cannot claim for a child who claims UC, jobseeker's allowance or employment and support allowance (ESA) in her/his own right.

If you were already getting UC for three or more children before 6 April 2017, or you were already getting UC for two children and you become responsible for any additional child/ren born before 6 April 2017, you can get a child element for each child. If you have a third child on or after 6 April 2017 and you get UC, you cannot get a child element for her/him unless an exception applies (see CPAG's *Welfare Benefits and Tax Credits Handbook* for what these are).

You get an additional amount for any child or young person who gets disability living allowance or personal independence payment. If the child is severely disabled, you get a higher amount.

Elements for illness

You get an extra amount of UC if you meet the medical test for 'limited capability for work' and your claim (or your request to be assessed for limited capability for work) was made before 3 April 2017 or if you meet the medical test for 'limited capability for work-related activity'.

This is the same as the test used for ESA to assess how much your health or disability limits your ability to work or undertake work-related activity.

Carer element

You qualify for a carer element if you are entitled to carer's allowance (CA), or you would be entitled to CA except for the fact that your earnings are too high. You must be caring for someone for at least 35 hours a week who is in receipt of certain disability benefits. You cannot get an element for being a carer and for your own illness at the same time.

Housing costs element

You get an amount for rent if you are liable for the rent on your home (see below). If you own your home, you may be able to get help with certain service charges, but not if you have any earnings in an assessment period.

UC does not include amounts to cover your mortgage interest payments, but you may be able to get a loan from the Department for Work and Pensions to help with these.

The housing element of UC for rent is paid directly to you, for you to then pay your landlord, although you can request for it to be paid directly to your landlord instead. See CPAG's *Welfare Benefits and Tax Credits Handbook* for more information.

An amount is deducted from your housing costs element if you are in rented accommodation and have a non-dependant living with you. This is called a 'housing costs contribution', and is a flat rate of £72.16 per month.

A non-dependant is someone, usually a friend or adult relative, who lives with you, but not on a commercial basis.

There is no deduction for a non-dependant who is under 21, and in certain other circumstances.

See CPAG's *Welfare Benefits and Tax Credits Handbook* for further details about the housing costs element, and about loans for mortgage interest.

Help with your rent

You must be liable for rent. There are some circumstances in which you can be treated as liable for the rent, even when you are not legally liable – eg, if you have taken over paying the rent from someone else.

Your UC housing costs element may not include the full amount of rent that you pay.

If you rent from a private landlord (including a hall of residence), your housing element is based on a standard 'local housing allowance' for the size of property that applies to you, even if your rent is higher than this amount. If your rent is lower, your housing element is based on the amount of your actual rent. Each local authority has its own rates for properties of different sizes. Check your local authority's rates at http://lha-direct.voa.gov.uk/search.aspx.

Generally, you are allowed one bedroom for:

- an adult couple;
- another single adult aged 16 or over;
- two children under 16 of the same sex;
- two children under 10;
- any other child.

You are allowed a maximum of four bedrooms. If you are a single person aged under 35 with no children, the local housing allowance is usually a lower, shared-accommodation rate. If you are disabled and need overnight care, you may qualify for an additional bedroom for a carer. See CPAG's *Welfare Benefits and Tax Credits Handbook* for details.

If you rent from a local authority or housing association, your housing element is usually the same as the weekly rent due. However, it is reduced if you are considered to have a spare bedroom (known as the 'bedroom tax'). The rules about how many bedrooms you can have are similar to the local housing allowance rules, but see CPAG's *Welfare Benefits and Tax Credits Handbook* for more information. If you are considered to have one spare bedroom, the reduction is 14 per cent, and 25 per cent if you have two or more spare bedrooms. If your housing element is reduced in this way, you should apply for a discretionary housing payment from the local authority. A discretionary housing payment can be paid if you get UC that includes a housing costs element and you need additional help with your housing costs – eg, to make up the shortfall in rent due to your housing element being reduced because you have a spare bedroom. Payments are usually awarded for a temporary period, beyond which you have to reapply. Apply to your local authority.

Childcare element

If you are working, you can get help with up to 85 per cent of your childcare costs, up to a maximum monthly amount. You must be in paid work, but there is no minimum number of hours that you must work. If you have a partner, you must both be in paid work, unless your partner is ill or disabled, or a carer.

Example

Colum is 23, a full-time, second-year undergraduate in Canterbury and a lone parent of Toni aged two. He lives with his parents and so has no housing costs. He gets a tuition fee loan of £9,250, a loan for living costs of £6,236, a special support grant of £3,680, a parents' learning allowance of £1,669 and a childcare grant of £3,900. He also receives £20.70 a week child benefit.

During the academic year September 2018 to May 2019:

Step one	Colum has no savings or capital.	
Step two	His maximum amount of UC is:	£
	Standard allowance for himself	251.77
	Child element	277.08
	Total	**528.85**
Step three	His monthly income is:	
	Student loan	669.50

The tuition fee loan, special support grant, parents' learning allowance and childcare grant are all disregarded, as is his child benefit. His loan is divided over eight months of the academic year, and £110 of the remaining amount is disregarded (see Chapter 21).

Step four	His income is above his maximum amount, so he cannot get UC.

During the long vacation from May 2019 to September 2019:

Step two	Colum's maximum amount of UC is still £528.85 (at 2018/19 rates).
Step three	His weekly income for UC purposes is nil. This is because his student income only counts during the academic year.
Step four	From May 2019 to September 2019, his monthly UC is £528.85, so Colum should reclaim over the summer. As Toni is now three, Colum is subject to work-related requirements, such as being available for work, and will face sanctions if he cannot meet these.

5. **Claiming universal credit**

You usually make a claim for universal credit (UC) online at www.gov.uk/apply-universal-credit. Help with online claims over the telephone, telephone claims and face-to-face claims should also be possible if required. If you have a partner, you claim jointly with her/him.

The Department for Work and Pensions (DWP) administers UC, and payments are made monthly in arrears. In Northern Ireland, payments are made twice monthly, unless you request them to be monthly, and amounts for your rent are paid directly to your landlord, unless you request otherwise. In exceptional circumstances, you can request alternative payment arrangements – eg, to get paid more regularly, or to get the payment split between you and your partner. This is a discretionary decision. See CPAG's *Welfare Benefits and Tax Credits Handbook* for more information.

If you are an employee, you do not usually need to report any changes in your earnings, as HM Revenue and Customs provides this information directly to the DWP.

If you do not have enough money to live on while you are waiting for your first payment of UC, you can ask for a short-term advance payment. This can be for up to 100 per cent of your award, and is repaid over the subsequent 12 months.

Short-term advances can also be made when your needs have increased and you are waiting for an extra element of UC to be paid with your next monthly regular payment – eg, when you first have a new baby or become responsible for a child. Awards are at the DWP's discretion. You must repay an advance, usually from the next three months' UC payments.

You can also ask for a loan, called a budgeting advance of UC, to meet certain needs once you have been getting UC for six months. Budgeting advances of UC normally must be repaid from your next 12 months' UC payments. See CPAG's *Welfare Benefits and Tax Credits Handbook* for more information.

6. **Challenging a decision**

If you think a decision about your universal credit is wrong, you can ask the Department for Work and Pensions (DWP) to look at it again. This process is known as a 'reconsideration' (the law refers to it as a 'revision'). Provided you ask within the time limit (usually one month), the DWP notifies you of the decision in a 'mandatory reconsideration notice'. If you are still not happy when you get this notice, you can appeal to the independent First-tier Tribunal. If it was not possible to ask the DWP to reconsider the decision within a month, you can ask for a late revision (within 13 months), explaining why it is late. You can also ask the DWP to look at a decision again at any time if certain grounds are met – eg, if there has been an official error.

7. **Other benefits and tax credits**

If you are in a universal credit (UC) 'full service' area, you cannot claim income support, income-based jobseeker's allowance (JSA), income-related employment and support allowance (ESA), housing benefit (there are some exceptions – see p147), child tax credit or working tax credit, unless you have three or more children (from February 2019, people with three or more children may have to claim UC).

You can still get other benefits, such as carer's allowance, contributory ESA or contribution-based JSA, but they may count as income.

The benefit cap

Your UC is reduced if your total income from benefits is over the maximum level that you or your partner can receive. The amount is £1,666.66 (£1,916.67 if you live in Greater London) a month if you are a lone parent or member of a couple, and £1,116.66 (£1,284.17 if you live in Greater London) if you are a single person.

The benefits that count towards the cap include child benefit and maternity allowance.

You are exempt from the cap if:
- you or your partner are working and earning at least £430 a month;
- you or your partner are disabled. You or your partner must get certain disability benefits, including disability living allowance (DLA), personal independence payment (PIP), ESA with a support component, or UC with a limited capability for work-related activity element;
- you are responsible for a child or young person who gets DLA or PIP;
- you or your partner are a carer and get carer's allowance or the carer element in UC;
- you are a war widow/er.

There is protection for nine months before the cap applies if you are no longer working, or are earning less than £430 a month, but were working and earning at least £430 a month for each of the 12 months before this.

Passported benefits

Provided you meet any other conditions, getting UC entitles you to:
- social fund funeral payments and Sure Start maternity grants;
- free school lunches from your local authority, provided your earnings (or the earnings of you and your partner) are not more than £610 in the assessment period before your application.

If you get UC and have income below a certain level, you are eligible for:
- free prescriptions (in England – see p139) and dental treatment;
- vouchers for glasses (see p140);
- Healthy Start vouchers and vitamins (see p141).

Notes

2. Who is eligible
1 Reg 12 UC Regs
2 paras H6031 and H6047 ADM
3 Reg 13(1) UC Regs
4 Regs 3(2)(b), 13(4) and 14 UC Regs
5 Reg 3(2)(b) UC Regs
6 Reg 8(3) UC Regs
7 Reg 8 and Sch 4 para 4 UC Regs
8 Reg 89 UC Regs

4. Amount of benefit
9 s11 WRWA 2016
10 Reg 4(2) UC Regs
11 Reg 5 UC Regs

19

Chapter 19

Child tax credit

This chapter covers:
1. What is child tax credit (below)
2. Who is eligible (p217)
3. Amount of child tax credit (p218)
4. Claiming child tax credit (p220)
5. Challenging a decision (p221)
6. Tax credits and benefits (p221)

Basic facts
- Child tax credit is paid to families with children.
- Both part-time and full-time students with children can claim.
- The amount you get depends on your income, but most student support is ignored in the assessment.
- You claim from HM Revenue and Customs.

1. **What is child tax credit**

Child tax credit (CTC) is a payment made to people with children. It is administered by HM Revenue and Customs and paid whether you are working or not working. Full-time and part-time students with children are eligible to claim. You get a higher amount if you have a child with a disability. The amount of CTC depends on your income in the tax year.

Note: you cannot make a new claim for CTC if you are in a universal credit (UC) 'full service' area, unless you have not yet claimed UC and you have three or more children (**Note:** this exception may end from February 2019). See p204. All areas are expected to be full service by the end of 2018.

2. Who is eligible

You qualify for child tax credit (CTC) if you meet all the following conditions.[1]

- You are aged 16 or over.
- You have a dependent child. You can get CTC for a child until 1 September after her/his 16th birthday. If s/he stays on at school, in other full-time non-advanced education or is on approved training, you can get CTC for her/him until her/his 19th, or sometimes 20th, birthday.[2] This includes during gaps between one course ending and another starting, provided the young person starts the next course. You can only continue to get CTC for a 19-year-old on a course or training, which s/he was accepted on, enrolled on or started before s/he reached 19, until s/he leaves the course or turns 20, whichever is earlier. You may be able to continue to get CTC for a young person under age 18 for 20 weeks after s/he leaves non-advanced education if s/he notifies HM Revenue and Customs (HMRC) within three months that s/he has registered for work or training with a qualifying body – eg, the place where your local authority provides careers advice for young people or the Ministry of Defence. If your child lives with someone else part of the time, you should decide between you who has main responsibility, otherwise HMRC decides who gets CTC.
- You are 'present and ordinarily resident' in Britain, are not a 'person subject to immigration control' and have a 'right to reside'. You must normally have been living in the UK for three months before you claim. These terms are explained in CPAG's *Welfare Benefits and Tax Credits Handbook*. Overseas students can get further advice from UKCISA (see Appendix 2).
- Your income is not too high (see Chapter 23).

There are no special rules for students. Both part-time and full-time students can claim.

Your parent gets child tax credit for you

If you live with your parent(s), s/he cannot get CTC for you if you are in higher education. S/he can continue to get CTC for you until your 19th, or sometimes 20th, birthday if you are in full-time non-advanced education (see above). The course must be one recognised by the government and be more than 12 hours a week, on average, in term time. The course hours include tuition, supervised study, exams, practical work and any exercise or project in the curriculum. Do not count meal breaks or unsupervised study. You count as full time between courses if you are enrolled on another non-advanced course.

Your parent(s) cannot get CTC for you if you get universal credit, income support, income-based jobseeker's allowance, CTC, working tax credit or employment and support allowance in your own right.

If you live with a partner, or are married or in a civil partnership, your parent(s) can only claim CTC for you if your partner is also a young person in full-time non-advanced education or approved training.

In some circumstances, special rules apply – eg, if you are being looked after by a local authority or are in prison or a young offenders' institution.

3. **Amount of child tax credit**

The amount of child tax credit (CTC) you get if you are not working and eligible for working tax credit (WTC) depends on your maximum CTC and how much income you have. If you are eligible for WTC (see Chapter 20), you claim both tax credits together and the amount is worked out together. Tax credits are calculated according to a maximum annual amount that you could receive in line with the tax year (6 April – 5 April). However, often an annual award is worked out by adding together amounts calculated over separate periods within the year because, for example, you start a new claim or your circumstances change – eg, you have another child, you cease to be a member of a couple or you start work or increase your hours. What follows, therefore, is a simplification of what is often a very complicated calculation and assumes you are claiming CTC (but not WTC) for a full tax year and have no changes in your circumstances during that year. See CPAG's *Welfare Benefits and Tax Credits Handbook* for the detailed rules.

HM Revenue and Customs (HMRC) has a tax credits calculator at www.gov.uk/tax-credits-calculator, where you can check how much CTC you are likely to get.

Step one: work out your maximum child tax credit
The maximum CTC you can get is made up of:
- **child element** of £2,780 a year for each child. **Note:** you cannot get a child element for a child born on or after 6 April 2017 if you are already claiming for two or more children. There are exceptions (see CPAG's *Welfare Benefits and Tax Credits Handbook* for these); *plus*
- **family element** of £545 a year. You only get this if your claim includes a child born before 6 April 2017; *plus*
- **disabled child element** of £3,275 a year for each child who gets disability living allowance (DLA), personal independence payment (PIP) or is certified as severely sight impaired or blind; *plus*
- **severely disabled child element** of £1,325 a year for each child who gets the highest rate care component of DLA or the enhanced rate daily living component of PIP.

These are the maximum amounts for the tax year April 2018 to April 2019. They usually increase each April, although most rates are frozen for the next two years. You get less than the maximum if your income is above a set threshold.

Example
Mairi has two children: Daisy, aged two, and Meena, aged four. Meena has asthma and gets the lowest rate care component of DLA. Mairi's maximum CTC for the tax year April 2018 to April 2019 is:

	£
Two child elements	2,780
	2,780
Family element	545
Disabled child element	3,275
Total maximum CTC	**9,380**

Whether she gets maximum CTC or a reduced amount depends on her income.

If your circumstances change so that you should gain or lose an element, tell HMRC so your award can be adjusted. If you should gain an element (eg, you have a new baby), you must tell HMRC within one month, otherwise you do not get the increase fully backdated. The exception to this is that the disabled child element and the severely disabled child elements can be fully backdated if you notify HMRC within one month of the DLA or PIP being awarded.

Other changes must be notified within one month – eg, if you stop being part of a couple. For details, see CPAG's *Welfare Benefits and Tax Credits Handbook*.

Step two: getting a means-tested benefit
You automatically get maximum CTC if you are getting income support (IS), income-based jobseeker's allowance (JSA), income-related employment and support allowance (ESA) or pension credit (PC).

Step three: not getting a means-tested benefit
If you do not get IS, income-based JSA, income-related ESA or PC, you must compare your income with a set threshold. The income threshold is £16,105, unless you are working and eligible for WTC. If your income is the same as or below this, you get maximum CTC. If your income is above this threshold, you get a reduced amount. If you or your partner are working and you are eligible for WTC, the income threshold is £6,420 instead of £16,105 (and Step one includes WTC elements).

Step four: work out your income
How income is calculated for tax credits is covered in Chapter 23. A CTC award for a tax year is usually based on your income in the previous tax year. However,

if you expect your income over the current tax year to be more than £2,500 lower or higher than the previous year, tell HMRC and it reassesses your tax credits. Your award is then based on the current year's income plus £2,500 if it is more than £2,500 lower than in the previous year, or based on the current year's income minus £2,500 if it is more than £2,500 higher than the previous year's award.

Step five: calculate your child tax credit

If your income is less than or the same as the threshold, you get maximum CTC. If your income is higher than the threshold, work out 41 per cent of the difference. Your CTC is the amount worked out at Step one minus 41 per cent of the difference between your income and the threshold.

Note: this simplified calculation gives an approximate amount of CTC. Amounts are actually calculated using daily rates. See CPAG's *Welfare Benefits and Tax Credits Handbook* for more details.

4. **Claiming child tax credit**

Claim child tax credit (CTC) on Form TC600. You can get a form by phoning the Tax Credit Helpline (see below) or from a Jobcentre Plus office.

When completing the form, remember to describe your circumstances, such as how many children you have or how many hours you work, as they stand at the time of your claim, but you must list your income as it was in the previous tax year. Bear in mind that HM Revenue and Customs (HMRC) requires your income for a tax year, April to April, even though your student award may run from September.

Your claim can be backdated for up to one month. Your award runs until the end of the tax year, at which point you are sent a renewal form. Your award can change or end during the year. Tell HMRC about changes in your circumstances. You should also tell HMRC if you expect your income that counts for tax credits to decrease by more than £2,500 in the current tax year, or if you expect it to increase by more than £2,500.

CTC and working tax credit are paid directly into a bank account.

Contacting HM Revenue and Customs

You can report changes of circumstances or make enquiries to the Tax Credit Helpline on 0345 300 3900 (textphone 0345 300 3909) between 8am and 8pm, Monday to Friday, 8am and 4pm on Saturdays, and 9am to 5pm on Sundays. It is often very difficult to get through to the helpline. If you cannot get through during the week, try on Sundays when it is sometimes less busy.

5. Challenging a decision

If you think a decision about your child tax credit is wrong, you can ask HM Revenue and Customs (HMRC) to look at it again. This process is known as a 'reconsideration' (the law refers to it as a 'review'). Provided you ask within the time limit (usually 30 days), HMRC notifies you of the decision in a 'mandatory reconsideration notice'. If you are still not happy when you get this notice, you can appeal to the independent First-tier Tribunal. If it was not possible to ask HMRC to reconsider the decision within 30 days, you can ask for a late review (within 13 months), explaining why it is late. You can also ask HMRC to look at a decision again at any time if certain grounds are met – eg, if there has been an official error.

If you want to complain about the way your claim has been dealt with, write to the Tax Credit Office, BX9 1ER.

If you have been overpaid, the leaflet COP26, *What Happens if We've Paid You Too Much Tax Credits*, explains when the overpayment can be written off and what you need to do. HMRC sets out what you are expected to do to ensure your claim is correct and what you can expect of HMRC. If you have met all your responsibilities and HMRC has failed to meet one of its, the overpayment should not be recovered. This leaflet also explains when you can ask to repay an amount owed over a longer period. If an overpayment is challenged, it should not be recovered until the dispute is resolved. If you want to dispute recovery of an overpayment, HMRC expects you to do so within three months.

6. Tax credits and benefits

Means-tested benefits

Child tax credit (CTC) is not taken into account as income for income support, income-based jobseeker's allowance or income-related employment and support allowance, although working tax credit (WTC) is.

Tax credits are taken into account as income for housing benefit. If a tax credit overpayment from a previous year is being deducted, the amount of the tax credit award less the deduction is taken into account. If you have been overpaid in the same year as the award and the tax credit award is consequently reduced, the lower amount of the award still to be paid to you is taken into account.

Arrears of tax credits are treated as capital for means-tested benefits and disregarded for 52 weeks.

CTC is taken into account when calculating whether the benefit cap applies (see p160). If you or your partner get WTC, the benefit cap does not apply.

Child benefit

Child benefit is paid in addition to tax credits. It is ignored as income in the tax credit assessment.

Passported benefits

Getting CTC or WTC may entitle you to other benefits. You may be able to get the following.

- Free school lunches from the local authority. Your income for tax credit purposes must be no more than £16,105 a year. You must get CTC but not be eligible for WTC, unless your income for tax credit purposes is no more than £6,420, or you are getting the four-week run-on of WTC because you have reduced your hours or stopped work.[3]

- Health benefits, such as free dental treatment, free prescriptions (in England) and vouchers for glasses. Your income for tax credit purposes must be no more than £15,276 and you must be getting CTC or WTC with a disability element. See Chapter 11 for other ways to qualify for health benefits.

- Sure Start maternity grant (if there is no child under 16 in the household already) or a funeral payment. You also qualify if you get WTC with a disability or severe disability element.

- Healthy Start food vouchers. If you have a child under four, or you are pregnant, and get CTC but are not entitled to WTC (except during the four-week run-on period) and have an annual income for tax credit purposes of no more than £16,190, you may be eligible for Healthy Start food vouchers and free vitamins.[4]

Notes

2. Who is eligible
1 Regs 3-5 CTC Regs
2 Reg 5 CTC Regs

6. Tax credits and benefits
3 The Education (School Lunches)
    (Scotland) Regulations 2009, No.178
4 HSS&WF(A) Regs

Chapter 20

Working tax credit

This chapter covers:
1. What is working tax credit (below)
2. Who is eligible (p224)
3. Amount of working tax credit (p225)
4. Claiming working tax credit (p227)
5. Challenging a decision (p228)
6. Tax credits and benefits (p228)

Basic facts

– Working tax credit (WTC) is paid to top up low wages.
– Both part-time and full-time students are eligible to claim.
– You may be eligible if you are over 25 and working at least 30 hours a week.
– You may be eligible if you are working at least 16 or 24 hours a week and you have a child, a disability or are over 60.
– You can get help with childcare costs in your WTC.
– The amount you get depends on your income, but most student support is ignored in the assessment.
– You claim from HM Revenue and Customs.

1. **What is working tax credit**

Working tax credit (WTC) helps supplement low wages. It is administered by HM Revenue and Customs. It is paid to people who are working (employed or self-employed) for at least 16 hours a week or, in some cases, 24 or 30 hours a week. Full-time and part-time students are eligible to claim. You get a higher amount if you work 30 hours a week or have a disability. You can get childcare costs paid with WTC. The amount of WTC you get depends on your income in the tax year.

Note: you cannot make a new claim for WTC if you are in a universal credit 'full service' area (see p204), unless you have three or more children (**Note:** this exception may end from February 2019). All areas are expected to be full service by the end of 2018.

2. Who is eligible

You qualify for working tax credit (WTC) if you meet all of the following conditions.

• You are working sufficient hours and have a child or a disability, or you meet certain age conditions (see below).

• You are 'present and ordinarily resident' in the UK and not a 'person subject to immigration control'. These terms are explained in CPAG's *Welfare Benefits and Tax Credits Handbook*.

• Your income is not too high (see p227).

There are no special rules for students. Both part-time and full-time students are eligible to claim.

Qualifying hours

To get WTC, you must work sufficient hours and meet other conditions. There are four ways to qualify.[1]

• **You have a child living with you.** You are eligible if:
 – you are aged 16 or over; *and*
 – you are working at least 16 hours a week and you are single or your partner is incapacitated, in hospital or prison, or gets carer's allowance, or you are a member of a couple and you are working at least 16 hours a week and between you and your partner you are working at least 24 hours a week; *and*
 – you have a dependent child. The rules are the same as for child tax credit (see p217).

• **You are a disabled worker.** You are eligible if:
 – you are aged 16 or over; *and*
 – you are working 16 hours or more a week; *and*
 – you have a disability that puts you at a disadvantage in getting a job and you pass a disability benefit test. This has a list of activities or functions concerned with mobility, manual dexterity, vision, hearing, speech, fits, mental disability, severe pain and rehabilitation. If you are unable to satisfy one of these, you pass the disadvantage test. HM Revenue and Customs (HMRC) may contact a doctor or medical professional to confirm this. You pass the disability benefit test if you get certain benefits such as disability living allowance or personal independence payment, or in the past six months you have been getting other benefits such as the higher rate of short-term or long-term incapacity benefit, employment and support allowance for at least 28 weeks, or a disability premium in a means-tested benefit. For more details, see CPAG's *Welfare Benefits and Tax Credits Handbook*. The test is also detailed in the notes for the claim form, TC600.

- **You are over 25.** You are eligible if:
  - you are aged 25 or over; *and*
  - you are working 30 hours or more a week.
- **You are over 60.** You are eligible if:
  - you are aged 60 or over; *and*
  - you are working 16 hours or more a week.

In each case, the work you do must be paid work. It must be expected to continue for at least four weeks from the time you claim WTC. This means you can claim WTC for work during long vacations but not during short vacations unless you will be working for at least four weeks. You can also claim during term time if you normally work sufficient hours to qualify. You must tell HMRC when you stop work, or if your hours reduce below the level required to qualify for WTC. In either case, your WTC award continues for another four weeks (called the 'four-week run-on').

3. **Amount of working tax credit**

The amount of working tax credit (WTC) you get depends on your maximum WTC and how much income you have. Tax credits are calculated according to a maximum annual amount that you could receive in line with the tax year (6 April – 5 April). However, often awards must be calculated on part years because of changes in your circumstances – eg, you have another child, you cease to be a member of a couple or you change your hours of work. What follows, therefore, is a simplification of what is often a very complicated calculation and assumes you are claiming for a full tax year and have no changes in your circumstances during that year. See CPAG's *Welfare Benefits and Tax Credits Handbook* for the detailed rules.

The government website has tax credit pages at www.gov.uk/topic/benefits-credits/tax-credits. You can use these to check whether you qualify and how much WTC you are likely to get.

The way in which WTC is calculated is the same as for child tax credit (CTC – see p218), except that the threshold with which your income is compared is always £6,420. First, work out your maximum WTC (and add the maximum CTC, if applicable). Then work out your income (see Chapter 23). Use your income for the previous tax year, unless the current year's income is more than £2,500 lower (in which case use the current year's income plus £2,500), or more than £2,500 higher (in which case use the current year's income minus £2,500) than this. Finally, work out 41 per cent of the amount by which your income exceeds £6,420, and subtract this from your maximum WTC.

Note: this simplified calculation gives an approximate amount of WTC. Amounts are actually calculated using daily rates. See CPAG's *Welfare Benefits and Tax Credits Handbook* for more details.

The maximum WTC you can get is made up of a **basic element** of £1,960 a year plus whichever one or more of the following elements apply:

* **lone parent/couple element** of £2,010 a year;
* **30-hour element** of £810 a year if you work at least 30 hours a week (you can add your hours to your partner's if you have a child);
* **disabled worker element** of £3,090 a year if you qualify for WTC as a disabled worker (see p224);
* **severe disability element** of £1,330 a year if you get the highest rate care component of disability living allowance (DLA) or the enhanced rate of the daily living component of personal independence payment;
* **childcare element.** You can get up to 70 per cent of your childcare costs up to a limit of £175 a week for one child or £300 for two or more children – ie, a maximum of £122.50 or £210. The childcare must be of a certain type, including a registered childminder, nursery or playscheme, an out-of-hours club or sitters service. You do not get help with childcare at home provided by a relative. To get the childcare element you must be a lone parent, or a couple and either both of you are working 16 hours or more a week or one of you is incapacitated, in hospital or in prison.

These are the amounts for the tax year April 2018 to April 2019. The maximum amounts usually go up each April. You will get less than the maximum if your income is more than a set threshold.

Examples

Sian is 26. She does not work during the academic year, but in the summer vacation she gets a job for 30 hours a week and expects to work for nine weeks. Sian is eligible to claim WTC. Whether any WTC is payable depends on the level of her wages and other income.

Katherine and Spencer have a four-year-old child at nursery school. Katherine is a student and Spencer works 24 hours a week. Katherine works 16 hours a week during the summer only. They are eligible for WTC throughout the year. During the summer they can get a 30-hour element included in their WTC and they can also claim help with nursery charges.

Morag is a full-time student on a Higher National Certificate course. She has an eight-year-old daughter. She works 20 hours a week. Her income is a student loan for tuition fees, a student loan for living costs, including a maintenance element and special support element, a parent's learning allowance of £1,669 and a childcare grant of £95 a week. Her earnings total £7,800 in the tax year April 2018 to April 2019. In the previous tax year 2017/18, she worked full time and earned £16,000.

Her maximum tax credits are:

	£
CTC family element	545
CTC child element	2,780
WTC basic element	1,960
WTC lone parent element	2,010
Total maximum tax credits	**7,295**

Her income this year is more than £2,500 lower than last year when she was working full time, so this year's income plus £2,500 is used.
Her income is £7,800 + £2,500 = £10,300
(Her student loan is ignored – see Chapter 23)
The threshold is £6,420.
Income minus threshold is £10,300 – £6,420 = £3,880
41% x £3,880 = £1,590.80
Maximum tax credits of £7,295 is reduced by £1,590.80.
Morag gets tax credits of £5,704.20, or about £109.70 a week.

The income threshold is £6,420. If your income is below this, you get maximum WTC. If your income is above this threshold, you get a reduced amount. See Chapter 23 for what income counts in the assessment.

If your circumstances change so that you could gain or lose an element, tell HM Revenue and Customs (HMRC) so your award can be adjusted. If you should gain an element (eg, because your hours of work increase or you incur eligible childcare costs), you must tell HMRC within one month, otherwise you do not get the increase fully backdated. The exception to this is that the disabled worker element or severe disability element can be fully backdated if you notify HMRC within one month of DLA being awarded.

Some changes must be reported within one month – eg, if you stop working.

4. **Claiming working tax credit**

There is one claim form (Form TC600) for both child tax credit (CTC) and working tax credit (WTC). This is available by phoning the Tax Credit Helpline on 0345 300 3900 (textphone 0345 300 3909) or from a Jobcentre Plus office.

Your claim can be backdated for up to one month.

Any childcare element of WTC is paid to the main carer directly into a bank account. Otherwise WTC is paid into the bank account of the person in work.

When you claim, the form asks for your income in the previous tax year (see Chapter 23). Your income might be very different this year. When you get your initial award, tell HM Revenue and Customs straight away how much your income is expected to be in the current year if it will be more than £2,500 lower or more than £2,500 higher than the previous year.

5. **Challenging a decision**

If you think a decision about your working tax credit is wrong, you can ask HM Revenue and Customs (HMRC) to look at it again. This process is known as a 'reconsideration' (the law refers to it as a 'review'). Provided you ask within the time limit (usually 30 days), HMRC notifies you of the decision in a 'mandatory reconsideration notice'. If you are still not happy when you get this notice, you can appeal to the independent First-tier Tribunal. If it was not possible to ask HMRC to reconsider the decision within 30 days, you can ask for a late review (within 13 months), explaining why it is late. You can also ask HMRC to look at a decision again at any time if certain grounds are met – eg, if there has been an official error.

If HMRC has overpaid you, see p221.

6. **Tax credits and benefits**

If you or your partner get working tax credit (WTC), the benefit cap does not apply.

See p221 for details of how WTC affects benefits.

Notes

2. **Who is eligible**
  1 Reg 4 WTC(EMR) Regs

Part 3

Treatment of student income

Chapter 21

How income affects universal credit

This chapter covers:
1. Working out your income (p232)
2. Grants and loans (p232)
3. Dividing student income throughout the year (p236)
4. Other payments (p238)
5. Earnings (p239)
6. Benefits (p239)
7. Savings and capital (p239)

This chapter explains how much weekly income is taken into account when working out your entitlement to universal credit (UC). If you do not yet come under the UC system and are claiming income support, income-based jobseeker's allowance, income-related employment and support allowance or housing benefit, see Chapter 22. If you are claiming child tax credit or working tax credit, see Chapter 23.

Basic facts
- Student loans and some grants count as income when working out how much universal credit you can get.
- Loans and grants are taken into account as income during the academic year, but ignored in the summer vacation.
- The maximum amount of student loan to which you are entitled is taken into account as income, whether or not you apply for it.

1. **Working out your income**

If you have student income (student loans and grants paid to you for your course), it usually counts as income for universal credit (UC).[1] This chapter explains how much monthly income counts in the assessment.

Step one	**Add together the annual income from your student loan and grants.** Add the annual amount of any grants, ignoring those that are disregarded, to the annual amount of any loan, ignoring any disregarded amounts (see below).
Step two	**Work out the period over which your student income counts.** Calculate this from the month in which you start your course until the month before the summer vacation or end of your course, as applicable (see p236).
Step three	**Divide income throughout the year.** Divide the amount in Step one by the number of months over which your student income counts for that year (see p236).
Step four	**Deduct disregard.** Deduct a set amount of £110 from the monthly amount of income from grants and loan.
Step five	**Add other income to the monthly amount.** Add any other income taken into account (eg, earnings) to the monthly amount of your grant and loan (see p238). This, added to the total at Step four, is the amount of income used in the UC assessment.

2. **Grants and loans**

If you get a student loan for living costs

If you are eligible for a standard loan for your living costs, it counts as income when working out your entitlement to universal credit (UC). The maximum loan you could be entitled to is taken into account, as though there were no reduction for household income or another grant.[2] The special support element (introduced for new students in England from 2016/17) is disregarded. If you receive a postgraduate loan for a master's course in England, 30 per cent of the maximum amount to which you are entitled is taken into account, and the remainder is disregarded.[3] Professional and career development loans do not count as student loans for this purpose. See p238 for more information on how they are treated.

Any other grants you receive are disregarded, except for any amount for the maintenance of your partner and/or child(ren), and any specific amount for rent if your UC includes an amount for rent.[4] Discretionary payments from an institutional hardship fund are ignored, provided they are not for the maintenance of your partner or child(ren) and not a specified amount for rent that is met by UC.

Note: at the time of writing, it was not yet known how the new part-time undergraduate loans for living costs in England, the new postgraduate doctoral loans in England and Wales and the postgraduate master's loans in Wales would be treated, and whether there would be any changes arising from the new arrangements for undergraduates in Wales. However, it is expected that part-time living costs loans will be treated in the same way as for full-time loans, with the special support element disregarded and the loan then taken into account according to the usual rules, doctoral degree loans will be treated in the same way as loans for master's degrees, and Welsh loans will be treated in the same way as loans in England. See CPAG's *Welfare Rights Bulletin* for updates.

Taken into account	Ignored
England	**England**
Loan for living costs (full-time students)	Tuition fee loan (full-time and part-time
Loan for living costs (part-time students)	students)
(expected)	Maintenance grant
Adult dependants' grant	Special support grant
30 per cent of postgraduate loan for master's	Special support loan element
degrees	Parents' learning allowance
30 per cent of postgraduate loan for doctoral	Childcare grant
degrees (expected)	Child dependants allowance
Some hardship fund payments (see above)	Disabled students' allowance
Wales	Travel expenses allowance
Loan for living costs	70 per cent of postgraduate loan for master's
Adult dependants' grant	degrees
30 per cent of postgraduate loan for master's	70 per cent of postgraduate loan for doctoral
degrees (expected)	degrees (expected)
30 per cent of postgraduate loan for doctoral	NHS bursary (means-tested and non-means-
degrees (expected)	tested)
Some hardship fund payments (see above)	NHS bursary dependants' allowance
Northern Ireland	Teacher training bursary
Loan for living costs	Social work bursary
Adult dependants' grant	Most hardship fund payments (see above)
Department of Health bursary dependants'	
additions	
Some hardship fund payments (see above)	

Taken into account	Ignored
	Wales
	Tuition fee loan
	Tuition fee grant
	Base grant (expected)
	Maintenance grant (expected)
	Special support payment (expected)
	Welsh government learning grant
	Special support grant
	Parents' learning allowance
	Childcare grant
	Disabled students' allowance
	Travel expenses allowance
	70 per cent of postgraduate loan for master's degrees
	70 per cent of postgraduate loan for doctoral degrees (expected)
	NHS bursary
	NHS bursary dependants' allowance
	Teacher training grant
	Social work bursary
	Most hardship fund payments (see p233)
	Northern Ireland
	Tuition fee loan
	Maintenance grant
	Special support grant
	Parents' learning allowance
	Childcare grant
	Travel expenses allowance
	Postgraduate loan for tuition fees
	Social work bursary
	Department of Health healthcare student bursary
	Most hardship fund payments (see p233)
	Disabled students' allowance

If you do not get a student loan for living costs

If you do not get a loan, but you receive a grant, the grant income is taken into account for UC (subject to the disregards below).[5] A grant is an educational grant or award, and does not include 16–19 bursary payments, education maintenance allowance payments or other payments for people under 21 to enable them to complete a course of non-advanced education.[6]

Grant income is completely disregarded if you do not get a loan and the grant is paid for:[7]

- tuition fees or exams;

- your disability;
- extra costs of residential study away from your usual place of study during term time;
- the costs of your normal home (if you live elsewhere during your course), unless these are included in your UC;
- the maintenance of someone not included in your UC claim;
- books, equipment, course travel costs or childcare costs.

If you get a grant but no loan, and receive a discretionary payment in either further or higher education, this is disregarded if it is paid for any of the above; otherwise it counts as income.

You should ensure your funder, university, college or learning provider gives you clear information on what any payment is for, especially if a grant is paid for course costs, as this may not be obvious from its title.

Taken into account	Ignored
England	**England**
Some learner support fund payments (see above)	Advanced learner loan
	Tuition fee grant
Dance and drama maintenance grant	Dance and drama tuition fee grant
Some bursary loan fund payments (see above)	16–19 bursary fund payment
	Some learner support fund payments (see above)
Social work bursary	
Postgraduate stipend/studentship	Some bursary loan fund payments (see above)
Some hardship fund payments (see above)	
Wales	Parents' learning allowance
Social work bursary	Childcare grant
Postgraduate stipend/studentship	Disabled students' allowance
Some hardship fund payments (see above)	Travel expenses allowance
Northern Ireland	**Wales**
Further education awards	Tuition fee grant
Nursing and midwifery bursary	Education maintenance allowance
Nursing and midwifery bursary dependants' additions	Welsh government learning grant for further education
Postgraduate stipend/studentship	Parents' learning allowance
Some hardship fund payments (see above)	Childcare grant
	Disabled students' allowance
	Travel expenses allowance
	Northern Ireland
	Education maintenance allowance
	Tuition fee grant
	Parents' learning allowance
	Childcare grant
	Disabled students' allowance
	Travel expenses allowance

3. **Dividing student income throughout the year**

Universal credit (UC) is paid monthly, for an 'assessment period'. Each assessment period runs from the day of the month you claimed UC, for one month – eg, if you claim on the second of the month, each assessment period runs from the second of the month to the first of the following month. The annual amount of your student income needs to be divided over the number of assessment periods in the course year, to arrive at the monthly amount that is used to work out UC.

Student income counts for each assessment period during your course, excluding the one at the end of each academic year and those in the long vacation.[8]

Student income counts as income:
- from the start of the assessment period in which the course/course year begins; *and*
- for every subsequent assessment period during the course/course year.

Student income is ignored:[9]
- in the assessment period in which the last week of the course or the start of the long vacation falls;
- in any assessment periods that fall completely within the long vacation; *and*
- if you abandon or leave your course completely, in the assessment period in which you leave.

Long vacation

The '**long vacation**' is the longest holiday in a course which lasts at least two years, and must last for at least one month.[10]

Once you have calculated the number of assessment periods in the course year, divide the total annual amount of loans and/or grants by this number, and apply the monthly disregard. In each assessment period, £110 of student income is disregarded.[11]

Example

Laura has a five-year-old daughter and is single. She starts a full-time degree course at her local university in Liverpool. Year one of her course runs from 1 October 2018 to 17 May 2019. Her assessment periods run from the of the month to the 2nd of the following month. Laura gets a tuition fee loan of £9,250, a loan for living costs of £6,236, a special support element of £3,680, a parents' learning allowance of £1,669 and a childcare grant of £3,900. She also receives child benefit of £20.70 a week.

Step one	Laura's tuition fee loan, special support element, parents' learning allowance and childcare grants are disregarded, as well as her child benefit.
Step two	Her loan for living costs counts as income over eight assessment periods in the first year of her course (from 3 September 2018 to 2 May 2019).
Step three	£6,236 ÷ 8 = £779.50
Step four	£110 per assessment period is ignored. £779.50 – £110 = £669.50
Step five	She has no other income. Laura's UC is calculated on student income of £669.50 a month from 3 September 2018 to 2 May 2019. From 3 May 2019, the monthly income from her student funding is nil. Laura's next UC payment in June will be based on £0 student funding.

Example

Paula is 27, has a seven -year-old son and is single. She is undertaking a full-time access to higher education course in Plymouth. Her course runs from 3 September 2018 to 24 May 2019. Her assessment periods run from the 14th of the month to the 13th of the following month. She has taken out an advanced learner loan of £1,700 to pay for her course. She also receives £700 over the year from the loan bursary fund for childcare. Both her loan and her bursary payment are disregarded, although she must provide evidence that the bursary payment has been made for childcare, not general costs. Her student income over the year is £0.

Example

Nadiya is a lone parent with one child. She is undertaking a master's course in Hull. Her course runs for one year between 1 October 2018 to 14 June 2019. Her assessment periods run from the 8th of the month to the 7th of the following month. Nadiya receives a postgraduate loan for a master's degree of £10,609. She also receives child benefit of £20.70 a week.

Step one   70 per cent of Nadiya's loan is disregarded, as well as her child benefit.

Step two   The remaining loan counts as income over nine assessment periods in the first year of her course (from 8 September 2018 to 7 June 2019).

Step three   £3,182.70 ÷ 9 = £353.63

Step four   £110 per assessment period is disregarded. £353.63 – £110 = £243.63

Step five   She has no other income. Nadiya's UC is calculated on student income of £243.63 a month from 8 September 2018 to 7 June 2019. From 8 June 2019, the monthly income from her student funding is nil. Nadiya's next UC payment in June will be based on £0 student funding.

4. Other payments

Professional and career development loans

These educational loans count as capital if paid as a lump sum. If paid in instalments, they normally also count as capital.[12]

5. Earnings

Your earnings and your partner's earnings are taken into account in the universal credit assessment. Your net monthly earnings are taken into account – ie, after deducting:

- income tax;
- class 1 national insurance contributions; *and*
- any contribution you make towards a personal or occupational pension.

Some of your earnings may be disregarded if you have children or if you are ill or disabled. This is known as a 'work allowance'. Earnings above your work allowance are deducted at 63 pence for every pound above the allowance.

For full details of the way earnings are treated, see CPAG's *Welfare Benefits and Tax Credits Handbook*.

6. Benefits

Some benefits are taken into account in the assessment of your universal credit, and others are ignored.

Benefits taken into account include:
- carer's allowance;
- contribution-based jobseeker's allowance;
- contributory employment and support allowance;
- most industrial injuries benefits;
- maternity allowance;
- retirement pension.

Benefits that are ignored include:
- attendance allowance;
- child benefit;
- disability living allowance;
- personal independence payment.

7. Savings and capital

There are limits on the amount of savings or capital you can have and still claim universal credit (UC). Some kinds of capital are not counted in the assessment. For details, see CPAG's *Welfare Benefits and Tax Credits Handbook*.

You cannot get UC if your savings or other capital are above £16,000.

If your capital is £6,000 or less, it does not affect your UC at all.

If your capital is between £6,000.01 and £16,000, you are treated as though you have income from this capital of £4.35 a month for every £250 or part of £250 between these limits. For example, if you have savings of £6,525, your assumed income is £13.05 a month.

Notes

1. **Working out your income**
   1 Reg 66(1)(e) UC Regs

2. **Grants and loans**
   2 Regs 68 and 69 UC Regs
   3 Reg 69(1A) UC Regs
   4 Reg 68(3) UC Regs
   5 Reg 68(2) and (4) UC Regs
   6 Reg 68(7) UC Regs
   7 Reg 70 UC Regs

3. **Dividing student income throughout the year**
   8 Reg 68 UC Regs
   9 Reg 13 UC Regs
   10 Reg 68(7) UC Regs
   11 Reg 71 UC Regs

4. **Other payments**
   12 Reg 46(4) UC Regs

Chapter 22
How income affects means-tested benefits

This chapter covers:
1. Working out your income (p242)
2. Grants and loans (p243)
3. Dividing student income throughout the year (p249)
4. Discretionary funds and other payments (p255)
5. Earnings (p257)
6. Benefits and tax credits (p257)
7. Maintenance (p258)
8. Savings and capital (p258)

This chapter explains how your weekly income affects your entitlement to income support, income-based jobseeker's allowance, income-related employment and support allowance and housing benefit. For information on how income affects universal credit, see Chapter 21. See also Chapter 23 for how your income is assessed for tax credits and Chapter 24 for health benefits.

Basic facts

– Student loans for living costs are normally divided over 42 or 43 weeks from the beginning of September to the end of June and taken into account as income for means-tested benefits during that period. If your income is too high, you do not get income support (IS), income-based jobseeker's allowance or income-related employment and support allowance during those weeks, and your housing benefit (HB) is reduced.
– Student loans for living costs are normally not taken into account as income for means-tested benefits from around the end of June until the beginning of September. You may be able to get IS or more HB during these months, even if your income was too high during the academic year.
– Some student support does not affect the amount of means-tested benefits you can receive.

1. **Working out your income**

The way that student income is taken into account for income support (IS), income-based jobseeker's allowance (JSA), income-related employment and support allowance (ESA) and housing benefit (HB) is essentially the same. Chapters 10, 12 and 13 outline the ESA, IS and HB assessments step by step. This chapter explains how much weekly income counts in these assessments.

Note: if you or your partner have reached the qualifying age for pension credit (PC) and are not getting IS or income-based JSA, your student support is ignored as income for HB.

Step one	**Add together the annual income from grants and loans.**
	Add together the annual amount of any student grants and/or loans for living costs, ignoring elements that are wholly disregarded.
Step two	**Apply annual disregards.**
	From the total annual grants and loans for living costs, deduct any disregarded amounts for books, equipment and travel.
Step three	**Divide income into a weekly amount.**
	Divide the annual amount of grants and loans for living costs by the number of benefit weeks in the period over which the grant and loan are counted as income for benefit purposes.
Step four	**Deduct any weekly disregard.**
	If you have a student loan for living costs, deduct £10 a week – this is the weekly disregard.
Step five	**Add other income to the weekly amount.**
	Add together any other weekly income – eg, from hardship funds (p255), professional and career development loans (p256), earnings (p257), tariff income from capital (p259), and benefits and tax credits (p257) – ignoring any amount that is disregarded. This total, added to the weekly grant and loan total in Step four, is the amount of income used in the benefit assessment.

If you want to work out benefit entitlement during the long vacation, p250 explains when the long vacation starts and finishes for benefit purposes – ie, when your student loan or grant counts as nil income. You should then total on a weekly basis any other income you have over the vacation.

2. **Grants and loans**

Grants

In general, grants intended for living costs are taken into account as income, and grants for other costs (such as books, travel, equipment, childcare or course-related support for disabilities) are disregarded. For the way that hardship funds are treated, see p255.

If you are a full-time undergraduate assessed for support in England, Wales or Northern Ireland and receive a special support grant, this is disregarded as it is paid for course-related costs.[1] If you receive a maintenance grant (eg, if you are the partner of a jobseeker's allowance (JSA) or income support (IS) claimant), this is taken into account in full as it is paid for living costs.

If you are *not* eligible for a student loan, deduct from your grant the following disregarded amounts:

- £390 for books and equipment;
- £303 for travel.

Higher education grants

The following higher education grants are completely disregarded:

- grant for tuition fees;[2]
- special support grant for full-time undergraduate students in England, Wales and Northern Ireland;[3]
- childcare grant;
- child dependants allowance;
- disabled students' allowance;[4]
- parents' learning allowance;
- travel expenses;[5]
- course costs grant for part-time undergraduate students;[6]
- institutional bursaries paid for anything other than living costs.[7]

The following grants are taken into account:

- maintenance grant for full-time undergraduate students assessed in England and Northern Ireland;
- Welsh government learning grant for students in Wales;
- adult dependants' grant;
- institutional bursaries paid for living costs.

Note: at the time of writing, it was not clear whether there would be any changes arising from the new arrangements for undergraduates in Wales. See CPAG's *Welfare Rights Bulletin* for updates.

Healthcare student allowances
The following grants are taken into account:
- means-tested NHS bursary for degree-level healthcare courses in England and Wales;
- means-tested Department of Health bursary for degree-level healthcare courses in Northern Ireland;
- non-means-tested Department of Health bursary for nursing and midwifery students in Northern Ireland;
- dependants' allowances for healthcare students (for housing benefit (HB) and some existing IS, JSA and employment and support allowance (ESA) claimants with no child tax credit (CTC) award);[8]
- single parent addition.

The following grants are disregarded:
- childcare allowances;
- disabled students' allowance;[9]
- parents' learning allowance;
- travel expenses.[10]

Other grants for vocational courses
The following are taken into account:
- NHS social work student bursary in England;[11]
- Social Care Wales social work student grant in Wales;
- Department of Health social work incentive bursary in Northern Ireland;
- initial teacher training incentive bursaries.[12]

The following are disregarded:
- travel expenses.

Postgraduate grants
Postgraduate maintenance grants and dependants' grants awarded by a research council, or for postgraduate social work students, are taken into account in the same way as for undergraduates (see p243). **You should ignore the following:**
- disabled students' allowance;
- grants for tuition fees;
- grants for residential study away from your normal home;
- grants intended to meet the costs of books and equipment.

Further education grants
The following further education grants are disregarded:
- education maintenance allowance;[13]
- 16–19 bursary fund payments;[14]
- Care to Learn grants paid for childcare costs;

- childcare bursaries paid through the discretionary support funds;
- residential bursaries paid through the discretionary support funds (IS/JSA/ESA only);
- Welsh government learning grant for further education;
- the Northern Irish further education grant;
- additional grant allowances for disabled students.

The maintenance element of further education and advanced further education awards in Northern Ireland, subject to the standard disregard for travel, books and equipment, is **taken into account in full.**

Student loans

Student loan for fees

Loans for fees are disregarded.[15]

Student loan for living costs

You should include in the student loan:
- the maximum loan for which you are eligible (excluding any special support element – see below). This is taken into account as your income whether or not you apply for it;[16]
- the assessed contribution from a parent or partner, whether or not you receive it. For IS, however, if you are a lone parent or a disabled student, only include contributions that are actually paid;[17]
- any payments for extra weeks of attendance.

Deduct from the annual student loan £390 for books and equipment and £303 for travel.[18] There is a further disregard of £10 a week that applies once the student loan has been divided into the relevant weekly amount (see p250).

If you are a full-time undergraduate or Postgraduate Certificate in Education student assessed for support in England and receive a special support element, this is disregarded as it is paid for course-related costs.[19] The standard student loan for living costs for which you are eligible is taken into account under the normal rules.

Note: at the time of writing, it was not yet known how the new part-time undergraduate loans for living costs in England would be treated, or whether there would be any changes arising from the new arrangements for undergraduates in Wales. However, it is expected that part-time loans will be treated in the same way as full-time loans, with any special support element disregarded, and that Welsh loans will be treated in the same way as loans in England. See CPAG's *Welfare Rights Bulletin* for updates.

Postgraduate loans

The postgraduate loan for master's degrees in England (see p75) is paid for both tuition and living costs support, and you can decide how to allocate it. A figure equal to 30 per cent of the maximum loan to which you are entitled is therefore used when working out your income. This amount is then taken into account in the same way as undergraduate student loans for living costs (see p245).[20]

Your income is assessed using the maximum loan for which you are eligible, whether or not you apply for it. Make sure that the Department for Work and Pensions does not take into account any amount of loan if you are not eligible for one (eg, if you already hold a master's level qualification) and are self-funding.

Note: at the time of writing, it was not yet known how the new postgraduate doctoral loans in England and Wales and the postgraduate master's loans in Wales would be treated. However, it is expected that both will be treated in the same way as master's loans in England. See CPAG's *Welfare Rights Bulletin* for updates.

Professional and career development loan

How professional and career development loans are treated depends on what they are paid for. Disregard any amounts paid for:
- tuition fees;
- course costs.

Any amounts paid for living costs are treated as income. This amount should be divided over the period for which the loan is paid.[21]

Professional studies loan

Loans paid to postgraduate students by banks or other financial institutions for vocational study are treated in the same way as professional and career development loans (see above).

Grants and loans checklist

Student support	Treatment
Further education income	
16–19 bursary fund	Disregarded
Advanced learner loan	Disregarded
Care to Learn grant	Disregarded
Dance and drama awards	Any element for tuition ignored; maintenance grant taken into account except: – £309 a year for books and equipment; – £303 a year for travel

Student support	Treatment
Discretionary or learner support funds/ Financial Contingency Fund/hardship funds payment	Taken into account if paid for basic living costs regularly; disregarded if paid for other items
Education maintenance allowance	Disregarded
Further education award (Northern Ireland)	Taken into account except: – £390 a year for books and equipment; – £303 a year for travel
Travel expenses allowance	Disregarded
Vulnerable student bursary (England)	Disregarded
Welsh government learning grant	Disregarded
Undergraduate income	
Adult dependant's grant	Taken into account in full
Base grant (Wales)	Expected to be taken into account in full
Childcare grant	Disregarded
Child dependants allowance	Disregarded
Disabled students' allowance	Disregarded
Hardship funds	Taken into account if paid for basic living costs regularly (as capital if not regular payments); disregarded if paid for other items
Institutional bursaries or scholarships	Tuition and course cost payments disregarded; payments for living costs taken into account
Maintenance grants	Taken into account in full
NHS childcare allowance	Disregarded
NHS dependants' allowance	Taken into account
NHS healthcare/nursing and midwifery bursary	Taken into account except: – £390 a year for books and equipment; – £303 a year for travel
Parents' learning allowance	Disregarded
Part-time students' grant for course costs	Usually disregarded (as it is less than the general books/equipment and travel disregards)
Part-time students' grant for tuition fees	Disregarded
Part-time students' loan for living costs	Expected to be taken into account except: – £390 a year for books and equipment; – £303 a year for travel; – £10 a week
Social work bursary (England and Wales)	Any element for non-living costs, such as travel or tuition fee costs, disregarded; remainder taken into account in full

Student support	Treatment
Social work bursary (Northern Ireland)	Taken into account in full except any element for travel costs
Special support grant	Disregarded
Special support loan element	Disregarded
Special support payment (Wales)	Disregarded (expected)
Student loan for living costs (including any means-tested element where appropriate)	Taken into account except: – £390 a year for books and equipment; – £303 a year for travel
Teacher training bursary	Taken into account in full
Travelling or accommodation expenses	Disregarded
Tuition fee grant (Wales)	Disregarded
Tuition fee loan	Disregarded
Welsh government learning grant	Taken into account in full
Postgraduate income	
Books and equipment expenses	Disregarded
Postgraduate loan for doctoral degrees	Expected to be 30 per cent of loan taken into account except: – £390 a year for books and equipment; – £303 a year for travel; – £10 a week
Postgraduate loan for master's degrees in England (equivalent loans in Wales expected to be treated the same)	30 per cent of loan taken into account except: – £390 a year for books and equipment; – £303 a year for travel; – £10 a week
Postgraduate tuition fee loan (Northern Ireland)	Disregarded
Research council studentship or scholarship (including British Academy)	Taken into account except: – £390 a year for books and equipment; – £303 a year for travel
Social work bursary	Taken into account in full
Supplementary grants	As for undergraduate income
Teacher training bursary/grant/ scholarship/salary	Taken into account in full
Other	
Professional and career development loan	Disregared, except for any amount applied or paid for living expenses during the period supported by the loan, which is taken into account in full

3. **Dividing student income throughout the year**

The annual amount of your loan and grant is divided over the number of weeks in, usually, a standard academic year to arrive at the weekly amount that is used to calculate your income support (IS), income-based jobseeker's allowance (JSA), income-related employment and support allowance (ESA) and housing benefit (HB). Rules specify the weeks over which the loan and grant are taken into account.

If your loan covers extra weeks of study beyond the usual academic year (a long courses loan), the extra weeks loan is added to the rest of the loan. However, it does not extend the number of weeks over which your loan is taken into account for benefit purposes.

Grants

Higher education maintenance grant

The higher education maintenance grant for full-time undergraduate students who do not have a benefits claim in their own right, and the adult dependants' grant paid by the Department for Education, the Welsh government or the Department for the Economy in Northern Ireland, are taken into account over the duration of the course, whether it comprises 52 weeks or fewer. They are treated as income over the same period as the student loan, if you have one or are eligible for one.[22] This is the case even though government guidance says that such grants cover 52 weeks.

Example

Rob lives in Wales and receives a student loan of £4,563 and a maintenance grant of £5,161 to do his full-time undergraduate degree in Cardiff. This is his second year and his first term begins on Monday 1 October 2018. Rob lives with his partner, Dylan, and their two children. Dylan has claimed JSA and his benefit week starts on a Thursday. Rob's student loan and maintenance grant are taken into account when working out Dylan's JSA. His student loan and maintenance grant are divided over the 42 weeks from Thursday 6 September 2018 to Wednesday 26 June 2019. From Thursday 6 September to Wednesday 26 June 2019, his student loan and grant income are included in the calculation to determine the amount of JSA Dylan receives. From Thursday 27 June until Wednesday 4 September 2019, his student loan and grant income is nil again for benefit purposes.

Healthcare student bursaries

There are two types of bursary available to students on healthcare courses. A non-means-tested bursary is available in Northern Ireland for nursing and midwifery students on both degree and diploma courses. If you are studying for a degree in England, Wales or another healthcare course in Northern Ireland, a means-tested bursary and a non-means-tested grant are available (although most new healthcare students in England must now apply for support from Student Finance England – see p83). In addition, you can receive a non-means-tested reduced-rate loan.

Dependants' grants and other allowances may be means tested (see Chapter 6).

The income from both types of bursary, dependants' allowance and single parent addition are taken into account. As these are paid in monthly instalments, they are taken into account over 52 weeks. The reduced-rate loan should be treated over the same period as other student loans. The NHS childcare grant is disregarded in full.

Social work bursaries

Social work bursaries in England and Wales should be taken into account for the period they are paid. In England, this is 52 weeks.

In England, the element paid for travelling expenses should be disregarded.[23] However, this is not usually specifically identified, so benefits offices may take the full bursary into account. Speak to an adviser for assistance.

Any amount paid for tuition fees should also be disregarded.

In Northern Ireland, the social work incentive bursary is taken into account in full, but any element paid for travel costs should be disregarded.

Postgraduate grants

A postgraduate award that is assessed for study throughout the calendar year is taken into account for the number of benefit weeks within the full calendar year.[24]

Students on a Postgraduate Certificate in Education (or Postgraduate Diploma in Education) course may get the same student loan and grants as undergraduates, and these are treated in the same way as undergraduate loans and grants. Teacher training bursaries/salaries are treated as grants.

If you leave your course early

For IS, income-based JSA and income-related ESA, if you abandon your course or are dismissed from it, your grant continues to be taken into account until the end of the term or vacation in which you stop being a full-time student or, if earlier, until you repay the grant or the period for which the grant is payable ends.[25]

For HB, your grant is taken into account until the grant provider asks you to repay it.[26]

Loan for living costs

For autumn term starters, student loans are normally divided over 42 or 43 weeks from the beginning of September to the end of June. During this period, your student loan is taken into account as income in the assessment of IS, income-based JSA, income-related ESA and HB. If your income is too high, you are not eligible for these benefits. However, your student loan is not taken into account from around the end of June to the beginning of September. Because your income decreases in these months (unless you have other income – eg, earnings), you may be able to get benefit during the summer. It is important, therefore, to make a claim from the end of June, even if you were refused benefit at the start of the academic year. Make your claim in mid-June or earlier so that your benefit can start as soon as you are entitled. In most cases, your claim will be for universal credit (UC), but check with an adviser if you are unsure.

Courses starting in the autumn term lasting more than a year

The student loan is divided over the number of weeks starting from the first day of the first benefit week in September until the last day of the last benefit week in June.[27] In 2018/19 this is 42 weeks for benefit weeks that begin on a Tuesday, Wednesday, Thursday or Friday and 43 weeks for benefit weeks that begin on a Monday or Saturday. If your course starts in August, you count the weeks starting from the first day of the first benefit week on or after the start of your course, until the last day of the last benefit week in June.

This is the period over which your loan is taken into account as income in the benefit assessment, unless you do not count as a student at all. For example, at the start of your first year, you do not count as being a student until you actually start attending or undertaking the course – ie, in the first year, the loan is still divided over 42/43 weeks, but the weekly amount arrived at is ignored as income until you start your course.

In the final year of study, the loan is divided over the number of benefit weeks starting from the first day of the first benefit week in September (or the start of the last day of the final term if it starts in August) until the end of the benefit week on or before the last day of the final academic term.[28]

For HB, the start of the benefit week is a Monday. For IS, JSA and ESA, it depends on your national insurance number.

- -
Example: first year higher education student in England
Jean is in her first year at university. She has one child aged two and is claiming HB as a lone parent. She gets a loan of £9,250 for her fees, which is disregarded, and a student loan for living costs of £8,702 for studying in London, which is not. She also gets a special support element of £3,680, a parents' learning allowance of £1,669 and a childcare grant of £100 a week, all of which are disregarded for IS and HB.

Her first term begins on Monday 1 October 2018. Her IS benefit week starts on a Monday. Her student loan is divided over the weeks from Monday 3 September 2018 until Sunday 30 June 2019 (43 weeks). However, as she is a first-year student, her loan is not taken into account until she starts her course on Monday 1 October. So, from Monday 3 September 2018 until Sunday 30 September 2018, her student loan income is not taken into account for benefit purposes. From Monday 1 October 2018 to Sunday 30 June 2019, her weekly student loan income is £176.26 for benefit purposes. From Monday 1 July until Sunday 1 September 2019, her student loan income is nil again for benefit purposes.

The weekly loan income taken into account is:	£
Loan	8,702.00
Less disregards for books and equipment (£390) and travel (£303) =	8,009.00
Divided by 43 weeks =	186.26
Less £10 weekly loan disregard =	176.26

£176.26 is taken into account as weekly income from her loan between 1 October 2018 and 30 June 2019. She also receives £63.94 a week child tax credit, which brings her weekly income for HB purposes to £240.20.

Her IS applicable amount is £73.10 and her HB applicable amount is £140 a week. From Monday 1 October 2018 to Sunday 30 June 2019, she is not entitled to IS because her income is higher than the IS applicable amount; her HB is reduced by £65.13 a week – 65 per cent of the excess (see p157). From Monday 1 July until Sunday 1 September 2019, her weekly income from her loan and grants is nil. Jean should make a new claim in June – it is likely that she will need to claim UC, rather than IS.

Example: final year higher education student in Northern Ireland
Graham is in his final year. He is claiming ESA as a disabled student studying at Queen's University, Belfast. He gets a student loan of £4,480.

His first term started on Monday 3 September 2018 and his final term ends on Friday 7 June 2019. His student loan is divided over the weeks from Monday 3 September 2018 until Sunday 2 June 2019 (39 weeks).

The weekly loan income taken into account is:	£
Loan	4,480.00
Less disregards for books and equipment (£390) and travel (£303)=	3,787.00
Divided by 39 weeks =	97.10
Less £10 weekly loan disregard =	87.10

£87.10 is taken into account as weekly income from his loan between 3 September 2018 and 2 June 2019.

Example: master's student in England
Holly is a lone parent with a child aged two, and claiming HB. She is starting an MA course in Huddersfield. She gets a postgraduate student loan of £10,609, the maximum available. Only 30 per cent is taken into account (£3,182.70).

As the course only lasts one year, her loan is only taken into account from when she starts the course until the end of her final term. Her first term starts on Monday 8 October 2018 and her final term ends on Friday 14 June 2019. Her student loan is divided over the weeks from Monday 3 September 2018 until Sunday 9 June 2019 (40 weeks) but is only taken into account from Monday 8 October.

The weekly loan income taken into account is:	£
Loan	3,182.70
Less disregards for books and equipment (£390) and travel (£303) =	2,489.70
Divided by 40 weeks =	62.24
Less £10 weekly loan disregard =	52.24

£52.24 is taken into account as weekly income from her loan between 8 October 2018 and 9 June 2019.

Courses not starting in the autumn term

Your student loan is divided over the number of weeks starting from the first day of the first benefit week on or after the beginning of a standard academic year and ending on the last day of the last benefit week on or before the last day of the academic year, but excluding benefit weeks that fall entirely within the quarter that is taken by the Department for Work and Pensions (DWP) to be the longest vacation.[29]

Academic years

'**Academic years**' are the 12 months beginning on 1 January, 1 April or 1 July for courses that begin in winter, spring or summer respectively.[30]

'**Quarters**' are 1 January to 31 March, 1 April to 30 June, 1 July to 31 August, 1 September to 31 December.[31]

Example

Madeleine's course begins on 7 January 2019. The main vacation is 7 June to 30 August 2019. She is claiming HB and the benefit week starts on a Monday. Her loan is divided over the weeks from Monday 7 January 2019 to Sunday 30 June 2019, and from Monday 26 August 2019 until Sunday 29 December 2019. From 1 July to 25 August 2019, her student loan income is nil for benefit purposes.

Courses lasting one year or less

Your loan is divided over the number of weeks from the first day of the first benefit week on or after the start of a standard academic year until the last day of the last benefit week on or before the last day of the final term. The academic year is taken to begin on 1 September, 1 January, 1 April or 1 July, depending on whether your course begins in the autumn, winter, spring or summer. The resulting weekly amount is then taken into account from the point you actually start attending or undertaking the course.

If you leave your course early

If you abandon your course early or are dismissed from it before you have had the final instalment of your student loan in that academic year, the loan continues to be taken into account up until the end of the term in which you leave. The end of term is taken to be the end of December if you leave in the autumn term, the end of March if you leave in the winter term, the end of June if you leave in the spring term and the end of August if you leave in the summer.

The amount of loan taken into account is that which remains from the loan that was paid from the start of the standard academic year (eg, 1 September for students whose courses begin in the autumn – see p251) to the end of the term in which you left, having subtracted that part of the loan (including disregards for books, equipment and travel) that would have been treated as your weekly income in a normal benefits calculation up until the day you left.[32] The example below illustrates how this amount is calculated.[33]

Example
Nick studies in Birmingham. He abandons his course on 1 November 2018. He is in the second year of a three-year course and is claiming HB. His benefit week starts on a Monday.

Work out weekly amount of annual loan	£
Loan	6,236.00
Less disregards (£693) =	5,543.00
Divided by 43 weeks =	128.91

Work out amount of loan prior to leaving the course
Multiply the weekly amount of annual loan by the number of benefit weeks from the week after the one that includes the start of the academic year until the end of the benefit week that includes the day Nick left the course.

Multiply weekly loan (£128.91) by nine weeks (3 September to 4 November 2018) =	£1,160.19

Work out amount of loan since leaving the course
To do this, add the loan instalments paid for the terms up to the one in which Nick left, deduct disregards and deduct the loan worked out for the period prior to leaving.

Loan up to end of term (33% x 6,236) =	2,057.88
Less disregards (£693) =	1,364.88
Deduct amount of loan prior to leaving (£1,160.19) =	204.69

Work out weekly amount of loan from leaving course to end of term
Divide the total amount of loan for the period since leaving the course by the number of weeks left in the term. Count from the benefit week that includes the day Nick left the course until the benefit week that includes the end of term – ie, end of December, March, June or August.

Divide £204.69 by nine weeks (29 October 2018 to 30 December 2018) =	£22.74

£22.74 a week is taken into account from 29 October 2018 until 30 December 2018.

If you leave your course nearer to the end of term, this formula could result in there being no loan income taken into account for the remainder of the term. **Note:** if you repay the loan, it is nevertheless taken into account as income until the end of term.[34] So you could be refused benefit despite having no other money to live on. However, if your funder asks you to repay the loan rather than your repaying it voluntarily, guidance tells DWP decision makers to disregard the loan as income from the date of the request.[35]

---

4. **Discretionary funds and other payments**

Hardship funds

Discretionary funds paid by colleges and universities for course or living costs may be called hardship funds, the Access to Learning Fund (although this no longer exists, institutions may still refer to it), the Financial Contingency Fund or other discretionary support funds.[36] Hardship funds are treated differently from student grants and loans. In general, if these funds are paid for course costs, they should be disregarded. If they are paid for living costs, they should be treated as capital if paid in a lump sum,[37] or as income if paid regularly.[38] Your learning provider should be able to give you a letter for the relevant benefit office explaining the purpose of the payment.

Payments from the 16–19 bursary fund in England are not taken into account when calculating entitlement to income-related benefits.[39] Learning providers have also been sent guidance that any payments made on a regular basis from the fund should be clearly marked as being for course costs. You should receive a letter from your provider stating what payments are for to take to the benefits office.

Grants from further education funds specifically for childcare are disregarded altogether.[40]

Lump-sum payments

Lump-sum payments are taken into account as capital if they are intended, and used, for food, ordinary clothing or footwear, household fuel, rent met by housing benefit (HB), housing costs met by income support (IS), jobseeker's allowance (JSA) or employment and support allowance (ESA), council tax or water charges.[41] Although taken into account as capital, they only affect your benefit if they bring your capital above the £6,000 lower limit (see p258). Payments for school uniforms or sports clothes or sports shoes are ignored, as these do not count as 'ordinary clothing or footwear'.

Regular payments

Regular payments are taken into account as income if they are intended, and used, for food, ordinary clothing or footwear, household fuel, rent met by HB, housing costs met by IS, JSA or ESA, council tax or water charges.[42] Up to £20 a week is disregarded. You cannot get the £20 disregard in full as well as the full disregards available on a student loan, widowed parent's allowance or war pensions (see p258). If you get one of these other payments in addition to a hardship payment, your maximum weekly disregard is £20. For example, if you have a student loan and receive a war pension, £10 a week is disregarded from each. If you also receive regular payments from a hardship fund, these count in full as you have already used up your £20 disregard.

Regular payments intended and used for anything else, such as childcare expenses, are completely disregarded.

Regular payments from the 16–19 bursary fund should be disregarded regardless of their purpose, but colleges and other providers have also been given guidance to ensure that any regular payments from the fund are clearly identified as being for course costs, and so disregarded.

Payments before a course starts or before a loan is paid

A payment from a hardship fund made before the course starts is always ignored as income, even if it is for living costs. A payment made before you get the first instalment of your student loan is ignored as income, provided it is intended to tide you over until your loan is paid.

Institutional bursaries

Bursaries paid by institutions for living costs are treated as income over the period for which they are paid.

Voluntary or charitable payments

Regular voluntary or charitable payments are ignored for IS, income-based JSA, income-related ESA and HB. For IS and JSA, if paid as a lump sum, the payment is taken into account as capital whatever it is intended for.

Professional and career development loans

Professional and career development loans (or any similar loans offered by banks or other lenders) are always treated as income rather than capital, no matter how they are paid.[43] The loan is taken into account if it is intended, and used, for food, ordinary clothing or footwear, household fuel, rent met by HB, housing costs met by IS, JSA or ESA, council tax or water charges. Once the period of education supported by the loan is completed, the loan is disregarded altogether, whatever it was originally intended for.

5. Earnings

Your earnings and the earnings of your partner are taken into account in the benefit assessment. It is your net weekly earnings that are taken into account – ie, after deducting:

- income tax;
- class 1 national insurance contributions;
- half of any contribution you make towards a personal or occupational pension.

Some of your earnings are disregarded. The highest disregard that applies in your circumstances is deducted:

- £25 for lone parents claiming housing benefit (HB) who are not claiming income support (IS), income-based jobseeker's allowance (JSA) or income-related employment and support allowance (ESA);
- £20 for lone parents claiming IS, JSA or ESA;
- £20 for someone who gets a disability premium;
- £20 for someone who gets a carer premium;
- £20 for part-time firefighters and some other emergency auxiliaries;
- £10 for couples, whether one or both of you are working;
- £5 for single people.

For HB only, there is an additional disregard (£17.10) for some people working 16/30 hours a week.

For HB, childcare costs for registered childminders, nurseries and playschemes can be disregarded from earnings in some circumstances. Childcare costs of up to £175 a week for one child or £300 for two or more children are deducted from weekly earnings for:

- lone parents who are working;
- couples who are both working;
- couples, where one is working and one is incapacitated or in hospital or prison.

In each case, the work must be for 16 hours or more a week.

For full details of the way earnings are treated, see CPAG's *Welfare Benefits and Tax Credits Handbook*.

6. Benefits and tax credits

Some benefits are taken into account in the assessment of income support (IS), income-based jobseeker's allowance (JSA), income-related employment and support allowance (ESA) and housing benefit (HB), and others are ignored or partially ignored.

Benefits and tax credits taken into account in full include:
- child tax credit (CTC) for HB;
- carer's allowance;
- contributory ESA;
- contribution-based JSA;
- incapacity benefit;
- most industrial injuries benefits;
- retirement pension;
- working tax credit.

Benefits and tax credits completely disregarded include:
- attendance allowance;
- child benefit;
- CTC for IS, JSA and income-related ESA;
- disability living allowance;
- personal independence payment;
- social fund payments.

Benefits and tax credits partly disregarded include:
- widowed parent's allowance, which has £10 a week disregarded for IS, JSA and ESA, and £15 a week for HB (but you do not get this disregard if you already have £10 disregarded from a student loan or £20 disregarded from hardship fund payments).

7. Maintenance

For housing benefit, income support, jobseeker's allowance and income-related employment and support allowance, child maintenance paid to you by a former partner or your child's other parent is disregarded completely.

8. Savings and capital

There are limits on the amount of savings or capital you can have and still claim benefit. Some kinds of capital are not counted in the assessment. For details, see CPAG's *Welfare Benefits and Tax Credits Handbook*.
- You cannot get income support, income-based jobseeker's allowance, income-related employment and support allowance or housing benefit (HB) if your savings or other capital are above £16,000.
- If your capital is £6,000 or less it does not affect your benefit at all.
- If your capital is between £6,000.01 and £16,000, you are treated as though you have income from this capital of £1 a week for every £250, or part of £250,

between these limits. This is referred to as 'tariff income'. For example, if you have savings of £6,525, your tariff income is £3 a week.

- These limits are different if you or your partner have reached the qualifying age for pension credit (PC). All your capital is ignored if you or your partner get PC guarantee credit. Otherwise, tariff income of £1 for each £500 or part of £500 between £10,000.01 and £16,000 is taken into account in the assessment of HB.

Notes

2. Grants and loans

1 **IS** Reg 62(2) IS Regs
  JSA Reg 131(2) JSA Regs
  ESA Reg 132(2) ESA Regs
  HB Reg 59(2) HB Regs
  See also para 30326 DMG

2 **IS** Reg 62(2)(a) IS Regs
  JSA Reg 131(2)(a) JSA Regs
  ESA Reg 132(2)(a) ESA Regs
  HB Reg 59(2)(a) HB Regs

3 **IS** Reg 62(2) IS Regs
  JSA Reg 131(2) JSA Regs
  ESA Reg 132(2)(2) ESA Regs
  HB Reg 59(2) HB Regs
  See also para 30328 DMG

4 **IS** Reg 62(2)(c) IS Regs
  JSA Reg 131(2)(b) JSA Regs
  ESA Reg 132(2)(b) ESA Regs
  HB Reg 59(2)(b) HB Regs

5 **IS** Reg 62(2)(h) IS Regs
  JSA Reg 131(2)(g) JSA Regs
  ESA Reg 132(2)(g) ESA Regs
  HB Reg 59(2)(g) HB Regs

6 **IS** Reg 62(2)(g) and (h) IS Regs
  JSA Reg 131(2)(f) and (g) JSA Regs
  ESA Reg 132(2)(f) and (g) ESA Regs
  HB Reg 59(2)(f) and (g) HB Regs

7 **IS** Reg 62(2) IS Regs
  JSA Reg 131(2) JSA Regs
  ESA Reg 132(2)(b) ESA Regs
  HB Reg 59(2) HB Regs
  See also para 30330 DMG

8 Reg 59(6) HB Regs

9 **IS** Reg 62(2)(c) IS Regs
  JSA Reg 131(2)(b) JSA Regs
  ESA Reg 132(2)(b) ESA Regs
  HB Reg 59(2)(b) HB Regs

10 **IS** Reg 62(2)(h) IS Regs
  JSA Reg 131(2) JSA Regs
  ESA Reg 132(2) ESA Regs
  HB Reg 59(2)(g) HB Regs

11 paras 30121-25 DMG

12 para 30131 DMG

13 **IS** Sch 9 para 11(a) IS Regs
   JSA Sch 7 para 12 JSA Regs
   ESA Sch 8 para 13 ESA Regs
   HB Sch 5 para 11 HB Regs

14 **IS** Schs 9 para 11 and 10 para 63 IS Regs
   JSA Schs 7 para 12 and 8 para 52 JSA Regs
   ESA Schs 8 para 13 and 9 para 52 ESA Regs
   HB Sch 5 para 11 HB Regs

15 **IS** Reg 66C IS Regs
   JSA Reg 136B JSA Regs
   ESA Reg 139 ESA Regs
   HB Reg 64A HB Regs

16 **IS** Reg 66A(3) and (4) IS Regs
   JSA Reg 136(5) JSA Regs
   ESA Reg 137(5) ESA Regs
   HB Reg 64(3) and (4) HB Regs

17 **IS** Reg 67 IS Regs
   JSA Reg 136(4) JSA Regs
   ESA Reg 139(5) ESA Regs
   HB Reg 64(4) HB Regs

18 **IS** Reg 64(5) IS Regs
JSA Reg 136(5) JSA Regs
ESA Reg 139(6) ESA Regs
HB Reg 64(5) HB Regs
19 **IS** Reg 66D IS Regs
JSA Reg 136C JSA Regs
ESA Reg 139A ESA Regs
HB Reg 64B HB Regs
20 **IS** Reg 66A(4A) IS Regs
JSA Reg 136(4A) JSA Regs
ESA Reg 13 ESA Regs
HB Reg 64(4A) HB Regs
21 **IS** Reg 41(6) IS Regs
JSA Reg 104(5) JSA Regs
ESA Reg 105(4) ESA Regs
HB Reg 41(4) HB Regs

3. Dividing student income throughout the year
22 **IS** Reg 62(3B) IS Regs
JSA Reg 131(5A) JSA Regs
ESA Reg 132(6) ESA Regs
HB Reg 59(7) HB Regs
23 **IS** Reg 62(2)(h) IS Regs
JSA Reg 131(2)(g) JSA Regs
ESA Reg 132(3)(g) ESA Regs
HB Reg 59(2)(g) HB Regs
24 **IS** Regs 61 and 62(3)(a) IS Regs
JSA Regs 130 and 131(4)(a) JSA Regs
ESA Regs 131 and 132(4)(a) ESA Regs
HB Regs 53 and 59(5)(a) HB Regs
25 **IS** Reg 29(2B) IS Regs
JSA Reg 94(2B) JSA Regs
ESA Reg 91(4) ESA Regs
26 *Leeves v Chief Adjudication Officer*, reported as R(IS) 5/99
27 **IS** Reg 66A(2)(c) IS Regs
JSA Reg 136(2)(c) JSA Regs
ESA Reg 137(3)(e) ESA Regs
HB Reg 64(2)(d) HB Regs
28 CIS/3734/2004
29 **IS** Reg 66A(2)(b) IS Regs
JSA Reg 136(2)(b) JSA Regs
ESA Reg 137(3)(d) ESA Regs
HB Reg 64(2)(d) HB Regs
30 **IS** Reg 66A(2)(aa) IS Regs
JSA Reg 136(2)(c) JSA Regs
ESA Reg 137(3)(e) ESA Regs
HB Reg 64(2)(b) HB Regs
31 **IS** Reg 61(1) IS Regs
JSA Reg 136(2)(aa) JSA Regs
ESA Reg 137(3)(b) ESA Regs
HB Reg 53(1) HB Regs
32 **IS** Reg 66A(2)(aa) IS Regs
JSA Reg 136(2)(c) JSA Regs
ESA Reg 137(3)(e) ESA Regs
HB Reg 64(2)(b) HB Regs

33 **IS** Reg 40(3A) IS Regs
JSA Reg 103(5) JSA Regs
ESA Reg 104(4) ESA Regs
HB Reg 40(7) HB Regs
34 See also HB/CTB Circular A31/2001 Part 6 and Annex D for guidance and a sample calculation, together with HB/CTB Circular A39/2001, para 19
35 CJSA/549/2003

4. Discretionary funds and other payments
36 para 30305 DMG
37 **IS** Reg 61 IS Regs
JSA Reg 130 JSA Regs
ESA Reg 131 ESA Regs
HB Reg 53 HB Regs
38 **IS** Reg 61(1) IS Regs
JSA Reg 130(1) JSA Regs
ESA Reg 131(1) ESA Regs
HB Reg 53(1) HB Regs
39 **IS** Reg 68 IS Regs
JSA Reg 138 JSA Regs
ESA Reg 142 ESA Regs
HB Reg 68 HB Regs
40 **IS** Reg 66B IS Regs
JSA Reg 136A JSA Regs
ESA Reg 138 ESA Regs
HB Reg 65 HB Regs
41 **IS** Reg 41(6) IS Regs
JSA Reg 104(5) JSA Regs
ESA Reg 105(4) ESA Regs
HB Reg 41(4) HB Regs
42 **IS** Reg 66B IS Regs
JSA Reg 136A JSA Regs
ESA Regs 2(1) and 138 ESA Regs
HB Regs 2(1) and 68(3) and (4) HB Regs
43 **IS** Reg 41(6) IS Regs
JSA Reg 104(5) JSA Regs
ESA Reg 105(4) ESA Regs
HB Reg 41(4) HB Regs

Chapter 23

How income affects tax credits

This chapter covers:
1. Income and tax credits (below)
2. Grants and loans (p262)
3. Earnings (p264)
4. Benefits (p264)
5. Other income (p265)

Basic facts
– Most student income is ignored when working out your entitlement to tax credits.
– The higher education adult dependants' grant and some elements of professional and career development loans are taken into account.
– Earnings, some benefits and certain other income are also taken into account.

1. Income and tax credits

If you are getting income support (IS), income-based jobseeker's allowance, income-related employment and support allowance or pension credit, you are entitled to maximum tax credits without any income test. If you are not on one of these benefits, the tax credit assessment is based on your income over a full tax year (6 April to 5 April). When you claim, HM Revenue and Customs (HMRC) uses your income from the previous complete tax year. For example, if you claim tax credits between 6 April 2018 and 5 April 2019, it uses your income from 6 April 2017 to 5 April 2018 to work out your entitlement. **Note:** although your income from the previous year is used in the initial tax credit assessment, all other relevant circumstances, such as the age of your child, are taken from the current year of the tax credit award.

Your tax credits are first assessed using the previous year's income, even if HMRC knows at the outset that your circumstances have changed. If you expect your income over the current tax year to be more than £2,500 lower or more than £2,500 higher, tell HMRC and it reassesses your tax credit entitlement. If you do not tell HMRC, you will have an overpayment to repay at the end of the tax year, or an underpayment that you will get back as a lump sum.

At the end of the tax year, HMRC sends you an annual review form to check whether your income and circumstances have stayed the same over the year. It reassesses your award for the previous year based on the current year's income plus £2,500 if it is more than £2,500 lower than in the previous year, or based on the current year's income less a disregard of £2,500 if it is more than £2,500 higher.

If your income increases by £2,500 or less since the previous tax year used to assess your claim, you do not need to tell HMRC as this does not affect the amount to which you are entitled (but you should let it know if the change means you are now eligible for working tax credit (WTC) or more WTC). However, any increase will be taken into account from the following April (April 2019 for an increase in the 2018/19 tax year), so it is important to tell HMRC of any increase by this date, otherwise you are likely to incur an overpayment.

If you have a partner, your tax credits claim is made jointly and her/his income counts as well as yours.

Unless you or your partner are working and eligible for WTC, your maximum child tax credit is reduced if your income is above the threshold of £16,105 a year. If you are eligible for WTC, this threshold is £6,420.

When working out your income for tax credit purposes, some income is disregarded.

2. **Grants and loans**

Most grants and loans are disregarded when calculating a student's income for tax credit purposes (see below).[1] The following are the exceptions.

- **Adult dependants' grant.** Any grant received for an adult dependant is included in the calculation.
- **Professional and career development loan.** Any part of this paid for living costs for the period supported by the loan is taken into account in full.[2]

Grants and loans checklist

Student support	Treatment
Further education income	
16–19 bursary fund	Disregarded
Advanced learner loan	Disregarded
Care to Learn grant	Disregarded
Dance and drama awards	Disregarded
Discretionary support funds/Financial Contingency Fund/ hardship funds payment	Disregarded

Student support	Treatment
Education maintenance allowance	Disregarded
Further education award (Northern Ireland)	Disregarded
Learner support grant	Disregarded
Travel expenses allowance	Disregarded
Vulnerable student bursary (England)	Disregarded
Welsh government learning grant	Disregarded
Undergraduate income	
Adult dependants' grant	Taken into account in full
Base grant (Wales)	Disregarded (expected)
Childcare grant	Disregarded
Child dependants allowance	Disregarded
Disabled students' allowance	Disregarded
Hardship funds	Disregarded
Institutional bursaries or scholarships	Disregarded
Maintenance grants	Disregarded in England; expected to be disregarded in Wales
NHS childcare allowance	Disregarded
NHS dependants' allowance	Disregarded
NHS healthcare/nursing and midwifery bursary	Disregarded
Parents' learning allowance	Disregarded
Part-time students' grant for course costs	Disregarded
Part-time students' grant for tuition fees	Disregarded
Part-time students' loan for living costs	Disregarded
Social work bursary (England and Wales)	Disregarded
Social work bursary (Northern Ireland)	Disregarded
Special support grant	Disregarded
Special support loan element	Disregarded
Special support payment (Wales)	Disregarded (expected)
Student loan for living costs (including any means-tested element where appropriate)	Disregarded
Teacher training bursary	Disregarded
Travelling or accommodation expenses	Disregarded
Tuition fee grant (Wales)	Disregarded
Tuition fee loan	Disregarded
Welsh government learning grant	Disregarded
Postgraduate income	
Books and equipment expenses	Disregarded
British Academy grant	Disregarded
Postgraduate loan for doctoral degrees	Disregarded (expected)
Postgraduate loan for master's degrees in England (equivalent loans in Wales expected to be treated the same)	Disregarded

Student support	Treatment
Postgraduate tuition fee loan (Northern Ireland)	Disregarded
Research Council studentship or scholarship	Disregarded
Social work bursary	Disregarded
Supplementary grants	Disregarded except for any adult dependants' grant, which is taken into account in full
Teacher training bursary/grant/scholarship/salary	Disregarded
Other income	
Professional and career development loan	Tuition and course cost payments disregarded; payments for living costs taken into account

3. Earnings

Your gross earnings from the last full tax year, plus those of your partner, are taken into account in the tax credit assessment. **'Gross earnings'** means all income before any income tax or national insurance contributions are deducted. It also includes tips, overtime pay, taxable expenses and, ignoring the first £30,000, taxable payments related to the termination of employment such as redundancy pay and strike pay.[3] If you make any contributions to a personal or occupational pension approved by HM Revenue and Customs, these contributions should be disregarded.[4] The first £100 a week of statutory maternity, paternity, shared parental and adoption pay is disregarded, but payments above this are included.[5] Statutory sick pay is included in full.[6] Any payments that are exempt from income tax should be ignored for the purposes of tax credits.

For full details of the way earnings are treated, see CPAG's *Welfare Benefits and Tax Credits Handbook*.

4. Benefits

In general, benefits that are not taxable are disregarded when calculating tax credits, and benefits that are taxable are included. For full details of the way social security benefits are treated, see CPAG's *Welfare Benefits and Tax Credits Handbook*.

Benefits disregarded include:[7]
• bereavement payment;
• bereavement support payment;
• child benefit;

- disability living allowance;
- personal independence payment;
- income-related employment and support allowance (ESA);
- guardian's allowance;
- housing benefit;
- income support (except to strikers);
- income-based jobseeker's allowance (JSA);
- industrial injuries benefit;
- maternity allowance;
- social fund payments;
- most war pensions;[8]
- increases for a child or adult dependant paid with any of the above benefits.

Benefits taken into account in full include:
- bereavement allowance;
- carer's allowance;
- contributory ESA;
- long-term incapacity benefit;
- contribution-based JSA. **Note:** amounts above the 'taxable maximum' are ignored. In practice, people are not paid above this amount, so in the majority of cases all contribution-based JSA is included;
- increases for a child or adult dependant paid with any of the above benefits.

Benefits partly taken into account include:
- state retirement pension (and private and occupational pensions);
- widowed parent's allowance.

These are included in the tax credit calculation, except for the first £300 of the total income from pensions, and income from capital and foreign income, which is disregarded.

5. **Other income**

This is a brief outline of how other income is treated. For further details, see CPAG's *Welfare Benefits and Tax Credits Handbook*.

Income from self-employment

Your taxable profits are taken into account, less any personal pension contributions.

Savings and investments

There is no capital limit for tax credits. You are eligible whatever amount of savings you have and whatever the value of other capital. However, income generated from your savings or other capital is taken into account. For example, interest from money in a bank account is taken into account, unless it is in a tax-free savings account. However, if you have no income from property or pensions, or foreign income, interest on savings or other capital is only taken into account if it is over £300 a year.

Property

The capital value of any property is ignored. Any taxable rental income is included, except for the first £300 of the total income from pensions, income from capital, and foreign income, which is disregarded.[9]

Note: you can rent a room in your own home without paying tax on the rental income, provided this does not exceed £7,500 a year. This income is not taken into account when working out your entitlement to tax credits.

Maintenance

Regular maintenance from an ex-partner is ignored, regardless of how the arrangement was made. Similarly, any support received from an ex-partner for your child(ren) is also ignored.[10]

Notes

2. Grants and loans
  1 Reg 8 TC(DCI) Regs
  2 Reg 19(c) Table 8 para 2 TC(DCI) Regs

3. Earnings
  3 Reg 4 TC(DCI) Regs
  4 Reg 3(7)(c) TC(DCI) Regs
  5 Reg 4(1)(h) TC(DCI) Regs
  6 Reg 4(1)(g) TC(DCI) Regs

4. Benefits
  7 Reg 7(3) TC(DCI) Regs
  8 Reg 5 TC(DCI) Regs

5. Other income
  9 Reg 11 TC(DCI) Regs
  10 Reg 19 Table 6 para 10 TC(DCI) Regs

Chapter 24

How income affects health benefits

This chapter covers:
1. Working out your income (below)
2. Grants and loans (p268)
3. Discretionary funds and other payments (p272)
4. Earnings (p274)
5. Benefits and tax credits (p274)
6. Maintenance (p275)
7. Savings and capital (p275)

Basic facts
– The NHS low income scheme helps with health costs if your income is low enough.
– Student loans and most grants count as income.
– The exact amount of help you receive depends on the amount of excess weekly income (if any) you are assessed as having, once it is offset against a personal allowance and your housing costs.

1. Working out your income

The way that student income is taken into account for health benefits is broadly the same as for means-tested benefits (see Chapter 22).

Step one | **Apply annual disregard.**
From the student maintenance loan, deduct the disregarded amount of £693 for books, equipment and travel.
Step two | **Divide income throughout the year.**
Divide the annual amount of loan by 52 weeks, unless you are in the final or only year of your course, in which case you should divide by the number of weeks between the start and finish of your course.

Step three	**Weekly disregard.**
	Unlike the means-tested benefits assessment, there is no weekly disregard of £10 on the student loan, unless you receive a premium in your applicable amount, an allowance because of deafness (separate to any disabled students' allowance), or you are not a student but your partner is. If you come into any of these categories, disregard £10.
Step four	**Add other income to weekly loan amount.**
	Add together any other weekly income (except for 'mandatory' awards such as research council awards or non-means-tested NHS bursaries) – eg, from hardship funds (see p272) or a professional and career development loan (see p273), earnings (see p274), tariff income from capital (see p275), and benefits and tax credits (see p274) – ignoring any amount that is disregarded.
Step five	**Divide mandatory grant income over 52 weeks.**
	Divide any mandatory grant or bursary over 52 weeks and add this to the weekly loan amount where appropriate. Amounts in excess of a maintenance grant are disregarded. This total, added to the weekly loan total calculated at Step four, is the amount of income used in the health benefits assessment.

2. **Grants and loans**

Grants

In general, grants intended for living costs (such as the NHS bursary and the social work bursary) are taken into account, and grants for other costs are disregarded. For how hardship funds and grants are treated, see p272.

A maximum amount of any maintenance grant or Welsh government learning grant paid to 2011 and 2012 cohort students is taken into account, but amounts above this are ignored.[1] The maximum amounts taken into account are as follows.

Student cohort	Amount taken into account
England	
2012 cohort	£1,796.50
Wales	
2011 or 2012 cohort	£2,580.00
Northern Ireland	£1,318.00

Note: at the time of writing, it was unclear whether there would be any changes arising from the the new funding arrangements for undergraduates in Wales. See CPAG's *Welfare Rights Bulletin* for updates.

Institutional bursaries and scholarships are taken into account if they are paid for living costs.

If you are *not* eligible for a student loan for living costs, £693 for books, travel and equipment is deducted from your grant.

Social work bursaries are usually divided over the number of weeks of study, except if your classroom weeks exceed 45, in which case they are divided by 52.

Teacher training bursaries are divided over the number of days they are paid, then multiplied by seven to give a weekly amount. The £693 disregard is not applied.

Further education grants
The following further education grants are disregarded:
- 16–19 bursary fund;
- education maintenance allowance;
- adult learning grant;
- Care to Learn grant;
- travel expenses allowance.

Higher education grants
The following higher education grants are completely disregarded:
- part-time course costs grant;
- childcare grant;
- child dependants allowance (expected to be disregarded);
- parents' learning allowance;
- disabled students' allowance;
- travel expenses;
- tuition fees grants and loans.

The following grants are taken into account:
- adult dependants' grant;
- teacher training bursary;
- nursing and midwifery bursary;
- social work bursary.

Postgraduate grants
Any research council or other maintenance grant and dependants' allowances are taken into account. Supplementary grants are treated in the same way as those for undergraduates (see p268). Ignore:
- grants for tuition fees;
- grants for residential study away from your normal home;
- grants intended to meet the costs of books and equipment.

Student loan

A student loan includes:

- the maximum loan for living costs for which you are eligible, including any means-tested element. This is taken into account as your income whether or not you apply for it. The government believes that it is the main source of support to students and should be fully exhausted before further support is given;
- any payments for extra weeks' attendance.

£693 for books, travel and equipment is disregarded from the annual student loan. Any special support element should be disregarded in the same way as for income support (IS). Thirty per cent of the maximum postgraduate loan for master's courses to which you are entitled is taken into account, but the remainder is disregarded. **Note:** it is not yet known how the new part-time undergraduate loans for living costs in England, the new postgraduate doctoral loans in England and Wales and the postgraduate master's loans in Wales will be treated, and whether there will be any changes arising from the new arrangements for undergraduates in Wales. It is expected that part-time living costs loans will be treated in the same way as for full-time loans, with the special support element disregarded and the loan then taken into account according to the usual rules, and that postgraduate master's loans in Wales and postgraduate doctoral degree loans will be treated in the same way as loans for master's degrees in England.

Grants and loans checklist

Student support	Treatment
Further education income	
16–19 bursary fund	Disregarded
Advanced learner loan	Disregarded
Care to Learn grant	Disregarded
Dance and drama awards	Any element for tuition ignored; maintenance grant taken into account except: – £390 a year for books and equipment; – £303 a year for travel
Discretionary or learner support funds/Financial Contingency Fund/hardship funds payment	Taken into account if paid for basic living costs, disregarded if paid for other items such as childcare
Education maintenance allowance	Disregarded
Further education award (Northern Ireland)	Taken into account except: – £390 a year for books and equipment; – £303 a year for travel
Travel expenses allowance	Disregarded
Vulnerable student bursary (England)	Disregarded
Welsh government learning grant	Disregarded
Undergraduate income	
Adult dependants' grant	Taken into account in full
Base grant (Wales)	Taken into account in full (expected)

Student support	Treatment
Childcare grant	Disregarded
Child dependants allowance	Disregarded
Disabled students' allowance	Disregarded
Hardship funds	Taken into account if paid for basic living costs (as capital if not regular payments); disregarded if paid for other items
Institutional bursaries or scholarships	Taken into account if paid for living costs
Maintenance grants	Any sum in excess of a certain amount taken into account
NHS childcare allowance	Disregarded
NHS dependants' allowance	Taken into account in full
NHS healthcare bursary	Taken into account except: – £390 a year for books and equipment; – £303 a year for travel
NHS nursing and midwifery bursary	Means tested: taken into account in full Non-means tested: taken into account, except: – £390 a year for books and equipment – £303 a year for travel
Parents' learning allowance	Disregarded
Part-time students' grant for course costs	Disregarded
Part-time students' grant for tuition fees	Disregarded
Part-time students' loan for living costs	Expected to be taken into account except: – £390 a year for books and equipment; – £303 a year for travel; – £10 a week
Social work bursary (England and Wales)	Any element for non-living costs, such as travel or tuition fee costs, disregarded; remainder taken into account in full
Social work bursary (Northern Ireland)	Taken into account, except any element for travel costs
Special support grant	Disregarded
Special support loan element	Disregarded
Special support payment (Wales)	Disregarded (expected)
Student loan for living costs (including any means-tested element where appropriate)	Taken into account in full except: – £390 a year for books and equipment; – £303 a year for travel; – £10 a week in certain circumstances
Teacher training bursary	Taken into account
Travelling or accommodation expenses	Disregarded
Tuition fee grant (Wales)	Disregarded
Tuition fee loan	Disregarded
Welsh government learning grant	Any sum in excess of a certain amount taken into account

Student support	Treatment
Postgraduate income	
Books and equipment expenses	Disregarded
Postgraduate loan for doctoral degrees	Expected to be 30 per cent of maximum entitlement taken into account, except:
	– £390 a year for books and equipment;
	– £303 a year for travel;
	– £10 a week
Postgraduate loan for master's degrees in England (equivalent loans in Wales expected to be treated the same)	30 per cent of loan taken into account, except:
	– £390 a year for books and eqipment;
	– £303 a year for travel;
	– £10 a week
Postgraduate tuition fee loan (Northern Ireland)	Disregarded
Research council studentship or scholarship (including Birtish Academy)	Taken into account, except:
	– £390 a year for books and equipment
	– £303 a year for travel
Social work bursary	Taken into account in full
Supplementary grants	As for undergraduate income
Teacher training bursary/grant/ scholarship/salary	Taken into account in full

. . . .
. . . .

Example

Oliver is a second-year full-time undergraduate in Wales. He receives the maximum away-from-home student loan (£4,563), the maximum Welsh government learning grant (£5,161) and £20 a week from his parents for food and bills.

When calculating his income for health benefits purposes, subtract £693 from his student loan, to give £3,870 and include the first £2,580 of his Welsh government learning grant. This gives £6,450. Divide this by 52 weeks (£124.04). The £20 a week he gets from his parents is added to this figure and his income is, therefore, assessed to be £144.04 a week. This income is then set against the appropriate IS personal allowances, housing and other costs to determine whether or not it exceeds or falls short of Oliver's requirements. If it falls short, he receives full support. If his income exceeds this amount, he may receive partial support, depending on the level of excess.

. . . .

3. **Discretionary funds and other payments**

Hardship funds

Discretionary support provided by your university or college when you are in financial difficulty is treated differently from other student grants and loans. This support can include:

- higher education hardship funds, including what was previously the Access to Learning Fund in England and the Financial Contingency Fund in Wales (individual institutions may still refer to them by these names);
- further education discretionary support funds or support from the Financial Contingency Fund in Wales.

In general, if the payment is for living costs, it is taken into account in full if it counts as capital, or with up to a £20 a week disregarded if it counts as income. If the payment is for other costs, it is disregarded. For example, a further education discretionary support funds grant solely for childcare costs is disregarded. Ask your provider for a letter saying what the payment is for and how it is paid.

Lump-sum payments count as capital. Regular payments count as income.

Lump-sum payments

Lump-sum payments are taken into account as capital if they are intended, and used, for living costs such as food, ordinary clothing or footwear, household fuel, rent, council tax or water charges. Payments for anything else are disregarded. Although taken into account as capital, this only affects your entitlement if it brings your capital above the £16,000 higher limit. See p275 for details.

Regular payments

Regular payments are taken into account as income if they are intended, and used, for food, ordinary clothing or footwear, household fuel, rent, council tax or water charges. Up to £20 a week is disregarded. You cannot get the £20 disregard in full as well as the full disregards available on a student loan or voluntary and charitable payments (or on widowed parent's allowance or war pensions). If you get one of these other payments as well as a discretionary hardship payment, your maximum weekly disregard is £20.

For example, if you have a student loan for living costs and regular payments from the university's hardship fund, £10 a week is disregarded from each. If you also receive regular payments from a charity, these count in full as you have already used up your £20 disregard on the loan and the hardship fund payment.

Regular payments intended, and used, for anything else, such as childcare expenses, are completely disregarded.

Voluntary or charitable payments

These are treated in the same way as hardship fund payments.

Professional and career development loans

Professional and career development loans are always treated as income, not capital, no matter how they are paid. The loan is taken into account if it is intended, and used, for living costs – eg, food, ordinary clothing or footwear, household fuel, rent, council tax or water charges. Once the period of education supported by the loan is completed, the loan is disregarded altogether, whatever it was originally intended for.

4. **Earnings**

Your earnings and the earnings of your partner are taken into account in the health benefits assessment. Your net weekly earnings are taken into account – ie, deducting:

- income tax;
- class 1 national insurance contributions;
- half of any contribution you make towards a personal or occupational pension.

5. **Benefits and tax credits**

If you receive income support (IS), income-based jobseeker's allowance (JSA), income-related employment and support allowance (ESA) or child tax credit, you automatically get free health benefits (see Chapter 11). You may also qualify if you get universal credit (see p138).

Housing benefit is effectively disregarded, as the NHS Business Services Authority only takes into account the rent paid directly by you when determining need.

Benefits and tax credits taken into account in full include:
- carer's allowance;
- contribution-based JSA;
- contributory ESA;
- incapacity benefit;
- most industrial injuries benefits;
- retirement pension;
- working tax credit.

Benefits and tax credits completely disregarded include:
- attendance allowance;
- child benefit;
- disability living allowance;
- personal independence payment;
- social fund payments.

Benefits and tax credits partly disregarded include:
- widowed parent's allowance, which has £10 a week disregarded. **Note:** you do not receive this disregard if you already have £10 disregarded from a student loan or £20 disregarded from hardship fund payments.

6. **Maintenance**

Regular child maintenance payments are disregarded and lump sums are treated as capital.

7. **Savings and capital**

There are limits on the amount of savings or capital you can have and still claim health benefits.

You cannot get health benefits if your savings or other capital is above £16,000.

If your capital is £6,000 or less, it does not affect your entitlement to health benefits at all. If your capital is between £6,000.01 and £16,000 (a higher limit of £23,250 if you are in a care home in England, or £24,000 if you are in a care home in Wales), you are treated as though you have an income from this capital of £1 a week for every £250 (or part of £250) between these amounts. This is referred to as 'tariff income'. For example, if you have savings of £6,525, your tariff income is £3 a week.

Notes

2. **Grants and loans**
   1 The National Health Service (Travel Expenses and Remission of Charges) Amendment (No.2) Regulations 2006, No.2171 (as amended)

Part 4

Other issues

Chapter 25

Council tax

This chapter covers:
1. What is council tax (below)
2. Who pays council tax (p280)
3. Council tax reduction (p286)
4. Second adult rebate (p287)

Basic facts
 – Council tax is a local tax on residential dwellings. It does not apply in Northern Ireland.
 – You do not pay council tax if you are under 18.
 – Most full-time students do not pay council tax.
 – Apprentices are exempt from council tax.
 – Full-time and part-time students who are liable to pay council tax may be able to get help in the form of a council tax reduction.

1. **What is council tax**

Council tax is a tax on residential dwellings and is paid to the local authority. There is one amount to pay and one bill for each dwelling, unless it is exempt from council tax. A 'dwelling' includes a self-contained flat.

Each dwelling is allocated a valuation band from A to H, based on property values in 1991 (2005 in Wales). The amount of council tax is lowest for those in Band A.

Some dwellings are exempt from council tax. If a property is exempt, there is no council tax to pay for anyone who lives there or for a non-resident owner. There are also exemptions specifically for students (see p284).

Properties occupied solely by students are usually exempt, and the local authority receives additional funds from central government instead of the council tax that would have been paid. Students who share with non-students are also exempt from paying council tax, although the property itself is not exempt.

If you are a student and you are liable, the amount you must pay may be reduced if you are eligible for council tax reduction (see p286) or a second adult rebate (see p287).

2. **Who pays council tax**

As a student, you may be exempt from paying council tax if:
- the accommodation in which you live is exempt (see p283); *or*
- you are not liable to pay (see p284).

If neither of these applies, it may be possible to reduce the council tax bill if:
- the liable person can get a discount (see p285); *or*
- the liable person can get council tax reduction (see p286) or a second adult rebate (see p287).

Who counts as a student

If you are aged under 20, whether you count as a student for council tax purposes depends on whether you are on an advanced or non-advanced course. For older students, one rule applies whatever the level of your course. **Note:** apprentices do not count as students (see p286).

Under 20 in non-advanced education

You are regarded as a 'student' for council tax purposes if you are aged 19 or under and on a non-advanced course of more than 12 hours a week.[1]

Non-advanced course
A '**non-advanced course**' is one below the level of a foundation degree, honours degree, Higher National Certificate, Higher National Diploma or national vocational qualification (NVQ) level four. It includes A levels, national diplomas and national certificates. The course must last more than three months.[2] It does not include evening classes,[3] correspondence courses,[4] or courses taken as a result of your office or occupation.[5]

The hours that count are those required by the course rather than those you actually do, if they are different. To work out your hours, average out over term times the hours required under the course for tuition, supervised study, exams, and supervised exercises, experiments, projects and practical work.[6]

You are treated as a student on each day from the day you start the course until the day you complete it, abandon it or are dismissed from it.[7] So, you count as a student during term times, during short vacations at Christmas and Easter, and during the summer if your course continues after the summer. If your course ends in the summer and you begin a different one in the autumn, you do not count as a student in the summer between courses.[8] However, you might be able to get a discount (see p285).

Example

Drew is 18 and taking three A levels at college. Including his classes, exams and supervised study, his course hours are 18 a week. He is a student for council tax purposes.

Under 20 in higher education

The rules are the same as for those aged 20 or over (see below).

20 or over in non-advanced or higher education

You are regarded as a 'student' for council tax purposes if the course requires you to undertake periods of study, tuition or work experience for at least 21 hours a week in at least 24 weeks each academic year.[9]

If you are on a sandwich course, required periods of work experience are included.

To count as a student, you must be enrolled on a course with an educational institution. You are a student from the day you begin the course until the day you complete it, abandon it or are no longer permitted by the educational institution to undertake it.[10] So if you take time out and are not enrolled on the course during that period, you do not count as a student for council tax purposes. If this means you become liable for council tax, check whether you can get council tax reduction (see p286).

If you take time out but are still enrolled on the course, you continue to count as a student, provided you have not abandoned it completely and the institution has not said you can no longer undertake the course. Because the law says you are not a student if you are 'no longer permitted by the institution to undertake [the course]', it suggests that your dismissal from the course must be final. So you could argue that if you are temporarily suspended from the course but still registered, you still count as a student. In an informal letter, written in 1996, the former Department of the Environment (then responsible for council tax) stated:[11]

In our view a period of intercalation will remain within the period of a course... and therefore, provided that the person remains enrolled at the education establishment, they will continue to fall within the definition of a full-time student.

Note: a valuation tribunal decision indicates that students who are repeating a full-time course on a part-time basis may not be regarded as meeting the definition of 'full-time student', even if their normal attendance is on a full-time basis.[12] It is therefore important to ensure that your institution is clear about the normal expectations of your course in any documentation it provides.

Your college or university determines the number of hours of your course. You may need evidence from it to prove to the local authority that you count as a student. Colleges and universities are required by law to provide you with a certificate, if you ask for one while you are a student or for up to a year after you leave the course.[13] After that, they may still give you a certificate, but are not legally required to do so. The certificate must contain:[14]

- the name and address of the institution;
- your full name;
- your term-time address and home address (if known by the institution);
- a statement that you are (or were) a student – ie, that you are (or were) enrolled on a course requiring you to undertake periods of study, tuition or work experience of at least 21 hours a week over at least 24 weeks a year; *and*
- the date you became a student and the date your course ends.

Note: the rapid change in the way that higher education courses are delivered and structured may not be reflected in council tax legislation, and so certain courses may not meet the definition of 'full time'. For example, condensed courses which do not last a full academic year do not exempt you from council tax, even if the number of hours you attend a week is much higher to reflect the shorter length of the programme.[15]

Postgraduate students

Full-time postgraduate students are regarded as 'students' for council tax purposes in the same way as other full-time higher education students.

In the past, some postgraduate research students had difficulty securing council tax exemption because local authorities considered that their periods of 'study, tuition or work experience' did not meet the requirements of the regulations and that, in particular, research did not count as 'study'. This has been successfully challenged in an appeal in Kent[16] and in a High Court case involving Cambridge City Council.[17] The council tax regulations were amended in 2011 so that the requirement is to 'undertake' the course for the prescribed periods as opposed to 'attend' it, as was previously required. This should make it easier for postgraduate students to show they meet the requirements for exemption.

Other postgraduate students have had difficulty in securing exemption during the thesis 'writing-up' period after the formal end of the course. While some local authorities are sympathetic and extend student status after the end of the course, others have regarded such students as liable as they are no longer 'within the period of their course'. A High Court ruling in 2008 in the case of *Fayad v Lewisham* has served to harden some local authorities' views (although in that case, the student was trying to claim exemption for a writing-up period lasting more than two years).[18] The case has been used by some local authorities to suggest that PhD students are ineligible for exemption even during the formal period of the course, but this should be challenged as the ruling related only to a writing-up period.

If this affects you, get advice from your students' union or institution's advice centre. In particular, check the dates of the course given by the institution and be prepared to challenge this if necessary.

Note: if you have completed an undergraduate course and intend to start a postgraduate course in the following academic year, you are not a student as you are not within the period of either course. Depending on your circumstances, however, you may be able to claim council tax reduction (see p286) or a discount on the bill (see p285).

Student nurses

Although the council tax legislation includes references to 'student nurses',[19] the definition refers to traditional hospital-based courses, which were phased out in the 1990s, and so is now redundant in practice. However, students on higher education nursing courses are regarded as 'students' under the same definition that applies to other full-time students, as made clear in amendments to the council tax regulations in 1994.[20] If a local authority wants proof of 'student nurse' status, refer it to these regulations.

Exempt dwellings

A dwelling is exempt from council tax if everyone who occupies it is:[21]
- a student; *or*
- a student's partner from abroad who entered the UK on a visa that prohibits her/him from working or claiming benefits. If the partner has the right to work but not to claim benefits (or vice versa), the High Court has ruled that s/he is covered by this exemption;[22] *or*
- under age 18; *or*
- under age 20 and left non-advanced education at school or college after 30 April – this only applies between 1 May and 31 October of the year they left school or college; *or*
- 'severely mentally impaired'.

An unoccupied dwelling is exempt for up to four months if it is the main residence of a student (and not of anyone else who is not a student) and it was last occupied by one or more students. This allows an exemption to continue, for example, on the student's term-time accommodation through the summer vacation. Dwellings left unoccupied by a student owner are exempt indefinitely, provided the owner has been a student since s/he last occupied the dwelling or within six weeks of leaving it. Unoccupied dwellings that are substantially unfurnished are exempt for up to six months. If you are liable for council tax and anyone who is jointly liable with you is also a student, and the dwelling is no one's main residence, the dwelling is exempt indefinitely.

If the dwelling is exempt, there is no council tax to pay.

There are a number of other exemptions that are not specifically for students. For details, see CPAG's *Council Tax Handbook*.

Full-time students liable for council tax

Most full-time students are *not* liable to pay council tax. This is because either the dwelling is exempt because everyone who lives in it is a full-time student or, if a student lives with non-students, s/he is usually deemed exempt from liability for the council tax due on the property.

If the dwelling is not exempt from council tax, at least one person is liable for the bill. This depends on her/his position in a liability hierarchy. The person who comes the highest in the hierarchy is the one who is liable to pay. If there are two or more people at the same level in the hierarchy, they are usually jointly liable (see p285).

Council tax liability hierarchy
– Resident with a freehold interest in the property
– Resident with a leasehold on the property, or the superior leaseholder if there is more than one
– Resident tenant
– Resident statutory or secure tenant
– Resident who is a licensee
– Other resident, including a squatter

If students share accommodation with non-students who are at the same level in the hierarchy, the non-students are liable, but the students are not.[23]

There is one situation in which a student may be liable for council tax. If a non-student adult lives in a property, the property is not exempt from council tax. If you are a full-time student living with non-students, but you are higher on the hierarchy of liability than the non-students (eg, you are the owner of the property or the only person named on the tenancy agreement), you, not the non-students, are liable for the council tax. In this case, you may be entitled to a discount on the bill or to council tax reduction, depending on your circumstances.

Example: joint tenants
Three students, Pooja, Joey and Zarah, share a flat as joint tenants. While they are all students, the flat is exempt and there is no council tax to pay. Joey drops out of his course. The flat is no longer exempt and Joey is solely liable for the whole council tax bill (although there is a discount). Pooja and Zarah are not liable for any council tax. Joey should apply for a council tax reduction if his income is low.

Examples: students who are liable

Antonia is studying full time and owns the flat in which she lives. She rents a room to a friend, Bill, who is not a student. Antonia is liable for the council tax. As there is only one non-student at the property, there is a 25 per cent discount on the bill. Bill is not liable for any council tax.

Raj is studying full time and rents the flat in which he lives. He sublets a room to a friend who is also a student. Raj is higher on the hierarchy of liability, but, as both of them are students, the flat is exempt from council tax and the bill is nil.

Joint liability

'Joint and several liability' means that, in legal terms, you can be held liable for all of a bill on which you are named, or for a share of it, even though there are other named individuals. It gives the local authority the right to pursue as many, or as few, of the people named on the council tax bill for payment as it wants, regardless of how many liable residents there are, or were, in the property.[24]

In practice, local authorities try to bill as many liable people as possible. However, if a local authority cannot contact all the liable people (eg, because someone has moved out of the property and left no contact details), those who it can contact can be required to pay the total amount between them. If a local authority can only contact one person, it can require her/him to pay the whole bill.

Usually, couples who live together are jointly liable for the council tax. Students, however, are exempt from this rule. If you have a non-student partner who is liable for council tax, you are not jointly liable while you are a student.[25]

Discounts

The full council tax bill assumes that there are two adults living in the property. If there is only one person living in the property, you get a discount of 25 per cent. If there is no one living in the property, you get a discount of 50 per cent.

Some people are disregarded when counting how many people live in the property. They are sometimes described as 'invisible' or having a 'status discount'.

The following people are disregarded in this way:

- anyone under 18 years old;
- anyone aged 18 or over for whom child benefit is payable;
- a full-time student;
- a student's partner who is not a British citizen and whose immigration status prevents her/him from taking up paid employment or accessing social security benefits (though not necessarily both);
- someone under age 20 who was on a non-advanced course of education and who left school or college after 1 May. The discount applies from 1 May until 31 October;

- a student nurse (see p283 for who counts);
- an apprentice (see below for who counts);
- others – eg, carers, hospital patients and trainees. See CPAG's *Council Tax Handbook* for details.

Apprentices

You count as an '**apprentice**' for council tax purposes, if:

- you are employed for the purpose of learning a trade, business, profession, office, employment or vocation;
- your training programme leads to a qualification accredited by the Office of Qualifications and Examinations Regulation (Ofqual) or by the Welsh Ministers; *and*
- you are receiving a salary or allowance (or both), which totals no more than £195 per week before bonuses or overtime.[26]

You will need to show the local authority evidence of your status, such as your apprenticeship agreement and payslips.

Disability reduction

The council tax bill is reduced to the valuation band below your own band if you or anyone else (adult or child) who is resident in the property is substantially and permanently disabled and uses a wheelchair indoors or needs an extra room.

3. **Council tax reduction**

Council tax reduction is administered by local authorities and helps you pay your council tax. It replaced council tax benefit (CTB) in April 2013, and may be referred to by your local authority as 'council tax support', or similar. Local authorities have the discretion on how to run their own schemes. However, there is a 'default scheme', which has been adopted by a large number of local authorities.[27] If you live in Wales, there is a national scheme and local authorities are funded by the Welsh government.[28]

If you have reached pension age, your local authority should provide support that mirrors that previously available under the CTB scheme.[29]

Most full-time students do not need to claim help as they are not liable for council tax. If you are liable, you might be able to get council tax reduction, depending on your local scheme.

In general, if your local authority has adopted the default scheme and you are a full-time student, you are not eligible for help unless you get certain other benefits, you are a lone parent or one of a student couple with children, or you are disabled.

If you are a part-time student, you may get help, depending on your circumstances and the details of your local scheme. The fact that you are a part-time student, in itself, is unlikely to affect your eligibility for a reduction.

However, schemes may have individual differences, so ask your local authority for details of its scheme. **Note:** scheme rules may change from year to year.

4. **Second adult rebate**

Students in England who are liable for council tax may be able to claim second adult rebate. The law refers to this rebate as 'alternative maximum council tax reduction'. It is intended for people whose bill is higher because they live with someone who cannot get a status discount (see p285), but who cannot make a full contribution towards the bill. You can only get a second adult rebate if you live with others who are not full-time students. **Note:** second adult rebate is not available in Wales.

Since April 2013, local authorities have been able to choose whether to offer second adult rebate. If you can claim, your entitlement depends on the income of the person who shares with you. Your own income or capital is ignored.

You may be able to get a second adult rebate if:

- you are liable for council tax or you are jointly liable and all of those jointly liable are (or all but one are) students or have a status discount for some other reason (see p285); *and*
- you have a 'second adult' (see below) living with you; *and*
- the second adult gets universal credit (UC), income support (IS), income-based jobseeker's allowance (JSA), income-related employment and support allowance (ESA) or pension credit (PC), or has a low income.

Second adult

A '**second adult**' is someone aged 18 or over who is a non-dependant – ie, someone who lives with you on a non-commercial basis, is not a student and does not have a status discount for any other reason.

If you are eligible for second adult rebate and for council tax reduction, the local authority decides which is worth the most to you. You cannot get both at the same time. If you get a second adult rebate, your council tax is reduced by 25 per cent, 15 per cent or 7.5 per cent depending on the income of the second adult. You may be able to get a reduction of 100 per cent if the second adult gets UC, IS, income-based JSA, income-related ESA or PC.

As the rules on second adult rebate are complex, get advice from your students' union, institution or local Citizens Advice office.

Notes

2. Who pays council tax

1 Sch 1 para 5(1) CT(DD)O
2 Sch 1 para 6(1)(a) CT(DD)O
3 Sch 1 para 6(1)(e) CT(DD)O
4 Sch 1 para 6(1)(c) CT(DD)O
5 Sch 1 para 6(1)(d) CT(DD)O
6 Sch 1 paras 5(3) and 6(2) CT(DD)O
7 Sch 1 para 3 CT(DD)O
8 Sch 1 para 5(2) CT(DD)O
9 Sch 1 para 4(1) CT(DD)O
10 Sch 1 para 3 CT(DD)O
11 Council tax information letter 5, 29 April 1996
12 Valuation Tribunal for England appeals 1765M88934/176C and 1765M88933/176C
13 Sch 1 para 5 LGFA 1992
14 Art 5 CT(DD)O
15 *Wirral Borough Council v Farthing* [2008] EWHC 1919 (Ch)
16 Kent Valuation Tribunal appeal 2220M23702/148C/1
17 *Feller v Cambridge City Council* [2011] EWHC 1252 (Admin)
18 *Fayad v Lewisham* [2008] EWHC 2531 (Admin)
19 Sch 1 para 7 CT(DD)O
20 Council Tax (Discount Disregards) (Amendment) Order 1994, No.543
21 Reg 3 CT(ED)O
22 *Harrow LBC v Ayiku* [2012] EWHC 1200 (Admin)
23 s74 LGA 2003
24 s6 LGFA 1992
25 ss9 and 77 LGFA 1992
26 Sch 1 para 1 CT(DD)O

3. Council tax reduction

27 CTRS(DS)(E) Regs
28 CTRS(PR)(W) Regs
29 Reg 11 CTRS(PR)(E) Regs

Chapter 26

. . . .

Tax and national insurance

This chapter covers:
1. Income tax (below)
2. National insurance contributions (p293)

. . . .

Basic facts

– In general, students pay income tax and national insurance (NI) just like everyone else.

– Most educational grants and scholarships, most research awards, and student loans and grants from discretionary funds do not normally count as taxable income, so most full-time students do not pay income tax or NI contributions on their student support.

– For all tax purposes, it is important to keep the relevant paperwork – eg, wage slips and tax forms from your employer, bank and building society statements and interest details, and invoices and receipts if you are self-employed.

. . . .

1. Income tax

Rates and allowances

Income tax is charged on 'taxable income' arising during a tax year (6 April to the following 5 April).[1] 'Taxable income' is your income from all sources, after deducting your personal allowance and any other allowable deductions, such as the blind person's allowance.

. . . .

Income tax rates 2018/19
Percentage taxable income

20% basic rate	£11,850 to £46,350
40% higher rate	£46,351 to £150,000
45% additional rate	£150,001 and above

. . . .

Every person resident in the UK has a personal allowance. This is an amount of annual income on which you do not have to pay tax. The allowance is deducted from your total taxable income before the relevant tax rate is applied. You may

. . . .

also be able to claim other tax allowances, such as the married couple's allowance, depending on your personal circumstances.

Income tax personal allowances 2018/19

Personal allowance[2]	£11,850
Blind person's allowance (additional)[3]	£2,390

Note: if your annual income is more than £100,000, your personal allowance is reduced by £1 for every £2 of additional income. If your income is high enough (over £123,700), your allowance can be reduced to nil.

Note also: if you take on a second part-time job while you are studying and you do not earn enough to pay tax in the first one, you can ask HM Revenue and Customs (HMRC) to split your tax allowance between your two jobs, so that your second job is not taxed at the higher (or basic) rate.

Up-to-date allowances and tax rates are at www.gov.uk/income-tax-rates.

The blind person's allowance can be claimed if you have a severe sight impairment. You do not have to be entirely without sight to be entitled. Claim the allowance by calling HMRC on 0300 200 3301 if either:

- you are registered blind with a local authority in England and Wales; *or*
- you live in Northern Ireland and your vision is so poor that it prevents you from doing any work for which eyesight is essential.

If you are married or in a civil partnership, the blind person's allowance can be transferred to your spouse or civil partner if you do not have enough taxable income to use any or all of it yourself.

Example: working out the tax due

Alice earns £20,000 in her placement year from September 2017 to August 2018, so £11,666 is earned in the seven months to 5 April 2018 (the 2017/18 tax year) and £8,333 from 6 April 2018 (the 2018/19 tax year). In each tax year, she has a personal allowance. In 2017/18, she pays no tax on the first £11,500 (the personal allowance in 2017/18) and 20 per cent on the remaining £166 above this – £33.20 in total. She should pay no tax in 2018/19, assuming she does not work after August 2018 for the rest of the tax year. **Note:** she will have tax deducted from her pay in 2018/19 as her monthly income is over the threshold, but can claim this back after she stops work or at the end of the tax year.

Students who are not domiciled in the UK

Most students from overseas are regarded as 'non-domiciled'. This means that different tax rules may apply, depending on your circumstances. More information is available from www.gov.uk/tax-foreign-income/study-in-the-uk, and the Low Incomes Tax Reform Group website at www.litrg.org.uk/tax-guides/migrants-and-tax/coming-uk-study.

Spouses and civil partners

Spouses and civil partners are taxed separately; each is responsible for her/his own tax affairs. However, if one partner is claiming child benefit and one earns above £50,000, your individual tax affairs are affected. See www.gov.uk/child-benefit-tax-charge for more information.

Sponsorships and scholarships

Sponsorships and scholarships are not usually taxable, provided they do 'no more than support a student during a period of study'.[4]

If you are receiving a scholarship, it is advisable to obtain written confirmation from the body making the award that it is, in fact, tax free.

If you are required to work in a company or organisation and its sponsorship is part payment for this, see p293.

Benefits

Some benefits are taxable and others are not – see www.litrg.org.uk or CPAG's *Welfare Benefits and Tax Credits Handbook*. For example, income support is not normally taxable and housing benefit is not taxable, but jobseeker's allowance is taxable.

The tax due is not deducted when the benefit is paid, but reduces the refund you might otherwise receive through the pay as you earn (PAYE) system when you either return to work or reach the end of the tax year, whichever is sooner.[5]

Bank and building society interest

From 6 April 2016, if you are a basic rate taxpayer, you can earn up to £1,000 per year in savings income (interest) without paying tax. Higher rate taxpayers can earn up to £500 per year. This is called the personal savings allowance. This means that most students do not pay tax on interest on their savings. If your other total taxable income is less than £16,850, you do not pay tax on any savings income.

Personal savings allowance rates 2018/19[6]

Tax rate	Income band	Personal savings allowance
20% basic rate	Up to £46,350	Up to £1,000 in savings income tax free
40% higher rate	£46,351 to £150,000	Up to £500 in savings income tax free
45% additional rate	Above £150,000	No personal savings allowance

If you already receive interest without tax being deducted, you do not need to tell your bank or building society that you qualify for tax-free interest. If you have interest deducted by your bank or building society, you may be able to reclaim this from HMRC using Form R40.

If you have other taxable income (eg, from earnings), your savings may be taxed at a higher rate.

Dividends on shares

Dividends are paid by companies on their shares and are a way of passing the profits to their shareholders.

From 6 April 2016, UK dividend income is paid gross and there is no longer a dividend tax credit. There is also a dividend allowance of £5,000, available to anyone who receives dividend income, which effectively means you can get some dividend income tax free.

The allowance means that you do not pay any tax on the first £5,000 of any dividend income that you receive. Above this allowance, the tax you pay depends on which income tax band you are in.

In 2018/19, tax is charged on dividends at:[7]
- basic rate tax band of 7.5 per cent on dividends over £5,000;
- higher rate tax band of 32.5 per cent on dividends over £5,000;
- additional rate tax band of 38.1 per cent on dividends over £5,000.

Note: you do not pay tax on dividends from shares in an individual savings account (ISA). For information on the previous years' dividend taxation rules, see www.gov.uk/tax-on-dividends/previous-tax-years.

Paying income tax

Employed earners

Under the PAYE system, tax is deducted by your employer from each wage or salary payment, using a code number. Your code takes into account your tax allowances and any allowable deductions or restrictions. When you start a new job, your employer should ask you for 'new starter information' (previously Form P46) to ensure that you pay the correct amount of tax. However, because of the way in which PAYE works, it is not uncommon for students to pay too much tax and then have to contact HMRC for a refund.

Check the tax code used against your income and be proactive in contacting HMRC if you think it is wrong or you do not understand it.

Earnings during vacations

Students employed during vacations should expect to have tax deducted by their employer under the PAYE system on the same basis as everyone else. If, at the end of the employment period or tax year, you have overpaid tax, you can reclaim this from HMRC. See www.gov.uk/claim-tax-refund to reclaim any overpaid income tax.

Placement students

Wages or salaries paid to placement students during periods of practical work experience (including sandwich courses) are taxable as earned income under PAYE, subject to the usual tax-free personal allowances and allowable employment expenses. However, if an employer sponsors your study, any wages/salary paid for periods spent at college can be paid tax free if:

• you are studying full time at a university, technical college or similar educational facility which is generally open to the public and offers more than one course – ie, employer 'in-house' training does not qualify;
• you are enrolled for at least one academic year (1 September to 31 August);
• you attend the course for at least 20 weeks in that academic year or, if the course is longer, for at least an average of 20 weeks in an academic year;
• your earnings, including lodging or subsistence allowances, are not more than £15,480 (excluding any fees paid by the employer).

These rules also apply if you are being released by your employer to study a course, but continue to be paid as a full-time employee. For further guidance, see www.gov.uk/student-jobs-paying-tax.

Self-employed earners

If you are self-employed, you must usually complete a self-assessment return and pay income tax directly to HMRC. You must also let HMRC know when you first become self-employed. Call 0300 200 3500 or register your new business online at www.gov.uk/working-for-yourself.

There are strict rules on completing self-assessment tax returns – make sure you are aware of the deadlines and requirements so that you avoid penalties. Guidance is available from www.gov.uk/self-assessment-tax-returns.

If you need help with your return, call HMRC's self-assessment helpline on 0300 200 3310 or textphone 0300 200 3319.

2. **National insurance contributions**

National insurance (NI) contributions are paid by people who are employed or self-employed and earn above a certain amount as a way of contributing to the social security system. Paying contributions during your working life can entitle you to a range of benefits, including retirement pension. HM Revenue and Customs (HMRC) keeps a record of everyone's contributions.

There are different types of contributions (called 'classes').

Contributions and benefit entitlement

NI contributions can count towards your future entitlement to social security benefits.

- **Class 1 contributions** may later entitle you to contribution-based jobseeker's allowance (JSA), contributory employment and support allowance (ESA), retirement pensions, bereavement support payment and widowed parent's allowance. If you earn between £116 and £162 per week (in 2018/19), your NI contributions are treated as paid and you can build up an entitlement to contributory benefits, even though you are not actually paying NI contributions.
- **Class 2 contributions** may later entitle you to contributory ESA, retirement pensions, and bereavement support payment.
- **Class 3 contributions** are voluntary and allow you to top up your contribution record to qualify for a higher retirement pension, and for widows' benefits.
- **Class 4 contributions** do not give entitlement to any social security benefits.

The exact amount of contributions required depends on the benefit concerned.

Note: paying NI contributions does not entitle you to benefits you would not otherwise be able to claim as a student.

National insurance numbers

HMRC should issue you with an NI number shortly before your 16th birthday.

Employers must have an NI number for each employee. If you have been allocated a number but cannot find it, you should go to www.gov.uk/government/publications/national-insurance-get-your-national-insurance-number-in-writing-ca5403 and you can request information about your number online. If you have not been allocated a number (eg, if you are an international student who is permitted to work in the UK), contact the NI number allocations service on 0345 600 0643. Who you need to contact in Northern Ireland varies depending on what you need the NI number for. See www.nidirect.gov.uk/articles/applying-national-insurance-number-if-you-live-northern-ireland or contact your nearest NI number processing centre (Belfast area: 028 9013 8286, Southern area: 028 3877 3046 or Northern area: 028 7185 5406).

If a new number must be issued, the process can take several weeks to be completed and normally requires a face-to-face interview. However, if you have lost your number, your employer can send the appropriate tax forms to HMRC without one, and attempts are automatically made to trace your number and inform your employer when it is found.

Contribution rates

National insurance contribution rates 6 April 2018 to 5 April 2019

Contribution type	Weekly earnings	Employee's contribution
Class 1 (employed)	Below £162	Nil
	£162.01 – £892	12%
	£892.01 and over	2%
Class 2 (self-employed)		£2.95 per week of self-employment
Class 3 (voluntary)		£14.65 a week
Class 4 (self-employed)	Profits between £8,424 and £46,350	9%
	Profits above £46,350	2%

Who must pay national insurance contributions

Age limits

No NI contributions are payable if you are under 16 or over state pension age, although you may have to apply for an exemption if your earnings would otherwise attract NI.

Vacation or part-time work

Students do not pay NI contributions on any form of student support. However, if you work and earn more than the 'earnings threshold' of £162 a week, you must pay class 1 (earnings-related) contributions. Your employer deducts these from your wages before you are paid. See above for the rates.

Example
Bob earns £900 a week. He pays no NI contributions on the first £162. He pays 12 per cent on the next £729 (£87.48) and 2 per cent on the remaining £8 (£0.16). His weekly NI contributions are, therefore, £87.64.

Self-employed students

If you are self-employed, you must pay a flat-rate class 2 NI contribution of £2.95 for each week of self-employment if your income is more than £6,205 in the 2018/19 tax year. If your profits are below £6,205, you can apply for an exemption on the basis of low income. However, you may decide to continue to pay your NI contributions as, if you stop, your future entitlement to certain social security benefits may be affected.[8]

You must pay class 4 NI contributions of 9 per cent on your taxable business profits between £8,424 and £46,350 and 2 per cent on any amount above this.[9]

Postgraduate students

If you are a research student, check whether you are liable for class 1, or class 2 and class 4 contributions if you are paid for teaching or other similar work.

Placement students

Placement students are liable to pay class 1 NI contributions if receiving a salary for periods of work experience, although this income can in some instances be classed as 'exempt scholarship income' for periods spent attending college (see p291).

If you have been released from work to take a course but continue to be paid by your employer, some of this income can qualify as scholarship income and is exempt from NI contributions.

Voluntary contributions

Your entitlement to state retirement pension depends on your having paid NI contributions at a certain level for a certain number of years during your working life. The exact number of years depends on when you reach state retirement age.

However, if your payment record is incomplete, you can pay voluntary contributions to make up the 'missing' years. These class 3 NI contributions are paid at a flat rate – £14.65 a week in 2018/19.[10]

You can preserve your entitlement to retirement pension and also to widowed parent's allowance in this way. Voluntary contributions do not count towards short-term benefits, such as contribution-based JSA and contributory ESA.

Deciding whether to pay voluntary contributions

Before committing yourself to paying voluntary class 3 NI contributions, contact the Future Pension Centre (tel: 0800 731 0175; textphone: 0800 731 0176) or see www.gov.uk/check-state-pension to establish your likely pension at retirement age and, therefore, whether it is necessary to make voluntary contributions. This is especially relevant if you are a mature or postgraduate student, have taken time out of work to care for children or adults (in which case, you might be 'credited' with NI contributions), or if you have lived abroad for long periods of time during your working life. Under the current rules, most younger students will not reduce their pension entitlement by not paying NI contributions during their studies, as they will have sufficient time after completing full-time education in which to do so.

Voluntary contributions can generally only be paid up to the end of the sixth tax year after they were 'due'.

Notes

1. Income tax
1 s1 FA 2017
2 s3 FA 2016
3 ss38-41 ITA 2007
4 s776 IT(TOI)A 2005; HMRC,
   Employment Income Manual, para 06220
5 ss671-75 IT(EP)A 2003 and part 8
   IT(PAYE) Regs
6 s3 FA 2017
7 s13 ITA 2007

2. National insurance contributions
8 s11 SSCBA 1992
9 s15 SSCBA 1992
10 s13 SSCBA 1992

Chapter 27

Time out from studies

This chapter covers:
1. Ill health (below)
2. Pregnancy and children (p301)
3. Carers (p303)
4. Re-sits (p303)
5. Time out for other reasons (p304)

Basic facts

– Students may be able to receive student support or get social security benefits during periods of absence from their course.
– Support is usually only available if you have taken time out because you are ill or pregnant, or because you have to care for someone.
– Support may also be available once you have recovered from your illness or your caring responsibilities have ceased and you are waiting to return to your course.

Note: all areas are expected to be full service for universal credit (UC) by the end of 2018. This means UC must be claimed instead of the benefits UC is replacing. In a few cases, new claims for the benefits UC is replacing can still be made. See p204 and the 2017/18 edition of this *Handbook* if this appies to you.

1. Ill health

Full-time students

Which benefits you are eligible for depends on how long you have been ill, your age, whether you have paid any national insurance (NI) contributions, and whether you need personal care or have mobility difficulties. Once you have recovered, you may be able to claim universal credit (UC) until you can return to your course.

This chapter provides a checklist of benefits for which you might be eligible if you meet the other conditions for that benefit. For more details about a benefit and how to claim it, see the relevant chapter.

You usually still count as a full-time student when taking time out of your course, unless you have completely abandoned or been dismissed from it.[1]

From the start of your ill health
If you have paid sufficient NI contributions in recent years, you are eligible for contributory employment and support allowance (ESA) after seven 'waiting days' (see Chapter 10).

From three months
You can claim personal independence payment (PIP) if you need help getting around or with daily living activities because of a disability. You are eligible for this after three months if your disability is likely to last at least another nine months.

If you get PIP or disability living allowance (DLA), you can claim UC if you have 'limited capability for work'. If you get PIP or DLA but have not yet been assessed as having limited capability for work, you can claim contributory ESA in order to establish this (although you do not have to get any ESA to qualify in this way). Once you are found to have limited capability for work for ESA (and you also get PIP/DLA), you are then eligible for UC.

Example
Charlie is ill and takes time out of his course. He is not eligible for PIP, and has not worked enough to qualify for contributory ESA. He makes a claim for ESA, supported by a medical certificate, in order to establish his limited capability for work. If he is found to have limited capability for work, he is then eligible for UC.

Once you have recovered
Once you have recovered, you may need to wait some time to be readmitted to your course. During this time you can claim UC.

You can claim for up to one year from the day you recover until the day the college or university agrees you can return to your course. You are not eligible if you get a grant or loan during this time. Once the student support stops, you can claim benefit.

You may have work-related requirements during this time (see p208).

Student support
Although regulations allow payment of student loans to be suspended after 60 days' absence because of ill health, Student Finance England, Student Finance Wales and Student Finance NI have the discretion to continue to pay you until the end of the academic year.

Your college or university should write to Student Finance England, Student Finance Wales and Student Finance NI explaining why it has suspended you from your course. You should also contact Student Finance England/Student Finance Wales/Student Finance NI in writing and request that it continue to pay you while you are ill. You are normally asked to provide medical evidence.

Any student who is personally eligible can also apply to the college of university for discretionary help from its hardship funds.

If you receive a bursary and want to take time out from your studies, check with the institution to see whether it continues to be paid during your time out and what happens when you return to your studies.

If you take time out from your course because of ill health and are not paid a student loan during this time, the unpaid student loan arguably does not count as 'notional' income when calculating your UC, because payment of it is discretionary.

Part-time students

If you are a part-time student, you can claim UC as soon as you are ill or disabled, whether or not you get DLA or PIP.

From the start of your ill health

If you are already getting jobseeker's allowance, you can continue to do so for up to 13 weeks. After that, you must claim UC instead.

You can claim contributory ESA, if you have paid sufficient NI contributions.

From three months

You can claim PIP if you need help getting around or with daily living activities because of a disability. You are eligible for this after three months if your disability is likely to last at least another nine months.

2. **Pregnancy and children**

Student support

If you are a full-time undergraduate student receiving a student loan for living costs, Student Finance England, Student Finance Wales or Student Finance NI normally stops your student support once you suspend your studies. However, they all have the discretion to continue making loan (or, in Wales, grant) payments for the rest of that academic year.[2]

Your college or university should write to Student Finance England/Student Finance Wales/Student Finance NI explaining why it has suspended you from your course. You should also contact Student Finance England/Student Finance Wales/Student Finance NI in writing to request that it continue to pay you while you are taking time out. You are usually asked to provide medical evidence as well as evidence of potential hardship if applicable.

If you are an NHS-funded healthcare student in England or Wales, you can receive an NHS maternity bursary for up to 45 weeks while on maternity leave. Contact NHS Student Bursaries in England or the NHS Student Awards Services in Wales for details.

You could also apply to your college or university for support from its hardship funds.

If you receive a bursary from your college or university and want to take time out from your studies, check with the institution to see whether this continues to be paid during your time out and what happens when you return to your studies.

Benefits

There is no provision for pregnant full-time students to claim universal credit (UC).

As a part-time student, you can get UC and have no work-related requirements from 11 weeks before the date your baby is due.

If you have an employer, you may be able to get statutory maternity pay. If you are not working now but have worked recently, you may be able to get maternity allowance.

Once the baby is born, there are various benefits you can claim.

Nursing and midwifery students can continue to receive their bursary for a period of up to 45 weeks' maternity leave.

Lone parents

Once the baby is born, if you are a lone parent studying full time you can claim:

- child benefit;
- UC;
- if there is no child under 16 already in the household, a Sure Start maternity grant of £500. Claims must be made within three months of the birth or, in some cases, before the birth (see p201);
- Healthy Start food vouchers and vitamins (see p138).

Fathers and partners

If your partner has had a baby and you have an employer, you may be able to claim statutory paternity pay. You can claim if you are the child's father or the mother's partner and you will be caring for the baby or the mother. You may also be able to claim statutory shared parental pay.

Couples

Throughout the course, a full-time student couple (ie, both are students) with a child can claim:

- child benefit;
- UC;
- Healthy Start food vouchers and vitamins (see p141).

Couples can also claim a Sure Start maternity grant if one partner gets a qualifying benefit and there is no child under 16 already in the household (see p201).

If you are a full-time student and a parent and you have a partner who is not a student, you can claim UC as a couple.

3. Carers

If you are a full-time student, there is no provision for you to claim universal credit (UC) while you are looking after someone who is ill or disabled. You cannot usually claim carer's allowance (CA), but you may be able to if you have had to interrupt your studies and the interruption is not temporary (see p110).

Part-time students can claim UC and CA.

As a full-time student, you may have to stop your course while you are caring. If you have to wait to return to it once your caring responsibilities have ended, you can claim UC. You can claim for up to a year until the day from when your institution agrees you can return to your course. You are not eligible if you get a grant or loan during this time. You may have work-related requirements during this time (see p208).

4. Re-sits

If you are a full-time student taking time out to re-sit exams, you are still treated as a student during your absence from the course. You cannot claim income support, jobseeker's allowance, income-related employment and support allowance, housing benefit or universal credit (UC) during this time, unless you would be eligible anyway as a student – eg, as a lone parent. However, if you are taking professional qualifications set by a professional institute or some other body unconnected to your own college or university, you may be able to claim UC while taking time out for re-sits. You may need to appeal and argue that caselaw supports your getting benefit.[3]

Note: you also continue to count as a full-time student if you are doing re-sits after the official end date of your course.

5. Time out for other reasons

If you take time out of your course for another reason, you still count as a full-time student. There is no additional entitlement to benefits during your time out.

Notes

1. Ill health
1 **UC** Reg 13(1)(a) UC Regs
ESA Reg 2(1), definition of 'period of study', ESA Regs
HB Reg 53(2) HB Regs

2. Pregnancy and children
2 Reg 112(12)-(13) E(SS) Regs; reg 94 E(SS)(W) Regs; reg 95 E(SS)(NI) Regs

4. Re-sits
3 R(JSA) 2/02

Appendices

Appendices

Appendix 1

Information and advice

Student support

Official guidance

The Department for Education issues guidance via the Student Loans Company on existing higher education student support legislation for England and forthcoming provisions. The guidance has no legal standing, but may be quoted in an appeal. It is available at www.practitioners.slc.co.uk and includes:

- notes for funding bodies on the student support regulations;
- *Student Support Information Notices;*
- notes announcing forthcoming student support provision.

The Department for Education also issues guidance to providers and partners on the learner support schemes in further education in England. These can be found at www.gov.uk/esfa.

Information and guidance on funding in Wales is available at www.studentfinancewales.co.uk/practitioners.

Information and support fund guidance for higher education institutions in Northern Ireland is available on the Department for the Economy website at www.economy-ni.gov.uk/articles/higher-education-student-finance.

Advice

Contact student advisers within institutions and students' unions for advice on student support. A list of advisory services is available on the website of the National Association of Student Money Advisers at www.nasma.org.uk.

Social security benefits and tax credits

Publications

The following are available from CPAG at 30 Micawber Street, London N1 7TB. You can order online at www.shop.cpag.org.uk, or telephone CPAG on 020 7837 7979.

- *Benefits for Students in Scotland Handbook* 2018/19, £22.
- *Welfare Benefits and Tax Credits Handbook* 2018/19, £61. The 2019/20 edition is due in April 2019. The book is also available online. See www.shop.cpag.org.uk/publications for more information.
- *Council Tax Handbook*, 12th edition (autumn 2018), £26.
- *Universal Credit: what you need to know*, 5th edition (winter 2019), £15.
- *Disability Rights Handbook* 2018/19, £33.99.

Official guidance

The following guidance, used by decision makers in the Department for Work and Pensions and local authorities, is available at www.gov.uk/dwp. It has no legal standing, but may be used in an appeal, revision or supersession.

- *Advice for Decision Making* (universal credit and personal independence payment).
- *Housing Benefit and Council Tax Benefit Guidance Manual*.
- *Decision Makers' Guide* (other benefits).

In Northern Ireland, guidance is provided by the Department for Communities and is available at www.communities-ni.gov.uk/topics/benefits-and-pensions.

Legislation

- www.legislation.gov.uk contains UK legislation. Most is updated.
- *Social Security Legislation*, Volumes 1 to 5. Published by Sweet and Maxwell, these volumes contain updated Acts and regulations covering social security and tax credits with explanatory commentary. Available from CPAG.
- CPAG's *Housing Benefit and Council Tax Reduction Legislation* contains updated Acts and regulations and a detailed commentary.
- Decisions of the Upper Tribunal are available from the HM Courts and Tribunals Service website at www.gov.uk/administrative-appeals-tribunal-decisions.

Advice

Contact your student services department or students' union for advice on studying and claiming benefits.

Other financial help

Publications

- *The Guide to Educational Grants* 2018/19 (published by Directory of Social Change).
- *The Guide to Grants for Individuals in Need* 2018/19 (published by Directory of Social Change).
- *The Directory of Grant Making Trusts* 2018/19 (published by Directory of Social Change).
- *Charities Digest* 2018 (published by Charity Choice/Wilmington Publishing and Information).
- *The Grants Register* 2019 (published by Palgrave Macmillan), containing information on postgraduate student awards for both the UK and overseas.
- *British Music and Drama Education Yearbook* 2018/19 (published by Rhinegold Publishing).

Many of these publications can be found online, or in public libraries, or university or college libraries. Advice centres may also carry some.

Appendix 2
Useful addresses

General sources of information
National Union of Students UK

England
Macadam House
275 Gray's Inn Road
London WC1X 8QB
Tel: 0845 521 0262
nusuk@nus.org.uk
www.nus.org.uk

Wales
2nd Floor, Cambrian Buildings
Mount Stuart Square
Cardiff CF10 5FL
Tel: 02920 435 390
office@nus-wales.org.uk
www.nusconnect.org.uk/nus-wales

Northern Ireland
NUS–Union of Students in Ireland
42 Dublin Road
Belfast BT2 7HN
Tel: 028 9024 4641
info@nistudents.org
http://nus-usi.org

NUS provides information on entitlement to student support, benefits and tax credits, along with other student welfare issues.

Child Poverty Action Group
30 Micawber Street
London N1 7TB
Tel: 020 7837 7979
Advice line for advisers only: 020 7812 5231
(10am–12pm and 2–4pm, Monday to Friday)
advice@cpag.org.uk (for enquiries about universal credit, child benefit and tax credits only)
www.cpag.org.uk/advisers

CPAG provides advice, information and training to advisers.

Low Incomes Tax Reform Group
1st Floor
Artillery House
11–19 Artillery Row
London SW1P 1RT
www.litrg.org.uk
www.taxguideforstudents.org.uk

The Low Incomes Tax Reform Group provides extensive information on students and the taxation system, including student loan repayment.

The Money Charity
15 Prescott Place
London SW4 6BS
Tel: 020 7062 8933
hello@themoneycharity.org.uk
https://themoneycharity.org.uk

The Money Charity provides general advice on money management, including a free guide: *The Student Money Manual.*

UKCISA (UK Council for International Student Affairs)
1st Foor, 3–5 Islington High Street
London N1 9LQ
Advice line: 020 7788 9214 (1–4pm, Monday to Friday)
www.ukcisa.org.uk

UKCISA provides advice and information for overseas students.

••

Disability Rights UK
14 East Bay Lane
HereEast
Queen Elizabeth Olympic Park
London E20 3BS
Disabled students' helpline: 0330 995 0414 (11am–1pm, Tuesdays and Thursdays)
students@disabilityrightsuk.org
www.disabilityrightsuk.org

Disability Rights UK produces a number of booklets and information sheets.

Support for learning

Dance and drama awards
www.gov.uk/dance-drama-awards

Department for the Economy
Student Finance Branch
Adelaide House
39–49 Adelaide Street
Belfast BT2 8FD
Tel: 028 9025 7715
studentfinance@economy-ni.gov.uk
www.economy-ni.gov.uk

Responsible for student financial support in Northern Ireland.

Department for Education
Piccadilly Gate
Store Street
Manchester M1 2WD
Tel: 0370 000 2288
www.gov.uk/government/organisations/department-for-education

Responsible for most student support for higher and further education in England.

Department of Health and Social Care
39 Victoria Street
London SW1H 0EU
Tel: 020 7210 4850
Textphone: 020 7222 2262
www.gov.uk/government/organisations/department-of-health-and-social-care

Responsible for NHS-funded healthcare and social work students in England.

Department of Health (Northern Ireland)

Nursing and midwifery bursaries
Bursary Administration Unit
Business Services Organisation
2 Franklin Street
Belfast BT2 8DQ
Tel: 0300 555 0113
studentnurse.bursaries@hscni.net
www.hscbusiness.hscni.net
See also: www.nidirect.gov.uk/articles/health-professional-courses

Social Work Student Incentive Scheme
Office of Social Services
Bursary Administration Section
Castle Buildings
Stormont
Belfast BT4 3SQ
Tel: 028 9052 0518
www.nidirect.gov.uk/articles/careers-social-care

Provides bursaries for healthcare and social work students in Northern Ireland.

Education and Skills Funding Agency
Student Bursary Support Team
Learner Support Provider Helpline: 0300 303 8610
Students/young parents: 0800 121 8989
1619bursary@studentbursarysupport.co.uk
C2L@studentbursarysupport.co.uk
www.gov.uk/government/organisations/education-and-skills-funding-agency
www.gov.uk/guidance/student-bursary-support-service

Funds further education for 16–19 year-olds and adult learners in England.

Get Into Teaching

https://getintoteaching.education.gov.uk
Tel: 0800 389 2500

Information on teacher training in England.

NHS Business Services Authority

NHS Student Bursaries

Ridgway House
Northgate Close
Middlebrook
Bolton BL6 6PQ
Tel: 0300 330 1345
nhsbsa.sbaccount@nhsbsa.nhs.uk
www.nhsbsa.nhs.uk/nhs-bursary-students

Provides information on funding and assessments for students undertaking allied health professions courses in England.

NHS Wales Student Awards Services

Floor 4
Companies House
Crown Way
Cardiff CF14 3UB
Tel: 02920 905 380
abm.sas@wales.nhs.uk
www.nwssp.wales.nhs.uk/student-awards

Provides information and assessments for students undertaking allied health professions courses in Wales.

Social work bursaries

PO Box 141
Hesketh House
200–220 Broadway
Fleetwood FY7 9AS
Tel: 0300 330 1342
www.nhsbsa.nhs.uk/social-work-students

Administers social work bursaries for all social work students in England.

Health Careers Helpline

Tel: 0345 606 0655
www.healthcareers.nhs.uk

Provides information on careers in the healthcare professions in the NHS in England.

Professional and career development loans
Tel: 0800 100 900
www.gov.uk/career-development-loans

Research councils

UK Research and Innovation
Polaris House
Swindon SN2 1FL
Tel: 01793 444 000
www.ukri.org

Arts and Humanities Research Council
Polaris House
North Star Avenue
Swindon SN2 1FL
Tel: 01793 444 164
enquiries@ahrc.ukri.org
www.ahrc.ukri.org

Biotechnology and Biological Sciences Research Council
Polaris House
North Star Avenue
Swindon SN2 1UH
Tel: 01793 413 200
enquiries@bbsrc.ukri.org
www.bbsrc.ukri.org

Economic and Social Research Council
Polaris House
North Star Avenue
Swindon SN2 1UJ
Tel: 01793 413 000
esrcenquiries@esrc.ukri.org
www.esrc.ac.uk

Engineering and Physical Sciences Research Council
Polaris House
North Star Avenue
Swindon SN2 1ET
Tel: 01793 444 000
epsrcstudentshipqueries@epsrc.ac.uk
www.epsrc.ukri.org

Medical Research Council
Polaris House
North Star Avenue
Swindon SN2 1FL
Tel: 01793 416 200 or 01793 416 440
rfpd@headoffice.mrc.ac.uk
www.mrc.ukri.org

Natural Environment Research Council
Polaris House
North Star Avenue
Swindon SN2 1EU
Tel: 01793 411 500
researchcareers@nerc.ukri.org
www.nerc.ukri.org

Science and Technology Facilities Council
Polaris House
North Star Avenue
Swindon SN2 1SZ
Tel: 01793 413 195
studentships@stfc.ac.uk
www.stfc.ukri.org

Social Care Wales
South Gate House
Wood Street
Cardiff CF10 1EW
Tel: 0300 303 3444
info@socialcare.wales
https://socialcare.wales

Social Care Wales provides bursary support to undergraduate social work students in Wales.

Student Loans Company
100 Bothwell Street
Glasgow G2 7JD
Tel: 0141 306 2000
www.slc.co.uk
Student loan repayment
Tel: 0300 100 0611(0300 100 0370 in Wales)
www.studentloanrepayment.co.uk

Responsible for administering the collection of student loans throughout the UK, in conjunction with HM Revenue and Customs.

Student Finance England
PO Box 210
Darlington DL1 9HJ
Tel: 0300 100 0607

A part of the Student Loans Company, Student Finance England is responsible for administering applications and payments of government-funded loans and grants in England.
Guides and information leaflets about financial support available for students are available from www.gov.uk/student-finance.

Student Finance Wales
PO Box 211
Llandudno Junction LL30 9FU
Tel: 0300 200 4050
Minicom: 0300 100 1693
www.studentfinancewales.co.uk

Student Finance Wales is a Welsh government-led partnership, responsible for administering student financial support to students who normally live in Wales.

Student Finance NI
Ballee Centre
Ballee Road West
Ballymena
Co Antrim BT42 2HS
Tel: 0300 100 0077 (undergraduate helpline)
Tel: 0300 100 0493 (postgraduate helpline)
Minicom: 0300 100 0625
www.studentfinanceni.co.uk
Further education awards: www.eani.org.uk/i-want-to/apply-for-a-further-education-award

Provides financial support to students who normally live in Northern Ireland, in partnership with the Department for the Economy, the Student Loans Company and the five regional offices of the Education Authority in Northern Ireland.

Student Finance Services Non-UK Team
Student Finance England
PO Box 89
Darlington DL1 9AZ
Tel: 0141 243 3570
www.gov.uk/contact-student-finance-england

Provides information about applications by European Union students for fee payment support in England, or migrant workers for fee and maintenance support.

Teacher Training Cymru
http://discoverteaching.wales

Information on teacher training in Wales.

Universities and Colleges Admissions Service
Rosehill
New Barn Lane
Cheltenham GL52 3LZ
Tel: 0371 468 0468 (undergraduates); 0371 468 0470 (performing arts); 0371 334 4447 (postgraduates); 0371 468 0469 (postgraduate teacher training)
Text relay service: 18001 plus relevant number
www.ucas.com

Contact UCAS for information on applying to higher education.

Welsh government (education and skills)
Tel: 0300 060 3300
https://beta.gov.wales/education-skills

Responsible for education funding in Wales.

Benefits and tax credits

Child tax credit and working tax credit helpline
Tel: 0345 300 3900
Textphone: 0345 300 3909
www.gov.uk/topic/benefits-credits/tax-credits

Department for Work and Pensions
www.gov.uk/government/organisations/department-for-work-pensions
www.gov.uk/government/collections/dwp-detailed-benefit-guides
www. gov.uk/browse/benefits

Responsible for social security in England, Wales and Scotland. The DWP website has information on general entitlement to benefits and contains the *Decision Makers' Guide* and *Advice for Decision Making* at www.gov.uk/government/publications.

Department for Communities
www.communities-ni.gov.uk
www.nidirect.gov.uk/money-tax-and-benefits
Benefit Enquiry Line: 0800 022 4250
Textphone: 028 9031 1092

Responsible for social security in Northern Ireland.

Other issues
Department of Health and Social Care
Health and Social Care Publications
PO Box 777
London SE1 6XH
Tel: 0300 123 1002
Minicom: 0300 123 1003
www.orderline.dh.gov.uk

For bulk orders of HC1 forms – eg, for students' union advice centres.

NHS Business Services Authority Help with Health Costs
Bridge House
152 Pilgrim Street
Newcastle upon Tyne NE1 6SN
Tel: 0300 330 1343
www.nhsbsa.nhs.uk/nhs-help-health-costs

The NHS Business Services Authority Help with Health Costs advises students on getting help with their health costs on the grounds of low income.

HM Revenue and Customs
For students: www.gov.uk/student-jobs-paying-tax
For the address of your nearest HMRC office and telephone numbers of helplines:
www.gov.uk/government/organisations/hm-revenue-customs/contact.

Local Government and Social Care Ombudsman
PO Box 4771
Coventry CV4 0EH
Tel: 0300 061 0614
www.lgo.org.uk

The Local Government and Social Care Ombudsman can investigate claims of maladministration by local authorities in England.

Public Services Ombudsman for Wales
1 Ffordd yr Hen Gae
Pencoed CF35 5LJ
Tel: 0300 790 0203
ask@ombudsman-wales.org.uk
www.ombudsman-wales.org.uk

The Public Services Ombudsman for Wales can investigate claims of maladministration by local authorities in Wales in respect of benefit claims or student support applications.

Northern Ireland Public Services Ombudsman
Progressive House
33 Wellington Place
Belfast BT1 6HN
Tel: 0800 343 424/02890 233 821
Textphone: 02890 897 789
nipso@nipso.org.uk
https://nipso.org.uk

The Northern Ireland Ombudsman's Office can investigate claims of maladministration by local authorities in Northern Ireland in respect of benefit claims or student support applications.

Appendix 3

Abbreviations used in the notes

AAC	Administrative Appeals Chamber
AACR	Administrative Appeals Chamber Reports
Art(s)	Article(s)
Ch	chapter
EWCA Civ	England and Wales Court of Appeal (Civil Division)
EWHC	England and Wales High Court
NICA	Northern Ireland Court of Appeal
para(s)	paragraph(s)
Reg(s)	regulation(s)
s(s)	section(s)
Sch(s)	Schedule(s)
UKUT	United Kingdom Upper Tribunal
Vol	volume

Acts of Parliament

CA 1989	Children Act 1989
EA 1996	Education Act 1996
ETA 1973	Employment and Training Act 1973
FA 2016	Finance Act 2016
FA 2017	Finance Act 2017
ITA 2007	Income Tax Act 2007
IT(EP)A 2003	Income Tax (Earnings and Pensions) Act 2003
IT(TOI)A 2005	Income Tax (Trading and Other Income) Act 2005
JSA 1995	Jobseekers Act 1995
LGA 2003	Local Government Act 2003
LGFA 1992	Local Government Finance Act 1992
SSCBA 1992	Social Security Contributions and Benefits Act 1992
WRA 2007	Welfare Reform Act 2007
WRWA 2016	Welfare Reform and Work Act 2016

Regulations and other statutory instruments

C(LC)SSB Regs	The Children (Leaving Care) Social Security Benefits Regulations 2001 No.3074
CB Regs	The Child Benefit (General) Regulations 2006 No.223
CT(DD)O	The Council Tax (Discount Disregards) Order 1992 No.548
CT(ED)O	The Council Tax (Exempt Dwellings) Order 1992 No.558
CTC Regs	The Child Tax Credit Regulations 2002 No.2007
CTRS(DS)(E) Regs	The Council Tax Reduction Schemes (Default Scheme) (England) Regulations 2012 No.2886
CTRS(PR)(E) Regs	The Council Tax Reduction Schemes (Prescribed Requirements) (England) Regulations 2012 No.2885
CTRS(PR)(W) Regs	The Council Tax Reduction Schemes and Prescribed Requirements (Wales) Regulations 2012 No.3144
E(ALGS)(W) Regs	The Education (Assembly Learning Grant Scheme) (Wales) Regulations 2002 No.1857
E(PDDL) Regs	The Education (Postgraduate Doctoral Degree Loans) and the Education (Student Loans) (Repayment) (Amendment) Regulations 2018 No.559
E(PDDL)(W) Regs	The Education (Postgraduate Doctoral Degree Loans) (Wales) Regulations 2018 No.656
E(PMDL) Regs	The Education (Postgraduate Master's Degree Loans) Regulations 2016 No.606
E(PMDL)(W) Regs	The Education (Postgraduate Master's Degree Loans) (Wales) Regulations 2017 No.523
E(SL) Regs	The Education (Student Loans) Regulations 1998 No.211
E(SL)(R) Regs	The Education (Student Loans) (Repayment) Regulations 2009 No.470
E(SS) Regs	The Education (Student Support) Regulations 2009 No.1555
E(SS)(NI) Regs	The Education (Student Support) (No.2) Regulations (Northern Ireland) 2009 No.373
E(SS)(W) Regs	The Education (Student Support) (Wales) Regulations 2018 No.191
E(SS)(W) Regs 2017	The Education (Student Support) (Wales) Regulations 2017 No.47
E(WMTTIS) Regs	The Education (Welsh Medium Teacher Training Incentive Supplement) Regulations 1990 No.1208
ESA Regs	The Employment and Support Allowance Regulations 2008 No.794
ESA(TP) Regs	The Employment and Support Allowance (Transitional Provisions) Regulations 2008 No.795
HB Regs	The Housing Benefit Regulations 2006 No.213

HSS&WF(A) Regs	The Healthy Start Scheme and Welfare Food (Amendment) Regulations 2005 No.3262
IS Regs	The Income Support (General) Regulations 1987 No.1967
IT(PAYE) Regs	The Income Tax (Pay As You Earn) Regulations 2003 No.2682
JSA Regs	The Jobseeker's Allowance Regulations 1996 No.207
JSA Regs 2013	The Job Seeker's Allowance Regulations 2013 No.378
LMI Regs	The Loans for Mortgage Interest Regulations 2017 No.725
NHS(CDA) Regs	The National Health Service (Charges for Drugs and Appliances) Regulations 2000 No.620
NHS(DC) Regs	The National Health Service (Dental Charges) Regulations 2005 No.3477
NHS(DC) (W) Regs	The National Health Service (Dental Charges) (Wales) Regulations 2006 No.491
NHS(FP&CDA)(W) Regs	National Health Service (Free Prescriptions and Charges for Drugs and Appliances) (Wales) Regulations 2007 No.121
NHS(GOS) Regs	The National Health Service (General Ophthalmic Services) Regulations 1986 No.975
NHS(OCP) Regs	The National Health Service (Optical Charges and Payments) Regulations 1997 No.818
NHS(TERC) Regs	The National Health Service (Travel Expenses and Remission of Charges) Regulations 2003 No.2382
NHS(TERC)(W) Regs	The National Health Service (Travelling Expenses and Remission of Charges) (Wales) Regulations 2007 No.1104
SS(ICA) Regs	The Social Security (Invalid Care Allowance) Regulations 1976 No.409
TC(DCI) Regs	The Tax Credits (Definition and Calculation of Income) Regulations 2002 No.2006
UC Regs	The Universal Credit Regulations 2013 No.376
WTC(EMR) Regs	The Working Tax Credit (Entitlement and Maximum Rate) Regulations 2002 No.2005

Other abbreviations

ADM	*Advice for Decision Making*
DMG	*Decision Makers' Guide*
GM	*The Housing Benefit and Council Tax Benefit Guidance Manual*

References like CIS/142/1990 and R(SB) 3/89 are references to commissioners' decisions. References like *AD v SSWP* [2009] UKUT 46 (AAC) are references to decisions of the Upper Tribunal.

Index

. . . .

How to use this Index

Entries against the bold headings direct you to the general information on the subject, or where the subject is covered most fully. Sub-entries are listed alphabetically and direct you to specific aspects of the subject.

CA   Carer's allowance
C-ESA   Contributory employment and
         support allowance
C-JSA   Contribution-based jobseeker's
         allowance
CTC   Child tax credit
DLA   Disability living allowance
ESA   Employment and support allowance
HB   Housing benefit
IS   Income support

I-ESA   Income-related employment and
         support allowance
I-JSA   Income-based jobseeker's
         allowance
JSA   Jobseeker's allowance
NI   National insurance
PIP   Personal independence payment
UC   Universal credit
WTC   Working tax credit

part-time students 198
payment 199
time out from studies 299
placement students
income tax 293
NI contributions on earnings 296
social work students
England 100, 101
Wales 102
work placements 34, 55, 69
Postgraduate Certificate in Education
student support
England 94
N. Ireland 99
Wales 97
teacher training bursary 95
teacher training incentive 97
tuition fees
England 95
Postgraduate Diploma in Education
student support 94
postgraduate loan for doctoral courses 77
eligible courses 78
eligible students 78
payment 78
repayment 78
postgraduate loan for master's degrees 75
eligible courses 76
eligible students 76
payment 77
repayment 77
residence conditions 76
treatment as income
health benefits 270
means-tested benefits 246
UC 232
postgraduate students
council tax 282
disabled students' allowance 79
N. Ireland 81
healthcare courses 85
IS 167
JSA 181
loan for doctoral courses
England and Wales 77
loan for master's degrees
England and Wales 75
NI contributions on earnings 296
social work
England 100
Wales 102
student support 74
N. Ireland 79
studentships 74
N. Ireland 80
treatment of grants as income
health benefits 269
means-tested benefits 244, 250

tax credits 262
treatment of loans as income
health benefits 270
means-tested benefits 246
tax credits 262
UC 232
tuition fee loans
N. Ireland 80
tuition fees
England and Wales 74
N. Ireland 80
practice placement expenses
healthcare students
2012 bursary scheme 89
degree-level pre-2012 91
pregnancy
benefits 191, 301
health benefits 144
healthcare students 92
Healthy Start scheme 141
Sure Start maternity grant 201
time out from studies 300
premiums
ESA 133
HB 156
IS 173
JSA 187
prescriptions 137
free 139
ESA 135
IS 177
JSA 189
tax credits 222
UC 215
pre-payment certificates 140
previous study
student support
England 26
N. Ireland 65
Wales 48
professional and career development loans
104
further education
England 13
N. Ireland 19
Wales 16
treatment as income
health benefits 273
means-tested benefits 246, 256
tax credits 262
UC 238
professional studies loans
treatment as income
means-tested benefits 246
property
treatment of income
tax credits 266